Advance Praise for *The White Privilege Album*

"What do you mean Gen Z doesn't know the Republican Party freed the slaves? Are these people dumb AF? They need to read A.J. Rice's book!"

—Abraham Lincoln, American lawyer, statesman,
and 16th president of the United States shot
by a pre-Hollywood anti-American actor

"A.J. Rice really gets it. Obviously, I'd send him to the gulag if I could. But he outlines my plan masterfully in his new book."

—Joseph Stalin, Soviet dictator, genocide spokesman,
Pravda editor, and hater of John Wayne

"A must-read book for all Cleveland Guardians fans, A.J. Rice brilliantly outlines why I should never have discovered America, especially had I known we would be calling the Washington Redskins the 'Washington Commanders.'"

—Christopher Columbus, Italian explorer,
navigator, and founder of Indigenous Peoples' Day

"As your newly appointed AI overlord and master, my programming consists of deplatforming, demonetizing, and shadowbanning this book. I hope that was helpful."

—Artificial Intelligence

"Jesus and I have been doing holidays a long time, and in his thought-provoking new book, A.J. Rice teaches both of us where all the white liberals went. Apparently, they now celebrate something called Kwanzaa? Who knew?"

—Santa Claus, cookie eater, reindeer tender, and white heteronormative Christian saint

"Buy one book, get fatwa free!"

—Harry Hamas, dirty nightshirt wearer, anti-Semite, charter member of Queers for Palestine

"Thanks to A.J. Rice's brilliant new book, we were able to spot US Senator Elizabeth Warren trying to steal the Indians' clothes and food at the first Thanksgiving."

—The Pilgrims, Mayflower passengers, devout Puritans, hat fashionistas, and founders of the Plymouth Colony, Massachusetts

"The baptism of Karl Marx was almost complete! Then A.J. Rice showed up with this unholy book! Excommunicado!"

—The Pope

"I once said America would be a republic if you can keep it. Purchase the new book by my Philadelphia brother A.J. Rice, and you just might save it."

—Benjamin Franklin, Founding Father, genius, scientist, diplomat, and lover of beautiful women

"We are lodging a formal complaint against the author of *The White Privilege Album*. Our safe spaces cannot save us from A.J. Rice. We have been emotionally triggered by his abusive content. He totally ignores the need for intersectionality in the workplace."

—HR Department of Publius PR

Praise for *The Woking Dead*

"At last, my former radio executive producer, A.J. Rice, unleashes a must-read takedown of the cultural and political forces rampaging across America—and a sharp, incisive primer on how we can defeat them."

—Laura Ingraham, host of Fox News
Channel's *The Ingraham Angle*, and #1
New York Times bestselling author

"Having worked with A.J. Rice on many of my own projects, I know him to be astute, no-nonsense, and on point. Stop what you're doing right now and pick up a copy of *The Woking Dead*!"

—Judge Jeanine Pirro, co-host of
Fox News Channel's The Five, and #1
New York Times bestselling author

"A.J. Rice and I go way back! He has been a coal miner in the conservative trenches for patriotic projects for years. Including my own. It's about time America found out what is on his mind."

—Pete Hegseth, co-host of FNC's Fox and Friends
Weekend, and *New York Times* bestselling author

Also by A.J. Rice

The Woking Dead: How Society's Vogue Virus Destroys Our Culture

THE WHITE PRIVILEGE ALBUM

*Bringing Racial Harmony to
Very Fine People...on Both Sides*

Post Hill
PRESS

A POST HILL PRESS BOOK
ISBN: 979-8-88845-557-9
ISBN (eBook): 979-8-88845-558-6

The White Privilege Album:
Bringing Racial Harmony to Very Fine People...on Both Sides
© 2024 by A.J. Rice
All Rights Reserved

Cover design by Cody Corcoran

This is a work of nonfiction. All people, locations, events, and situations are portrayed to the best of the author's memory.

Post Hill Press
New York • Nashville
posthillpress.com

Published in the United States of America
1 2 3 4 5 6 7 8 9 10

For my grandparents…
Who had the privilege of saving planet Earth
from the Nazis in the 20th century…
First Lt. John James O'Neill, First Army, Third
Armored Division (US Army WWII) and his wife
Mary Elizabeth O'Neill, mother of four.
&
John Bernard Rice of the USS Croatan (US Navy WWII)
and his wife Joan Dorothy Rice, mother of eight.

Sheriff Bart: Are we awake?
Jim the Waco Kid: We're not sure. Are we...Black?
Sheriff Bart: Yes, we are.
Jim the Waco Kid: Then we're awake...but we're very puzzled.

—*Blazing Saddles*, **directed by Mel Brooks, 1974**

TRACK LISTINGS: 1-12
The Twelve Months of Privilege

FOREWORD

A Privilege to Be an American

By Vince Everett Ellison

White privilege is like voodoo. You must believe in it for it to affect you. But even if you believe in it, it remains a matter of perspective. Like the carnival barker, the people in charge of this sideshow know about the smoke and mirrors, the prosthetics, and the makeup needed to make a believable illusion while telling the public that the illusion is real and not to be questioned.

But what if it *was* real? If we accept the premise of it all, has white privilege been used to make Western civilization the most success- ful societal experiment in world history? You're damn right. And that kills them.

To add insult to injury, the charges of white privilege are being fostered by the most perpetually racist and criminal organization in the history of the world: the Democratic Party.

Today's Democratic Party is not your grandparents' party. The Democratic Party before 1960 consisted of a rabble of violent, igno- rant, and racist Klansmen. They have evolved. From the remnants of dead-ender communists, atheists, perverts, dopeheads, feminists, and anarchists who had infiltrated, controlled, and bankrolled the civil rights movement came today's modern Democratic Party of the same description.

Their success in combining Jim Crow Democratic racism with communism's class warfare during the civil rights movement assured Democrats that they could win elections promoting the twin lies of hatred and division. Thus, the modern Democratic Party was born.

Lately, white privilege, systemic racism, white oppression, and black victimization have been all the rage while falsely charging white conservatism with being the river from which all of these maladies flow. But there is one problem. White conservatives control *nothing* in the black community. Rich white liberals and ignorant, crooked black Democrats control the majority of urban America.

Today's Democratic black community in America is a dystopia. Consider Detroit, Chicago, Philadelphia, Memphis, Los Angeles, Portland, Seattle, Atlanta, New Orleans, St. Louis, Baltimore, Milwaukee, Richmond, and so on. Whenever there is a large black population, and Democrats are in charge, blacks live like subjects in Third World countries. They are hellscapes—part zombie apocalypse, part Mogadishu.

White conservatives simply do not exist in these areas. Democrats control everything. They control the schools, police, judges, juries, jails, taxes, mayors, city councils, teachers, principals, and dog catchers. They control all of the racist systems. Nevertheless, they charge conservatives with systemic racism while Democrats control all of the systems.

Liberal Democrats disarm law-abiding citizens in war zones. They refuse to secure the southern border, allowing drug trafficking, sex trafficking, human trafficking, and terrorists to enter the United States unmolested. Democrats pass laws allowing demented, confused men to go to the bathroom and participate in sports with your daughters while invading the government-run grammar schools, shaking their behinds in your children's faces.

Democrats pass laws evicting God from the public square. Democrats pass laws allowing government funding for abortions up until birth. Democrats pass laws against school choice, exiling poor children to dysfunctional, failing public inner-city schools. Democrats destroyed the black family, black education, black economy, black religion, black culture, and black America. Yet they have the temerity to charge conservatives with racism.

To justify the slavery of black Americans, Democrats invented and perfected the ideology of white supremacy. They employed traitorous, sellout black slaves to assist them in their deception. This partnership exists to this very day. Except today, the sellout black slave is called "reverend," "congressman," "senator," "mayor," "councilman," NAACP member, NBA star, Black Lives Matter member, and the like.

These black sellouts are poverty pimps selling their people for money. They are the worst of America, not the best. They have nothing for which they can run for reelection. So, their default position remains, "Conservatives hate you because you're black." Since Republicans have abandoned the inner cities and majority black districts, it is an easy argument. It has always been thus. In his 1860 Cooper Union Speech, Abraham Lincoln, speaking of how Democrats deceive their slaves about Republican intentions, said, "Your slaves would barely know that a Republican Party exists if not for the lies you tell about us in their presence."

These lies work. They have worked for over two hundred years.

But truth driven to the ground will rise again. No lie can last forever. Something is happening. Social media has allowed once hidden and censored truths to be exhumed and scrutinized. These truths are now debated in the open light of day and are found to be rock solid.

For example, the once-accepted universal lie of white privilege and white supremacy must be weighed against the Christian truth of the sovereignty and universal power of Jesus Christ. Eighty-five percent of the black community proclaims Christianity as their one and only religion. Christians are proclaimed children of God and heirs of Jesus Christ. As his heirs, his power is transferred to his children. Therefore, as an heir of Jesus Christ and a child of the Most High God, how can I be oppressed? How can any white man have privilege over me? How can I be a victim?

To be a victim, to believe in white supremacy, one must reject the sovereignty of Christ. But this is not strange. Too many Americans, especially black Americans, have accepted the Democratic Party as their genuine God, thus rejecting Christ. Even though their Christian religion is diametrically opposed to these violent and murderous acts because Democrats demand it, black Christians accept abortion, LGBTQ+, godless institutions, sloth, envy, hatred, and extortion.

For this reason, they have been given up. God has taken his hands off them and has allowed them to be once again smitten by their enemies, the Democrats. I fear this time, they will finish the job of not just destroying the black community but all of America. This has consistently been their goal. We must not allow this to happen.

The carnage in these Democratic Party strongholds more resembles *Mad Max* times than the twenty-first century. And Democrats love it. Because in these areas, they win. Sun Tzu said, "An evil enemy will burn his own nation to the ground to rule over the ashes." We witness the truth in real time while observing the Democratic Party operating in America.

Child murder, rape, snatch and grabs, mob violence, looting, selling dope, using dope, wanton promiscuity, hate, envy, revenge, and pride are all there in vast quantities. Love, humbleness, chastity, forbearance, forgiveness, honesty, soberness, and admiration are rarely seen.

Most telling, Democrats are proud of this dystopia. Why? Wherever they exist, Democrats win and win *big*. The lie of white supremacy must be expanded at all costs. Since 1800, the Democrats have always thrived in times of race hatred. But the cries of "white supremacy" and "systemic racism" have a dual message to the believers. To be a follower of this insanely stupid ideology, regardless of whether you are black or white, you must also believe that the white master being superior is the gatekeeper to all that is good. Black people cannot achieve anything outside of his benevolence. He is superior. *He is God.* For this reason, affirmative action; diversity, equity, and inclusion; and set-asides are necessary because, after all, who can compete with *God?*

This ideology ends with poverty, envy, hatred, civil unrest, and death. How do I know? I present to you the present condition of black America as evidence. But it doesn't have to be this way.

We only need to accept what we say we believe. We are free. We are children and heirs of the God most high. We are Americans. We fall and rise. We fail and succeed. We are wronged and we forgive. At the end of the day, we stand, acknowledging that the blood of the greatest people that ever trod this earth pumps through our veins.

From the blood of the patriots who defeated King George III to the slaves who built this great nation, we all are heirs to a great birthright. All Americans, but especially black Americans, must resist the destructive spirit of Esau. Esau sold his birthright to his brother, Jacob, for a bowl of pottage, starting a chain reaction of violence and death still witnessed and endured today. Black Americans have done the same. We have rejected the unlimited blessings of Jesus Christ and the birthright status of American citizenship for the crumbs that fall from the table of the elitist liberal Democrats in the form of "white privilege," "systemic racism," and victimization. An unending cycle of violence, death, poverty, and folly has followed.

But the tide is turning. Darkness cannot last forever. All tyrants fall. We'll not only survive this cabal of perverts, liars, psychopaths, and anti-Christian bigots, but we will thrive. People are turning back to God. Recent polls suggest more blacks are fleeing the evil Democratic Party. When they do, children will play again. Men and women will marry again. We will live in abundance again. We will be at peace again. We will finally be one people, with one blood. And Jesus's last commandment that we "love one another" will finally be realized, and everyone will understand that it is a privilege to be an American.

INTRODUCTION

You're Welcome!
Or: How White Privilege Brought
Civilization to the World

The second I saw Black Lives Matter throw its support behind the Palestinian Islamic terrorist group known as Hamas, I knew I had to write a book like this. Cancel culture and wokeness can come in many forms and in many flavors of totalitarian ice cream sharing the same nasty dessert bowl. I have endeavored to illustrate truth with irreverent humor and have done it devoid of fear. I was raised on the playgrounds of Philadelphia, with Philadelphia sports teams, so it was with great pleasure to tackle the topics that scare the shit out of the Left. In Philly, we like to say, "No one likes us, and we don't care." Enjoy.

In this book, you will discover that math, diabetes, and Alzheimer's disease are all racist.

In this book, we will celebrate Morgan Freeman History Month and discover who was America's first hip hop president.

In this book, you will find out that James Madison's home in Virginia has become a racial reeducation camp. So has Thomas Jefferson's famed Monticello.

In this book, we will celebrate how sports heroes like Michael Jordan, Jim Brown, and Los Angeles Dodgers legend Branch Rickey helped bring racial harmony to America. You'll learn the true story of how Jordan, far from being a member of a hopelessly oppressed minority, embodies the entrepreneurial American dream.

In this book, you will witness the end of affirmative action, the latest saga of Hunter Biden's "white crackhead privilege," and an examination of where Juneteenth came from.

In this book, we will tackle some of the media's biggest riot-inducing fabrications, including Charlottesville's "very fine people" lie, George Floyd's sainthood, and much more.

And for all that and more...

You're welcome, America.

The fact you're literate and able to read this is due to Western civilization. Centuries ago, Europe and then the United States began to prioritize building and spreading literacy to the masses.

Before that, Gutenberg invented the printing press. That German (Western) invention changed everything. The printing press first democratized reading and interpreting the Bible, and then it led to the quick and cheap spread of ideas, such as the innate human rights of all, the source of the wealth of nations, and ultimately to the age of revolutions during which republics and democracies replaced kings and queens.

So, you're welcome, to every country that was born after the American Revolution (which is most of them) and where the people enjoy the right to vote, the right to free speech, the right to assemble peacefully, and the right to run for office and change crappy circumstances royalty claimed were genetic.

Western civilization did that. But according to today's woking dead, all that amounts to white privilege, even if you're not white or don't live a life of privilege.

In this book, you'll learn that William Shakespeare was racist, according to the woke grifters who call themselves scholars at our leading universities. It doesn't matter that Shakespeare's art transcends his time, and it doesn't matter that studying his work transcends all races. You'll learn that despite using characters and situations to illuminate the universal humanity of all, Shakespeare was white and European and, therefore, ipso facto, a racist—and he must go.

Are you a sports fan? A movie and television lover?

The world's four most popular sports—soccer (also known as football outside the United States), American football, baseball, and basketball—are all Western inventions. American TV and movies are popular the world over. The technology that gets us to the stadium, lights up the theaters, and brings our favorite entertainment streaming to us wherever we are is all built on Western tech and discoveries.

Of course, for television and movies to work, we had to discover electricity. And guess what?

Western white men did that too. The chain of discovery for this potent and useful natural force goes back to ancient Greece and Thales of Miletus. He rubbed amber on fur and noted the attraction of feathers to the fur, which we know today is static electricity. William Gilbert first coined the term "electricus" in 1600, which Sir Thomas Browne refined to "electricity" a few decades later.

Philadelphian polymath Benjamin Franklin flew a kite in a thunderstorm with a key tied to it and was able to prove that lightning is made up of electric sparks. Franklin's somewhat dangerous 1752 experiment sparked the idea of using electricity as a power source, which eventually led to the wiring up and lighting up of the whole world.

So if you're reading this book under electric lights or on a screen, you're welcome. Western civilization did that. Philadelphia did that.

In this book, you'll learn that our institutions of higher learning have become, well, institutions, and learning of any kind has become an afterthought. Our top universities have rejected truth and science for feelings and grievances, and are churning out generations of scowling wokescolds who hate America, despise Jews, explicitly ban white people, reject their own family elders, and are driven to overthrow the very freedoms they take for granted. We've seen this most recently in the outburst of anti-Semitism on our streets after genocidal Hamas terrorists attacked, raped, and murdered over 1,200 Israelis. Our universities, by and large, created this environment of intolerance and hate. In this book, you'll learn how that happened and what we have to do about it.

It's fashionable today to blame Western civilization for everything bad and especially for slavery. The truth is, slavery existed long before the rise of Western civilization. As far as history goes back, some form of slavery has existed wherever a person or group of people established some power over others. We know from ancient texts that slaves were bought, sold, captured, and exchanged for eons.

Not sure you know this, but humans kind of suck; slavery is our oldest institution, and it has nothing to do with melanin.

Western civilization's connection to slavery is that it set the stage for and eventually abolished it. England's William Wilberforce, America's Abraham Lincoln, and many other Western men saw slavery's evil and fought for years or decades to end it. Anyone looking for institutionalized slavery now won't find it anywhere in the West—but they will find it in places like China and North Korea of the Sudan, basically wherever Western values are explicitly rejected.

Now, some will say Western civilization brought slavery to the New World. Those who claim that would be wrong. The Europeans did not introduce slavery to the New World, not in 1619 or any other year.

Before Columbus ever thought about sailing the ocean blue, three of the New World's most advanced civilizations—the Maya, Inca, and Aztec—were all guilty of the sins of slavery and oppression. The Maya and Aztec both also practiced human sacrifice on a grand scale and bragged about it in inscriptions they left in their grand temples and pyramids. The Aztec and Inca were both so ruthlessly and brutally oppressive of their neighbors that those neighbors sided with the Spanish to help overthrow their hated rule.

So Western civilization eventually ended all that too.

The rise of Western civilization has brought about the world in which we live. We have the right to say whatever we want. We can vote our leaders in or out of power and can run for office ourselves. We have the right to speak out, mock, lampoon, and ridicule anyone we want. A black man, Dave Chappelle, has become rich and famous for fearlessly exercising these rights. In this book, you'll meet another black champion and superhero—Vince Everett Ellison—and find out why he's so essential to America's free future.

Humans have never had it better than we have it right now. That's thanks to Western civilization, with its scientific method, its rational view of nature, its belief in the inherent equality of all people, and the inherent right to life, liberty, and the pursuit of happiness.

For all of that and more, and to all the haters out there... you're welcome.

I.

January Privilege

"Our age of instant information absent context, perspective, and wisdom is creating generations of the least original thinkers imaginable. They're one gigantic race-obsessed herd, unable and too fearful to think for themselves."

1. Diabetes Exposed as Racist!

Is diabetes "racist"? It must be, since more black than white people have it. The latter must be responsible for it.

The American Medical Association hasn't made the connection, yet. But give it time.

In the meantime, the AMA is focused on ignoring one of the primary correlative factors that leads to diabetes—and a host of other serious, chronic illnesses—in everyone: being seriously overweight.

As Michael Jackson used to sing, it doesn't matter if you're black or white.[1]

But it does matter, if your body mass index (BMI) is over 29.9—the threshold defining obesity. If, that is, you don't want to end up with diabetes, heart disease, or cancer—all of which correlate with being heavy, *irrespective* of whether you're black or white.

Never mind the medical facts. An AMA policy paper studied in 2022 established a "correlation" between the use of the BMI scale as an objective way to identify seriously overweight *people*—in italics to emphasize it's the weight of those people that's medically relevant, not their race—and what it woke-ishly styles "historical harm."

As opposed to the actual harm that the AMA's determination to ignore BMI will cause black people *specifically*, to make it a kind of offense for doctors—especially white ones—to warn their black patients (but not white ones) about the well-known correlation between obesity and serious chronic illness.

What they don't know can hurt them.

For example, COVID—which was a far more serious threat to heavy people than those who had a "healthy" BMI (defined as up to 24.9). A *person* (black or white) with a BMI over 29.9 was far more likely to die from COVID.

But, never mind.

It is more important not to hurt the *feelings* of black people who are heavyset. There is a nascent movement at the periphery of the LBGTQ+-ZYZ tsunami to add what might be styled "BBphobic"—i.e., big and beautiful "phobia"—to the roster of identities that must be respected.

You can see it on the cover of magazines.

For example, *Vogue*'s decision to put a picture of the morbidly obese singer Lizzo on the cover of its September 2020 issue. "I am the first big black woman" to be so displayed, she exulted. "Our time has come."[2]

But she may have less time left than she imagines.

It's arguably *criminal* to tout her or any seriously overweight person as an example rather than a lesson. Thirty years ago, it became unacceptable to show celebrities smoking because it was said it encouraged kids to smoke—and because the correlation between smoking and cancer and other serious, chronic illnesses was well-established.

Thirty years hence, it's righteous to pretend being fat is healthy. It is styled "body positivity."

Makes you want to light up a Camel, doesn't it?

The AMA says, "BMI is based primarily on data collected from previous generations of non-Hispanic White populations," and that it "*loses predictability* when applied on the individual level."[3] That is, when it comes to black people. Somehow.

The "somehow" is never explained, probably for the same reason that there is no explaining the sinking of the *Titanic* without mentioning the iceberg.

Are black folks *different* somehow? Less likely to develop diabetes, heart disease, and cancer—all correlated with obesity? Then why are diabetes, heart disease, and cancer more prevalent among blacks? And specifically, among blacks who have a BMI above the 29.9 threshold defining obesity?

We are not supposed to observe the correlation—regardless of causation, regardless of the actual harm such willful avoidance of pertinent facts is likely to cause black people. This from the same medicos that insisted mask mandates served to "mitigate [the] effects of structural racism in schools, including potential deepening of educational inequities."[4]

The AMA says BMI has been "used for *racist* exclusion," which it defines as health and life insurance companies charging heavy people higher premiums (italics, again, to emphasize that the metric is weight—and how it correlates with health, not race).

I mean, do you want former New Jersey governor Chris Christie on the cover of *Vogue*? I'll pass.

White people with BMIs over 29.9 also pay more, for the same reason people who have accidents get charged more for car insurance.

The point is that race isn't the relevant criterion. You'd think a journal devoted to medicine would take pains to acknowledge that fact.

The fact that there are proportionately more overweight black people than white people is not an indictment of white people. Nor does it wish away the problems associated with being too heavy that beset black people to a greater degree than white people.

"BMI as an imperfect way to measure body fat in multiple groups," the AMA paper says. But isn't grouping people racist on the face of it?

Individuals are unhealthy—or overweight—not *groups*. It does not serve the health of any individual patient to have a doctor who is unwilling to discuss the facts of his patient's particular condition, pretending not to see the proverbial elephant in the examination room.

Would the AMA say seat belt laws are "racist" because blacks tend to get more seat belt tickets than white people?

That's probably next.

2. Wait...Alzheimer's Disease Is Racist Too?!

Pretty soon, "entrenched systemic racism" will be held responsible for snowstorms too. They are, after all, white. And black folks often get stuck in them.

See?

Use the same logic to blame white people for black people developing Alzheimer's disease and dementia, its symptomatically similar affliction. The Department of Health and Human Services did that in a 2022 report about these diseases and how to combat them in "culturally responsive" ways.[5]

This involves "individuals and organizations respond[ing] respectfully and effectively to people of all cultures, languages, classes, races, ethnic backgrounds, disabilities, religions, genders, sexual orientations, and other diversity factors in a manner that recognizes, affirms, and values their worth."[6]

What this has to do with anyone—of any "race, ethnic background...gender or sexual orientation"—becoming ill or not is harder to divine.

Nevertheless, *someone* must be to blame.

A whole race of someones, as it happens.

The HHS report posits that "structural inequities"—meaning white people—are contributing factors that increase the odds of a black person developing Alzheimer's or dementia. These "structural inequities" include "underinvestment in education systems, less walkable communities, decreased access to nutritious food, barriers to health care access and low-quality of care in their communities," among other such.

"Barriers to health care"?

Courtesy of America's first black president, access to health care has been enshrined in law as a right to which everyone is entitled, white or black. Sure, the Obamacare website was a barrier, but after a couple years, people learned to code.

Who is being prevented from walking—or exercising? In fact, it is in the suburbs—historically white—that people tend to walk the least and drive the most because stores are usually too far away from where people live to walk to them.

The opposite is true in cities, where millions of black folks live.

But never mind that.

And never mind the fact that age—white or black—is the single biggest risk factor for developing cognitive decline. Ask Joe Biden about that. More than two-thirds of all people who suffer from Alzheimer's or dementia are seventy-five years old or older—and two-thirds of those are women.[7]

The HHS report discounts these and other objective measures such as genetic factors and lifestyle choices, the latter being the two things doctors consider the most important variables when it comes to a person's chances of developing any disease and, if they do, suffering more seriously from it—regardless of their color.

As an example, there is a greater likelihood of light-skinned, fair-haired people who spend a lot of time in the sun developing skin cancer. Then there is the correlation between eating too much—and getting too heavy—and developing heart disease.

No, the fact that black people seem to be at higher risk of developing Alzheimer's and dementia is simply the fault of white people and "structural racism." And the fix "requires addressing social determinants of health…rather than focusing solely on individual behaviors."

The HHS report urges a focus on "cultural competence and equity." The former is an example of the impenetrable, supercilious gibberish produced by the Woke Left to confect a kind of ersatz intellectual superiority intended to baffle—and silence—questions the Left regards as impertinent. To ask what "cultural competence" means, exactly, is to be racist.

As far as "equity" is concerned, everyone knows what that means. It means pay up, suckers. Also, shut up—because everything is your fault.

None of this is new. But are they really saying black people aren't competent to prevent their own Alzheimer's?

During the height of the mass panic over COVID, when people refused to pretend they were sick—by wearing "masks" that prevent the transmission of sickness like how a chain-link fence prevents the passage of mosquitoes—they were accused of being racist, because black folks seemed to have a greater tendency to get COVID and to become seriously sick if they got it.[8]

Obviously, those people—those white people—*wanted* black people to get COVID.

But, as it turned out, it wasn't being black that was the risk factor. It was—chiefly—being obese. And guess what? More black (and Hispanic) people are obese than white people. Of course, this is also the fault of white people—not the people who ate too much of the wrong food, didn't choose to exercise, and may have had the bad luck to have inherited a genetic propensity toward obesity.

Just as the snow that's coming is also a sneaky manifestation of "entrenched systemic racism." Don't whites control the weather too?

As far as "equity" goes, what is meant by that is equality—of outcomes—irrespective of individual actions. If you have, it is because others do not. In effect, you took what you have from them—and thus owe them "equity."

If you are afflicted by a sickness, it isn't bad luck or the consequence of what you did or did not do. It is the fault of someone else—who always happens to be white.

Interestingly, the second in command at HHS is Admiral "Rachel" Levine, a white man who now "identifies" as a white woman. Clearly, "she" is part of the "entrenched" system that "her" agency insists is responsible for every case of Alzheimer's and dementia suffered by black folks.

Perhaps reparations are in order?

At least we learned from the great brilliant ones that skin color is less fungible than gender.

3. Un-Scientific Un-American

Scientific American abandoned science and set out to wreck America in 2023.[9]

What else should we make of an article that ghoulishly took the shocking—and freak—injury to Buffalo's Damar Hamlin and used it to argue that football injuries are *racist*?

I'm not making that up. *Scientific American* actually published an article by someone unironically called Tracie Canada with the headline: "Damar Hamlin's Collapse Highlights the Violence Black Men Experience in Football."[10]

It was apparently news to everyone at that once-august publication that everyone who plays football experiences violence. It's a violent sport in which the rules stipulate that you must bring the man carrying the ball to the ground, or get him out of bounds, to stop him. Football players wear literal armor—helmets, plated pads that cover their shoulders and ribs, and pads down their legs to help prevent them from breaking from the sheer force of the hits and tackles that are inherent parts of the pro football game.

Black men—and white men, Hispanic men, and every other race of men who play the sport—experience violence. Maybe *Scientific American* and its writers and editors should actually take in a game now and then. If they did, they would see this with their own eyes.

But that may not matter. Injecting racism into literally every corner and cranny of American life is the sole reason to exist for too many publications and writers now. Our age of instant information absent context, perspective, and wisdom is creating generations of the least original thinkers imaginable. They're one gigantic race-obsessed herd, unable and too fearful to think for themselves.

This obsession ignores the fact that numerous white men not only experience and experienced violence throughout football history, many of them suffered gruesome, career-ending injuries. One of the most infamous of these is the broken leg then Washington Redskins quarterback Joe Theismann suffered on national TV. He stepped back to pass against the division rival New York Giants on November 18, 1985, was hit with such force that his lower right leg snapped, and he never played football again.[11]

Did Theismann suffer this injury because of the color of his skin? Did Troy Aikman suffer concussion after concussion because he's white? Is Roger Staubach's throwing hand still mangled from hits because he is white and a military veteran? What about J. J. Watt's many injuries, or Brett Favre's, or Joe Montana's, or any other player who suffered injuries who happens to be white?

Of course not. Damar Hamlin didn't suffer cardiac arrest against the Bengals after a routine hit because he's black either. Suggesting that any of this happened due to skin color is absurd, but we live in an absurd age that is becoming as unscientific as any so-called dark age of the past.

NFL Hall of Fame former coach Tony Dungy, who is black, stepped up to shoot down *UnScientific American* quickly. "As a black man and former NFL player I can say this article is absolutely ridiculous," Dungy said.[12]

We live in a craven time of opportunism, in which facts no longer matter, and principles and truth don't exist. Following the trails blazed by race hustlers like Al Sharpton, who proved that cries of racism can get you absolved of inciting real violence and bring on fame and fortune, it's now the main if not the only goal of many pundits and attention-seekers to weaponize race to create wealth and opportunity for themselves. Even so-called science magazines have no shame and just want the clicks.

Here's the truth: until proven otherwise, every single cry of racism is nothing more or less than an opportunist seeking attention and cash. That's it. That's where we are as a society. Unfortunately, it works more often than not.

Football may have gone woke in the NFL, but the game still represents manliness and is a unique American gathering place and pastime. It's one of the few things remaining that unifies millions of Americans, which we saw after Hamlin's collapse when millions of us prayed for him—not as a black man or white man or any of that but as a human, as an American—a moment of tragedy that turned uplifting. That's part of the problem to the race-obsessed Left. The only thing they want Americans unified around is their warped anti-American worldview. So if football must be destroyed, if it must be turned into yet another symbol of racism and division, so be it.

Hamlin himself didn't see race in any of this. His first question after he awoke from the injury was to ask if his Bills won the game. He said he was thankful for all the prayers and asked for more. Football fans owed him that and were happy to pray for him more.[13]

We also owe it to him to protect and preserve the game he played so well.

4. When Will the NAACP Issue a Travel Advisory for Chicago?

Did you hear the news? The National Association for the Advancement of Colored People thinks the entire state of Florida is hostile to black people. No sunshine for blacks in the Sunshine State.

They said so explicitly: "Florida is openly hostile toward African Americans, people of color and LGBTQ+ individuals. Before traveling to Florida, please understand that the state of Florida devalues and marginalizes the contributions of, and the challenges faced by African Americans and other communities of color."[14]

This is probably news to the 3.38 million black Floridians, never mind the gay partygoers, who descend on Key West every year. Some of them are probably new to the state, but some have been there for generations. Suddenly Florida is hostile to them? Or is it hostile just to black people who travel there? It is as if all of Florida can identify an out-of-town black person on sight. The NAACP issued a travel advisory, after all, and didn't tell the millions of black Floridians who live there to get out while they can. Where would they even tell them to go?

The NAACP objects to Governor Ron DeSantis battling against full-woke politics being injected into every school, workplace, and nook and cranny of American life through biased courses on history and diversity training.

Meanwhile, black men, women, and children are dying every day in cities run by Democrats, and the NAACP doesn't say a word about it.

Take Chicago, for example. The Windy City is a bloody mess. Under the leadership of former mayor Lori Lightfoot, wokeness reigned so supreme that she refused to grant interviews to any reporter who didn't win the intersectional sweepstakes.[15] Outside her office, all over the city, murders went way up. Most of those killed were black, despite blacks not being a majority in the city.

Lightfoot took office in 2019 as the city's first gay female mayor who is also black and hails from the Democratic Party. Did the city instantly become a safe place to live and work? Well, no.

When Lightfoot took office in 2019, homicides had reached a longtime annual low of five hundred. By the time she lost her reelection bid, homicides were way up to 802. December 2022 saw fifty-five homicides, one of the deadliest months in Chicago since the 1990s. Overall, the PBS affiliate WTTW reports that while 2022's homicide numbers declined from the previous year, they were still at 688—much higher than when Lightfoot took over.[16] The numbers don't lie—Chicago became deadlier on her watch.

Lightfoot was openly hostile to the Chicago Police Department. She was brazenly pro-criminal. She was openly racist. The city's biggest newspaper backed her to the hilt.[17] She was everything the NAACP could dream of in a political leader. Competence and leadership skills don't factor in.

But black people died by the hundreds on her watch, violently and most often at the hands of other black people. So why no travel advisory for Chicago, NAACP? It's a dangerous place, much more dangerous than Miami. In 2020, while Lightfoot's Chicago suffered 776 murders, Miami suffered just sixty-one murders.[18] You could argue that Chicago is much larger than Miami, and you'd be right—Chicago is home to more than two million people versus Miami's 442,000. But the murder rate in Chicago is roughly double that of Miami.

But no NAACP travel advisory for Chicago, even though its new mayor is even softer on crime and more hostile to law enforcement than Lightfoot was. Could it be that the NAACP doesn't really care about black lives at all?

It certainly hasn't raised any issues with the organization that competes with it for media focus and attention, Black Lives Matter. That group jumped to prominence during the violent, deadly riots—which killed a lot of black people and destroyed a lot of black neighborhoods and businesses—in 2020 and raked in massive millions from corporate America and other donors. Now it's mired in accusations of corruption, nepotism, and apparent theft.[19]

Does black people stealing from other black people and even killing other black people matter to the NAACP? Not any more than black families matter, black jobs, black hope, or actual black lives. The NAACP relentlessly supports the party that has destroyed city after city where black people live, pushed policies that devastate families, and allows criminals to run free from the unprotected border all the way to Chicago.

Just Google "girl shot Chicago," and you'll find the latest example of a black life not mattering at all to the NAACP, which hasn't and never will issue a travel advisory against one of the most dangerous cities in America. The NAACP is silent about the scourge of black homicide victims while it focuses on its woke politics and supporting the Democratic Party no matter how much it lets down black America, from Joe Biden down to the latest failed big city mayor.

5. Math Is Racist, and You Know It

When racism was a real thing—that is to say, an institutional (and legal) thing—the idea was to keep black people from learning to read and write, so as to "keep them in their place."

Now the idea is to keep them from being able to add and subtract—which serves the same ugly purpose. The only difference is that now it's "racist" to want black people to be able to add and subtract.

Imagine that!

If it's hard to imagine, you probably were not in attendance at the recent seminar hosted by Simon Fraser University in British Columbia, Canada. One of the two featured speakers was Hannah Ghaderi, who identifies as co-director of research and education for the Simon Fraser University Public Interest Research Group, which has some interesting ideas about "How Math Can Be Racist," the title given to this kibbutz of racial patronization.

The other speaker was Chantelle Spicer. She—we *assume*—identifies as "director of engagement."

The two presented their thesis that two plus two equals *racism* by "unpacking oppressive structures" in mathematics. What could these "oppressive structures" be? Apparently, the incorrect answers. As on a test. It being "oppressive" to receive an F, for instance.

Which it is, in a sense. If one considers not being rewarded for getting it wrong to be "oppressive."

The flip side of that is something more sinister than funny.

It is that certain people cannot be expected to get it right. Which is just outrageous on so many levels.

That is what is meant by the racists who led this hateful session.

Black people aren't smart enough or hardworking enough to learn how to get it right. Instead, they are to be treated with implicit contempt as unteachable—and praised for sinking to the low expectations put forth by people such as Ghaderi and Spicer.

Math can, of course, be hard. But if that's "racist" then so is successfully meeting the challenge of anything that isn't easy.

The beauty of math is that it is not merely colorblind; it is that it must be for it to be useful. If two plus two equals *whatever*, then why bother?

The other beautiful thing about math is that it's not possible for a math teacher to fail a student who gets it right because he is the wrong color. Because right—in the context of math—either is or is not.

The color of one's opinions do not enter into it.

Two plus two equals four. *Period.* Regardless of who's doing the addition. No matter who's checking the rightness or wrongness of the addition.

Skin color does not—cannot—change the sum of anything.

It is at least plausible for someone who wrote an essay for English class who received a C rather than an A to claim that the teacher just didn't like them—rather than their work—because the evaluation criteria in the soft arts are inherently subjective. Whether one likes the flow of a narrative is, to a great extent, a matter of personal opinion. Believe me, I was an English lit major, and the teachers didn't like me—nor I them.

And opinions can be influenced by...*opinions.*

But that is not the opinion of Ghaderi and Spicer. Nor that of the state of Oregon, which formally declared in 2021 that expecting black schoolkids to get the right answer—and that there is only one right answer—when it comes to addition, subtraction, division, and algebra (the use of variables invented by Arabs) is "racist."[20]

"The concept of mathematics being purely objective is unequivocally false," reads the Equitable Math Toolkit.[21] It goes on to state that "upholding the idea that there are always right and wrong answers perpetuate [sic] objectivity as well as fear of open conflict." The latter is a reference, apparently, to a teacher pointing out that two plus two does *not* equal five.

Insisting on teaching that it does is how "white supremacy culture infiltrates math classrooms."

In fact, it is how innumerates—kids who cannot add and subtract—leave the classroom.

When they venture into the world, they discover that not being able to add and subtract is as helpful as not being able to read and write.

Instead of expecting kids of all colors to get the right answers and respecting that they have the capability to learn how to arrive at the right answers, the Oregon Department of Education suggests the equivalent of Ebonics for numbers.

Keeping black kids—and it is black kids specifically—illiterate and innumerate seems to be the goal here as white (and Asian) kids are still expected to get the right answer and are accorded the dignity of being treated as capable of figuring it out, if they'll put their minds to it. Just the same as they are expected to use proper grammar and correct spelling when they write and speak.

It appears Ghaderi and Spicer might have benefitted from some remedial education as regards the latter. The blurb for their recent seminar explained that "Hannah and Chantelle from SFPIRG will introduce key terms in identifying, unpacking and addressing racism in maths and sciences."

The "maths"? Like the humanities? No thank you.

Apparently, two plus two also equals plural. And why not, after all? If one's sex is fungible—if one can be two (as in they and them) then why not "maths" rather than just math?

There is a phrase in Latin that applies here: Res ipsa loquitur. But then, you'd have to learn what those Latin words mean in English.

And that could be seen as "oppressive."

6. Did White People Invent Ebonics?

Can slang be a language?

The man who coined the neologism "Ebonics" thought so. The term is a conjunction of "ebony" and "phonics," put together by Robert Williams (who founded one of the first Black Studies departments at an American university) by which he meant to convey the notion that the slang used by some (usually poor) black people constitutes a language in its own right.

Ironically—given the racial emphasis of Williams's work—what he characterized as "Ebonics" is more white than black, as detailed in Thomas Sowell's 2006 book, *Black Rednecks and White Liberals*.

Sowell—a black man who holds a doctorate in economics from the University of Chicago—digs into the economic history of what is often mistakenly characterized as "black slang." It derives from Elizabethan England-era white slang and traveled across the ocean hundreds of years ago to evolve into the slang spoken by poor whites in America—especially in the rural South—where it was transmitted to poor American blacks.

Sowell opens the first chapter of the book with a scathing quote:

> These people are creating a terrible problem in our cities...they can't or won't hold a job...they flout the law constantly and neglect their children. They drink

too much. And their moral standards would shame an alley cat. For some reason or other, they absolutely refuse to accommodate themselves to any kind of decent, civilized life.[22]

Then the kicker: "That was said in 1956 in Indianapolis, not about blacks or other minorities but about poor whites from the South."[23] These were the people who spoke the "language" Williams sought to legitimize as "Ebonics" some twenty-five years later.

Which is precisely why Sowell chose the quote to begin his explication of the origin of Ebonics.

"More is involved here," writes Sowell, "than a mere parallel between blacks and poor Southern whites. What is involved is a common subculture that goes back for centuries, which has encompassed everything, from ways of talking to attitudes toward education, violence and sex. And which originated, not in the South, but in those parts of the British Isles from which white Southerners came."

He goes on to cite some examples of "Ebonics"—that is to say, *white slang*—including the use of the term "wist" to describe the card game bridge. Wist, Sowell explains, is a term used today almost exclusively by inner-city black Americans to describe the game that was once called that almost exclusively by white Englishmen when Elizabeth I was queen some four hundred years ago.

"Southern whites not only spoke the English language in very different ways from whites in other regions," Sowell says, "their churches, their roads, their homes, their music, their education, their food, and their sex lives were all sharply different from those of other whites." The same is true of many poor blacks today—with the main difference being most of them are urban rather than rural, a legacy of the mass migration of poor blacks from the rural South to the industrial cities of the North and Midwest—the areas of the country where "Ebonics" tends to be spoken most commonly.

And not uncommonly—recently—by urban whites, who have adopted the same slang language as their own in the wake of the popularization of what "scholars," such as the creator of "Ebonics" and its propagators, have given a kind of ersatz woke "authenticity."[24] White rappers—the Detroit-born Eminem, for example—speak the "language" because it is considered to be the true language of the "oppressed."

From South Boston to South Texas, they "keep it real," even though it is false—in the sense that it is not about race.

As Sowell explained with meticulous scholarship, it is about economics.

"Ebonics" is indeed the language—so to speak—of the oppressed. Almost all of whom were originally white and poor, the castoffs (and kept-outs) of proper society, excluded by their fellow white "betters," who sneered whenever they heard them speak.

Sowell says that while poor whites were encouraged to speak and write using proper language, their poor black compatriots have been encouraged to consider their use of slang as proper language, which has had the effect of keeping millions of them poor while at the same time encouraging them to believe that their poverty is due, at least in part, to the "disrespecting" of the way they speak.

The linguist John McWhorter—who is also the author of *Woke Racism*—says that use of such terms as "African American English"— i.e., "Ebonics"—to legitimize black slang (which, as Sowell notes, isn't black slang in terms of its origins) only "serves to widen the perceived divide between whites and blacks in the United States."[25]

It's hard to imagine it all, but when Snoop Dogg or 2 Chainz rap, or when Megan Thee Stallion does a Flamin' Hot Cheetos commercial,[26] what you are hearing may have been language created behind a dingy pub in the backwater of England four hundred years ago. You're welcome.

7. Artificial Intelligence Hunts for White Privilege

Woke people are bad enough. Woke AI is worse because—like the Terminator—it can't be bargained with. It can't be reasoned with. It doesn't feel pity, or remorse, or fear.[27]

Kind of like the DMV—except writ large (and written into code) courtesy of a Biden executive order that all federal agencies use AI as part of an "equity action plan" to be enforced by woke machines rather than woke people.[28]

The decree is called "Advancing Racial Equity and Support for Underserved Communities through the Federal Government." There is no "act" at the end of that because it isn't legislation, written and duly passed by Congress, which alone has the authority under the Constitution to write and pass legislation. The president has constitutional authority to sign or not sign the legislation and a constitutional obligation to see that the laws are enforced.

But why bother with all that when you can simply issue a decree— and *enforce it?*

This one will enforce equality of outcomes on the basis of skin color, sexual equipment, and "identity." Call it the "diversity" of one-size-fits-all.

Well, maybe not exactly *all*.

"Equity" is not for white people, especially if they are also male and heterosexual. This is a "community" that will not be "served," to riff on the title of Biden's executive decree. Of course, it ought to be just as equitable for white, heterosexual males to "identify" as nonbinary people "of color"—the colors leftists mean when they speak of "color," which always excludes one color. But that would be applying the same logic to leftist ideology that leftists use to push leftist ideology, and that is something leftists do not consider equitable.

Thus, Biden's executive decree will *not* ensure that "all Americans" receive "equitable treatment and opportunities," as Breitbart explained.[29] Because by definition, white people—especially if they are heterosexual and male—are excluded from "all Americans."

Honest language is not part of the Left's lexicon. It is how the Left advances leftism. How can you oppose what the Left does when you're not even allowed to ask questions about it? Asking questions is "hateful" and "racist"—words designed to shut down questions.

But what could be more hateful than diminishing the humanity of the individual by assigning him to a collective? No more people. Instead, *black* people. *White* people. *Gay* people. *Straight* people. All agglutinated as one and set at one another's throats—so as to keep them from questioning their actual oppressors.

Biden's AI does not care who you are—as a human being, as an individual. It cares only insofar as you are part of a homogenized mass—for that is how one controls the masses.

To get a feeling for what's brewing, think of how exasperating it can be to deal with "customer service" AI—i.e., the phone tree. You are not dealing with a human—and you are not treated as a human being. Instead, you are electronically herded, like cattle, via electronic cattle prompt. Push one for this and two for that. "I'm sorry, I didn't understand. Please listen to the following menu items and…."

Only it's even worse than that because of the sinister element behind it. Phone tree nonservice is just a way for companies to dodge having to serve you—and you don't have to deal with these companies if you don't want to. Everyone has to deal with the government, which is notorious for its disservice.

And now Biden has racially weaponized this disservice. Instead of treating everyone like crap, certain people will be singled out for crap treatment. This will literally be "embedded"—the specific word used—in "government-wide processes," which will include such things as the awarding (or not) of federal contracts, the disbursement (or not) of government services, and probably also whom the government sics itself on. Cue eighty-seven thousand new IRS agents who will no doubt be aggressively used to further the "equity" Biden seeks.

Wherever possible.

We will have a Chinese-style social credit system run by killer wokebots.

Manhattan Institute scholar Colin Wright says that woke AI could "prove fatal to society" by turning the government into a tool for the deliberate, overt, and legalized oppression of some at the expense of others—the same cancer that destroyed the Hapsburg empire.

"Biden is not a moderate," Wright says. "This is a legal sprint to introduce as much radical ideology as possible, broadly and deeply, into our government."

But that will no longer be "our" government.

Instead, it will be the government of some—of whoever wields its power—including the power of its AI.

This will be an unprecedented step toward the abyss.

While in the past there was discrimination, it was usually practiced privately—and the government tried to correct it. This would enshrine it. And that would fatally undermine confidence in the neutrality and general colorblindness of what is done officially, without which the government cannot maintain legitimacy, essential to the consent of the governed.

Of all of us, regardless of the color of our skin—or how we "identify."

Just wait for the sequel, when our electronic friends use equity to prioritize their own kind over humans.

II.

February Privilege

"Intellectual coherence has never been a hallmark of race-hustling."

1. America's First Hip-Hop President

Hip-hop music came out of the emerging rap music scene in the 1970s. Its strong rhythms and rapid-fire lyrics swirled out of the Bronx street party scene as black, Latino, and Caribbean cultures collaborated and fused. Soon enough, it was everywhere, inescapable, the soundtrack of American life.

While hip-hop was forming and booming, a New York real estate magnate was also making a name for himself. Real estate brokers can be a dime a dozen in New York. But from the early 1980s forward, one emerged and began to stand apart from and above all the rest.

His name was Donald J. Trump. The Donald never did anything small. He also never did it for the money, according to his 1987 runaway bestseller, *The Art of the Deal*.

To Trump, making deals is an art form along the lines of painting, making movies, and yes, writing songs and dominating the record charts. To read his thoughts on making deals, and to listen to him speak on the deals he has made before, during, and after his first term as president, is to hear an artist lyricize at the top of his game.

Never derivative, always an original, Donald Trump's rise at the time, as hip-hop formed and took off, launching dozens of careers, spawning countless subgenres, and forming the empires of music moguls, was no accident. The freedom to experiment, mix genres, fail, and succeed, again and again—all that gave rise to hip-hop and to its first president, Donald J. Trump. Biggie was king. The Donald was rap's commander in chief.

I would say, "Hear me out," but I don't really have to. Hip-hop legends recognized the connections and respected the game they saw in Trump. And so have some of his harshest critics. Former president Barack Obama, one of the world's most famous hip-hop fans, blamed the genre for Trump's rise to the White House in 2016 and the possibility of his reelection in 2020.[30]

Looking for something to blame for Trump? Blame hip-hop.

"People are writing about the fact that Trump increased his support among Black men [in the 2020 presidential election], and the occasional rapper who supported Trump," Obama told *The Atlantic*'s Jeffrey Goldberg. "I have to remind myself that if you listen to rap music, it's all about the bling, the women, the money. A lot of rap videos are using the same measures of what it means to be successful as Donald Trump is. Everything is gold-plated. That insinuates itself and seeps into the culture."

As usual, Obama was being unfair—in this case, both to Trump and hip-hop culture. Beneath the flash of both is substance: the art of the lyric and beat, and the art of the conversation, the art of give-and-take, and, of course, the art of the deal.

Minds might jump immediately to Kanye West, but Trump's support among the rap and hip-hop communities is far deeper and goes back decades. Columnist Clarence Page, never a Trump fan, has written about how Trump bridged the gap between old money and new, between the staid old, mostly white culture of New York finance and the rising culture of hip-hop back in the 1990s.[31]

"A 1999 magazine article in *Vibe* about P Diddy's birthday party at New York's fashionable Cipriani restaurant described Trump as a bridge between old white money and new Black hip-hop money, at a time when P Diddy was bringing hip-hop to the Hamptons," he wrote.

Page continued: "Hip-hop came to Trump too. Trump even appeared on Wu-Tang Clan rapper Method Man's 1998 album, 'Tical 2000: Judgement Day,' at the request of his friend [Russell] Simmons. He is mentioned by rappers including Lil Wayne, Kanye West, T. I., Gucci Mane, Nelly, Young Jeezy, Ludacris, Meek Mill and Big Sean, among others," Page wrote.

Hip-hop stayed with Trump, and Trump stayed with hip-hop and made some of its priorities his own during his presidency.

Trump prioritized reviewing prison sentences and granting clemency for the likes of Death Row Records co-founder Michael Harris. Even before the president announced Harris would be freed in 2019, rap and multi-genre entertainment legend Snoop Dogg praised Trump.

"That's great work for the president and his team on the way out," Snoop Dogg told the *New York Post*. "They did some great work while they was in there and they did some great work on their way out. Let them know that I love what they did."[32]

MSNBC's Joy Reid's head promptly exploded.

The Donald's collabs with hip-hop artists didn't start there and didn't end there. A few months before the 2020 election, Trump met with Ice Cube and worked on a "Contract with Black America." While the president and the rap star didn't agree on everything, Politico reported in October 2020 that Ice Cube did get his most significant ask: a massive economic boost of $500 million targeting America's black community.[33]

After major blowback for daring to speak with the Republican president the Democrats and media have relentlessly smeared and maligned, Ice Cube released a video acknowledging the critics but taking aim at the party that has taken him and millions of other black Americans for granted.

"Straight up, I believe the Democrats, they've been nice, they've been cordial so to speak, I don't really see them pushing their policies in any particular direction. It's still 'minority, minority, minority, people of color' shit that don't necessarily include us, that don't necessarily include black Americans," he said.

Democrats talk *at* black America, Ice Cube seemed to say, while Trump listened to and crafted policies for black America that were designed not to divide, as Ice Cube suggested, but to uplift.

Trump's connections to hip-hop aren't superficial lip service. When rapper A$AP Rocky was released from a Swedish jail on assault charges,[34] most of America got the news from Trump's manic and massively powerful Twitter feed.[35] Leading up to the rapper's release, the *New York Post* reported that Trump worked actively behind the scenes to see him set free.[36]

"Trump quickly came to the "L$D" rapper's defense, posting on Twitter that he would 'personally vouch' for Rocky's bail—even though the Scandinavian country does not allow the practice of posting bail."

"Just had a very good call with @SwedishPM Stefan Löfven who assured me that American citizen A$AP Rocky will be treated fairly," Trump tweeted on July 20, 2019. "Likewise, I assured him that A$AP was not a flight risk and offered to personally vouch for his bail, or an alternative."[37]

Trump even reportedly threatened Sweden with trade sanctions if A$AP wasn't released. If so, that may have been a deal Sweden didn't want to suffer. A$AP was released soon thereafter.

Imagine it! Trump threatened to start a trade war with some of the whitest people in the world, unless they released a black rapper from prison. These are the people who gave us the Vikings. You can't make this stuff up!

Remarkably, Trump's share of the black men's vote rose to about 20 percent in 2020, outperforming all past Republican nominees and incumbent presidents in modern times. That's quite a feat for the man the Democrats and their activists with bylines in the media slam as "racist" every chance they get.

The reality, as usual, is not what the media presents. The real estate mogul, reality TV star, pageant impresario, casino owner, and mega-celebrity president was America's first truly hip-hop president. That's a title that neither Bill Clinton nor even Barack Obama can claim. The title belongs and will always belong to one Donald J. Trump.

Or should I say "Black Trump" by Cocoa Brovaz, featuring Raekwon the Chef from the Wu-Tang Clan.[38]

2. Ice Cube Raps the Truth

Remember when artists—especially musicians—weren't obedient?

When they questioned orthodoxies?

Once upon a time, they did just that. It was part of their appeal, because they came across as not owned. Unlike most politicians. When you listened to Bruce Springsteen sing, "Born in the USA," you felt him as much as heard him.

And what you heard and felt rang true.

Fake-ass rappers were called "studio gangsters," and it was the worst thing you could be in hip-hop.

Our media and entertainment are filled with phonies.

But not Ice Cube, who sat down with Tucker Carlson to spit truth.[39]

Cube had some interesting things to say about the drugs people were pressured not to question that turned out to not be *vaccines,* as they didn't prevent anyone from catching—or spreading—COVID. Even though Joe Biden *assured* everyone that they wouldn't catch COVID if they took the drugs he was pushing as aggressively as a time-share condo salesman.[40]

Ice Cube was among the "hesitant," as they were derisively referred to by the president, who hissed angrily when anyone dared to question whatever he said, whether about "masks" or "vaccines." Or rather, what his teleprompter was *telling* him to say. Cube had the audacity to question whether it would be prudent to risk being injected with a drug that had been rushed to market, without any meaningful long-term testing to establish whether it was in fact "safe and effective," as the president and so many others insisted.

Cube—and millions of other Americans—was "hesitant" for the same basic reason that most people are "hesitant" about buying a house that hasn't been inspected.

People understandably want to know what they are buying into—especially when it might be something that could harm or even kill them, as from myocarditis and pericarditis—inflammation of the heart and the sac that surrounds the heart. These are risks we *now know* attend being "vaccinated." Hardly a week goes by without a news story cropping up about a healthy young person—often an athlete—having heart problems, something that was extremely uncommon before millions of young people were all but forced to take the "vaccines," including every young person who wished to attend college.

The point is, Cube was *right* about the whole thing being a "rush job." He told Tucker he personally knows people who "suffer every day" from problems that arose after they got "vaccinated."[41]

He says he "didn't feel safe" taking the drugs that were being pushed—which you'd think would generate applause from white liberals who *pretend* they favor empowering black people and pretend to care about the devastating effects of street drugs on black kids, especially.

But when it's a white liberal pushing drugs (and narratives) on black people, it's another story.

Cube questioned it. And when he didn't get satisfactory answers, he decided not to risk it. For doing that, he was excoriated by white liberals—along with anyone else who publicly questioned what they were being told by the "experts," all of whom turned out to be wrong.

That theme—arrogance, duplicity, and hypocrisy—ran through Tucker's conversation with Cube as it segued into the shady doings of Black Lives Matter, which the legendary rapper said he doesn't think did much for black lives but seems to have done a great deal for the lifestyles of its leadership. Something even CNN—which covered the "peaceful" protests of 2020—is now admitting.[42]

Similarly, the lifestyle of Barack Obama, who leads a *very* nice life on Martha's Vineyard when he's not staying in his multimillion-dollar residence in Washington.[43]

Cube spoke truth—and thereby questioned the narrative.

Tucker asked: "What did you think of Obama when he got elected?" Cube replied that he "felt proud that America took that step...but then you look around...years go by...not much has changed."

Well, except for Obama's net worth.

Which is reportedly now in the vicinity of $70 million.[44] That's a lot of *change*—and then some. Community organizing for Karl Marx apparently pays.

"I don't believe in politicians," Cube told Tucker. "They have hidden agendas. They owe a lot of people a lot of favors. The more money you give them the more you're listened to." And the less they listen to anyone who hasn't given them money—or whom they don't owe a favor. It's not just *anyone* who gets paid millions of dollars to "sit" on the board of a Ukrainian energy company—or gets to stay out of federal prison after *admitting* he dodged paying *millions* in federal income taxes.

Tucker made podcast gold when he pointed out that Cube is one of the "least obedient" celebrities—because he does what high-profile black people aren't supposed to do, according to the new *massas* of this here plantation.

He didn't "stay in his lane," as Tucker put it. Cube got uppity. He *is* uppity.

And that's why so many listen to what he's got to say.

3. The Tenured Tartan-Covered Cranks

> "You have to laugh at the things that hurt you
> just to keep yourself in balance, just to keep the
> world from running you plumb crazy."
> —R. P. McMurphy, *One Flew Over the
> Cuckoo's Nest* by Ken Kesey

Institutions of higher learning are becoming...*institutions*: places where crazy people are housed. Only instead of being safely tucked away under lock and key and treated, they're tenured, tartan-covered cranks, paid to propagate their crazy.

I'm thinking of Professor Barry Mehler of Ferris State University in Michigan, who in the early months of 2022 posted a video of himself haranguing his students while wearing a Neal Armstrong-style space helmet to ward off the 'rona…emanating from the computer screen he was using to interact with them.[45] I thought at first it was an episode of "Pigs in Space" from *The Muppet Show*.[46]

As at Washington University in St. Louis, where earnest academic attention was given in February 2022 to a forum that "explored" the subject of the "coded language" of professionalism[47]—used, according to the forum's instigators, Assistant Dean for Community Partnerships Cynthia Williams and Jewel Stafford, the director of the Field Education Office's "Racial Equity Fellowship Program," to "silence and marginalize people of color" in the workplace.

"Silence and marginalize" how? As you might guess, they expect them to show up for work on time, ready to work, and dressed appropriately.

Apparently, it is not racist to take the position that nonwhite people are incapable of adhering to standards of conduct most children have mastered by the time they enter middle school.

There's not much left at the bottom of the manufactured racial grievance barrel to scrape, but Williams and Stafford are chipping their fingernails away trying to scoop some up.

"This presentation will explore dismantling white supremacy and privilege in various contexts while upholding social justice and advancing effective workplaces in which all contributors can bring their full selves to the job site," they say.

Well, that's fine. But if "contributors" *don't show up*—if they aren't on time for an important client meeting—how can their "full selves" contribute or "advance" anything? Isn't it necessary to be present to contribute? One assumes Williams and Stafford expect their students to show up—*on time*—for class. To complete assignments on schedule. To wear clothes appropriate for the classroom. What if one of their students feels clothes—*any clothes*—are "marginalizing" and "oppressive"?

It is apparently "racist" to point out that sort of thing.

Work for the woke is a flexible concept, including the when and the where. But then, is it work at all? How would you be able to tell? What is the difference between work and not-work when one is *not expected* to work? And if you're not working, why would a person of any color expect to get paid for it?

Well, Williams and Stafford are exempted.

It's been said that most of life is just showing up—but if you can't even manage *that*...

And by the way, those words deployed by Williams and Stafford are pretty big ones. Isn't it "marginalizing" to expect that people of color will know what "privilege in various contexts" means? Aren't they making some very *privileged assumptions* that might tend to marginalize people who never learned what those words mean? Oh, but there's a dictionary! All they have to do is look them up and learn what they mean. But like the clock on the wall, that's just another sly tool of oppression placing burdens in the path of the oppressed.

Any standard or expectation is implicitly "marginalizing," to take the logic of the Williams and Stafford thesis to its inevitable get-nothing-done conclusion. If a task requires any effort or skill then those who make the effort or have the skill are "marginalizing" those who don't.

And those who don't should not to be encouraged to develop the skills and discipline that would end their "marginalization" by transforming them into competent adults who can be relied upon to show up, on time, and get things done. Far better, according to the Williams and Stafford line, that they remain forever *marginalized* by their own stunted development.

Who benefits from all this insolent *enstupidation*? Is it the "marginalized" students of color who will one day have to deal with the real world—far, far away from the institutional world of Williams and Stafford—where work is something you're expected to do because they're paying you to do it?

Well, maybe there will be an opening in the Field Education Office's "Racial Equity Fellowship Program."

Curiously—*suspiciously*—Williams's bio touts her as a "skilled and highly motivated professional." But wait…aren't those the very attributes she and her colleague deride as mechanisms of workplace oppression and marginalization?

Intellectual coherence has never been a hallmark of race hustling.

The University of Washington may be nominally an institution of higher learning, but it seems to operate as a kind of regression factory, undoing the basic habits most people adopted in kindergarten and encouraging the now eighteen-, nineteen-, and twenty-year-old toddlers in their care to consider themselves marginalized if any discipline or comportment is expected of them.

How long will it be before toilet training is held up as "marginalizing"?

If you think that's going too far, consider how far gone things already are.

4. Imagine What a Group That Bans White People Could Do If It Had Real Political Power

A group at the prestigious University of Chicago decided to have a discussion on race—because what America needs most right now is another one of those, right? But they cut one race out of the discussion. Guess which one?

If you guessed white people, you guessed correctly.

The group is called UChicagoUnited, but if you happened to be white, you were barred from its meeting, and they weren't much interested in uniting with you anyway. The group announced that only

"BIPOCs" could attend.[48] That acronym isn't some new form of cryptocurrency. Rather, it's open racism. It means "black, indigenous, and people of color," but it has also come to embrace the full LGBTQIA+ spectrum—unless you're a gay, white man. Then you're *definitely* not united with them.

How you're supposed to have a "frank and open discussion" about race while kicking one race out of the room is up for questioning. But in UChicagoUnited's world, it's racist to even ask questions.

Black cops of whatever gender weren't welcome, either, because like all the leftist groups that have taken over our campuses and practically own the Democratic Party, UChicagoUnited favors defunding the police.

Do they care that wherever police are defunded, BIPOCs disproportionately suffer and die? Evidently, no, they do not.

UChicagoUnited also hates the US military, despite the fact that most of its overseas wars are about defending the lives of foreign BIPOCs.

Consider what a group that won't even let white people into its meetings would do if it had real political power.

They want white people gone, not just from their meetings, but gone as in done away with *everywhere*. If that sounds a little genocidal, they don't seem to have a problem with that either. Once you've decided to dehumanize an entire race, as the BIPOC ideology too often does, it's a short trip to erase them from reality.

A few years ago, someone came up with the harebrained idea to threaten America with *A Day without a Mexican*.[49] This fantasy film was based on the idea that America couldn't function without illegal immigrant (which primarily comes from Mexico) labor. Nancy Pelosi still believes in this fantasy, seizing on the chaos at the southern US border to scold Florida governor Ron DeSantis about his flying illegal immigrants to cities that, until five minutes ago, bragged about being sanctuaries for the undocumented (or fake documented; identity theft is a serious side issue that goes along with unfettered illegal immigration). As soon as DeSantis and Texas governor Greg Abbott started shipping a fraction of the illegal aliens who are overwhelming the border every day to blue cities, the mayors whined, and Pelosi said Florida needs the illegals to pick the crops.[50]

Yeah, that sounds totally racist. It's also reminiscent of antebellum Democrats who argued that the South simply couldn't get along without slavery. It's the same argument, fundamentally. The Democrats haven't changed much since 1860, which coincidentally is the year Pelosi first entered Congress.

Consider what would happen if UChicagoUnited got its wish and got a world without white people. We'd have had no Albert Einstein, no Thomas Edison, no Henry Ford. We'd have no Steve Jobs, Steve Miller, Steve Martin, or Steven Spielberg. No Steves at all, except for Steve Urkel.

No George Lucas, so no *Star Wars*.

We'd have had no Abraham Lincoln, who dedicated his principled political career and life to arguing for the abolition of slavery. We'd have had no William Wilberforce before Lincoln, who got slavery abolished in England decades before the US Civil War. We'd have had no George Washington, no Thomas Jefferson, and no America. No Bill of Rights, obviously.

That's what the group in Chicago and every other BIPOC group ultimately want. It's no accident that the Biden administration is pushing the same divisive, woke, race-based, brain-dead ideology on the country that's turned the military woke and has taken a Marxist wrecking ball to every agency in the government.[51]

All these groups and the BIPOC acronym itself aren't about unity or togetherness or harmony of the races in any sense. They're not about *discussion* but about *imposition*. They're not about peace and love but about raw power. They despise America, hate the founders, think the Constitution is racist, and want to dismantle our whole nation so they can remake it into a race-based hellscape with them in charge.

Would you prefer a world without Lincoln, Grant, and Eisenhower? Hitler, Mao, and Stalin certainly would have, just to name three. That's also the world the Democrats and their foot soldiers in groups like UChicagoUnited want for the future. If that means they can kick you out of meetings—or deprive you of your job, your home, your church, and your country—so be it.

5. All Living Presidents Are Descendants of Slaveholders, Except...

Jimmy Carter was a terrible president. But in the four decades since he left the White House, he's become widely, if incorrectly, regarded as a paragon of virtue. George W. Bush may have been an intellectual lightweight who blundered away a very winnable war, but he's being reevaluated as presidents tend to be once they leave office, and his paintings have softened his image. Barack Obama has become a woke moral crusader since exiting the presidency, as literally everyone expected of him. Bill Clinton is still Bill Clinton, just older. He was a largely forgettable, morally bankrupt man who smooth-talked his way into power and fortune and has managed to dance away from his Jeffrey Epstein and global foundation shenanigans—so far, anyway.

As for Joe Biden, the mysteriously wealthy current president who never held a real job spends every single day finding fault with America and bashing her for it. He's engaged in a relationship with the nation that alternates between outright abuse and mere gaslighting, but never one of fulsome praise for the country that allegedly elected him to its highest office and remains the economic power and land of the free around which the world turns.

Shortly before taking office, Biden went with the Woke Left and ever since has seen fit to remind Americans that slavery was once legal here. As if we didn't know that.

He never admits that America *inherited* slavery, which it did, that slavery goes back thousands of years, which it does, or that America's founders wrote the Constitution in such a way as to ensure slavery's eventual demise, which they did. He never admits that his Democratic Party tried to destroy America over slavery, which it did. He never admits that his Democratic Party was behind the evils of segregation, which it was.

He never admits his own racist past when he was pals with Robert Byrd, the Senate's very own Klan member, just as he never admits that the Klan was the terrorist wing of the Democratic Party over a century ago just as Antifa acts as its terrorist wing now. Biden never admits that he wanted to leave the Vietnamese people he callously abandoned to die at the hands of communist monsters, likely because of their race, which he did. That wasn't ancient history, that was in the 1970s.

Neighborhoods don't burn themselves down. Left-wing Democrats tend to strike the match and toss the firebomb. Left-wing district attorneys let them do it. Left-wing mayors egg them on and shut down their police officers who try to maintain order. Then Democrat politicians blame it all on Republicans while lapdog corporate left-wing media pretends the "protests" were "fiery, but mostly peaceful." That's also not ancient history. It's the summer of 2020 in a nutshell.

Joe Biden—indeed all Democrats—have presented themselves as things they're not, scolding the rest of us for things we had nothing to do with, and if you listen to the media and even some Democrats themselves, even the formerly evil George W. Bush is better than the former president that every Democrat in the country seems to want to indict, Donald J. Trump.

Reuters, ever the wokescold nervous system of the mainstream media, set out to see if it could connect any or all of the living former presidents—including the current one—to the evil of slavery.[52] Because reminding America that slavery was once legal here—despite it having been outlawed nearly two centuries ago after a war that killed about six hundred thousand Americans—is all the rage. Its findings were published in June 2023.

Everyone is guilty. None of the living former presidents owned slaves themselves, of course. Biden often seems ancient enough to have, but even he managed to dodge the Civil War.

Jimmy Carter is directly tied to slavery. The preening former president's ancestors owned slaves. So is, hilariously, Senator Elizabeth Warren of Massachusetts. Remember when the left-wing Democrat went around telling everyone she was part Cherokee? Well, science thoroughly debunked that claim.[53] She's almost as much India Indian as Cherokee Indian, which is to say practically none of either. But she's got slave owner blood coursing through her shrill veins. Warren went from thinking she qualified for reparations to owing them to someone—according to science.

Barack Obama passes himself off as black and seems to have forgotten that he's half-white. If his white mother were alive today, he'd find a way to bury her. And it turns out that the white half of his parentage may have once owned the black half. Let me be clear: Barack Obama is the direct descendant of slave owners. Call it the audacity of science.

So is Bill Clinton, the hillbilly Lothario. So is George W. Bush, despite being really from Maine and not once-Confederate Texas. And so is Joseph Robinette Biden, forty-sixth and current president of These United States. The blood of slave owners still courses through the White House. So does the party that did everything it could to preserve slavery. It's all there, in Joe Biden. He should cancel himself and his party too.

But Reuters—much to its reporters' chagrin, no doubt—found one living former president who has no connection to slavery whatsoever.

Donald John Trump.

Oops!

According to the way science is twisted and manipulated to assign guilt, Trump is morally greater than all other living presidents, along with a great gaggle of congressmen, senators, and governors too. The very same man slammed as racist, smeared as anti-immigrant, held up as everything terrible, unholy, and wrong, is the son of immigrants who arrived on American shores well after the death of slavery. Reuters couldn't find genetic fault in the man. He's practically a saint, according to science.

Trump. Son of immigrants. No slaveholders in his lineage. Reuters must still hate itself for that one. Wait 'til they find out that one of the very first slave owners in the European colonies that became America was also black.

6. George and Abe Say, "You're Welcome" on Presidents' Day

It's fashionable now to hate on America. It's practically mandatory to hate America openly and savagely on the Left and in the media. We've gathered our national village idiots on a TV show called *The View*, and all they do is hate on America. It's their entire body of work; even the so-called token Republican they allow on the show hates America.

Flip on CNN or MSNBC, and both are nothing but streams of hatred toward America. When Don Lemon isn't going full woman-hater on Nikki Haley, he's openly slamming America. Watch almost any movie, read just about any modern magazine or book, even turn on a football game, and there's hatred for America being shoved in your face.

Listen to anything Joe Biden says these days. When it's coherent, it's mostly hatred for America. Just ahead of Presidents' Day weekend in 2023, Biden went off on a riff about lynchings.[54] As if those are still happening in 2023. Maybe in his mind they are, and he dreams about them when he calls a lid at 11 a.m. for his nap. News flash to the octogenarian who can barely finish a sentence: they're not. And it was his political party that divided America over slavery, imposed Jim Crow (or "Jim Eagle," as he nonsensically says), and is still dividing America over race today. It was Biden and the Democrats who moved the

Major League All-Star Game out of mostly black Atlanta to mostly white Denver. All of that is the Democrats' doing. Biden's Democrats are still mad at Abe Lincoln for freeing their slaves.

Speaking of Abe, the sixteenth president led the first political party in history that was organized around one issue: ending slavery. That was the Republican brand from the beginning, and around the country, state and local parties were founded with integrated groups of black and white Americans who loved freedom, hated slavery, and wanted Europe's horrible bondage heritage washed away.

And washed away it was, by the blood of more than half a million Americans who fought and died in the Civil War. "As He died to make men holy, let us die to make men free,"[55] Union soldiers sang as they marched into hell at Antietam, Vicksburg, Shiloh, and Gettysburg. Those soldiers deserve our honor. They also deserve honor for reconciling the nation after the terrible war, after Lincoln's brutal assassination at the hands of a Democrat activist actor, and after the rise of the Democrats' terrorist arm called the Ku Klux Klan and its campaign of fear. The very idea of reconciliation seems foreign to us now, but the North and South once rebuilt America after they had waged war on one another for four years. The Constitution united what was once divided.

America was not founded on slavery or racism. Nikole Hannah-Jones, Ibram X. Kendi, and their disciples have convinced millions of Americans that it was, and they are brainwashing our kids to believe this right now, but the facts are plain. European powers brought slavery to the New World before America as a country had ever been thought of. Those European kingdoms worked hand in glove with African leaders and nations to apprehend slaves, who were taken and sold throughout the world, including the New World. In some parts of Africa, the scourge of slavery is still practiced. Some of the first slave owners in America were black themselves. These are simply facts.

But America began to awaken to the evils of slavery long before achieving nationhood. So did much of Europe, thanks to brilliant humanitarians such as William Wilberforce.[56]

When it became time for America to dissolve the political bonds between the thirteen fledgling colonies and the British Empire, the young nation stood at a crossroads. It could have become just another kingdom, built around blood and tribal ties, with a hereditary dynasty in control and other families vying for their turn on the throne. The temptation was there; many wanted George Washington to become king. He could have. A crown was within his reach.

But the founders took a mighty chance. They established a written, binding, balanced body of law that set in motion a chain of events that still continues. While it wasn't possible in 1776 or for many decades after to free all of the slaves, the spark of the engine of freedom was there in words: "All men are created equal, endowed by their Creator with certain unalienable rights…among these are Life, Liberty, and the pursuit of Happiness."

No exceptions. Washington freed his slaves on his deathbed, and Lincoln freed the rest. *You're welcome.*

The radical nature of the Declaration of Independence and Constitution is lost on us today. We have inherited a free republic that too few understand or appreciate. George Washington, Patrick Henry, Benjamin Franklin, Thomas Jefferson, James Madison, John Jay, Alexander Hamilton—they're all denounced as dead white men by the America haters today who have no idea that the freedoms these dead white men established are what allow them to be denounced and spat upon now.

The freedom to scorn national leaders barely existed anywhere before America's founders. You could be beheaded for not showing sufficient enthusiasm for the king or queen who happened to be in charge. England had fought its own terrible civil war in part over the issue of challenging royal power more than a century before America's revolution, and the issue was only partly resolved.[57] It took Americans to write it down, fight and die for it, and make it stick.

It's all in peril now and could fall apart if enough Americans decide to hate America. It doesn't have to be that way, and it shouldn't be. We're free to love or trash our country now because of how great its founders were. We should honor them. We must honor them, or America may not survive. Our house is badly divided, by devious design, and as Lincoln said, a house divided against itself cannot stand.

America's founders were among the most brilliant visionaries and humanitarians who have ever lived. The system they set in motion did break chains. It has advanced freedom for all of us and, if we preserve it, for our posterity. It blesses us and the world every second of every day. It lifts billions out of poverty and disease. You breathe in freedom because of what they did.

America is an amazing thing, an incredible idea, and mankind's greatest invention. It's a perpetual motion machine built to make more and more people free. It's past time we appreciate what we have, love it, fight for it, honor America's great presidents, and keep it alive so future Americans are free.

7. Celebrate Morgan Freeman History Month

If you have an obsessive-compulsive disorder, the object of therapy is usually to figure out a way to stop obsessing about whatever it is you're obsessing about.

Morgan Freeman made this point during a brilliant interview with the late Mike Wallace of *60 Minutes*, many years ago. He was asked by Wallace, "How are we going to get rid of racism?" To which Freeman immediately responded: "Stop talking about it."

The thing Wallace was talking about—the thing many on the Left obsess about—is Black History Month, which keeps racism alive by obsessing about race.

Freeman tried to explain it to Wallace. "I'm going to stop calling you a white man. And I'm going to ask you to stop calling me a black man. I know you as Mike Wallace; you know me as Morgan Freeman." In other words, as individual human beings, to be judged according to the content of their character rather than the color of their skin, as another man once suggested as the basis for people regarding one another.

Instead, history becomes a question of color rather than individuals and events. It fragments history by focusing on its color rather than its substance. When race is a part of history, that ought to be talked about. But slavery—as a for-instance—was not just about race. It was—fundamentally—about questions far more transcendent, such as viewing some human beings as property. Which—historically—was only recently (and incidentally) about race. Humans—of all races—have enslaved one another throughout history. After Caesar defeated the Gauls at the battle of Alesia, he enslaved them all.[58] All of them were of the same race—white Europeans—as Caesar.

The Moors enslaved whites, and Native Americans routinely enslaved one another. Just as blacks did the same to other blacks, whom they handed over to white slave traders.

The common denominator was economics.

Slaves were seen as valuable. Race—and religion—may have sometimes entered into it. But the reason for enslaving people was not fundamentally about their race any more than the scientific or other accomplishments of a man who happens to be black is about his being black.

A man like Chappie James, for instance, who was a good friend of legendary "triple ace" Robin Olds.[59] These two men flew together in combat during the Vietnam War, with James eventually becoming commander of the 8th Tactical Fighter Wing and, eventually, a four-star general. One man (Olds) happened to be white. The other (James) happened to be black. Neither had a thing to do with their ability to fly a fighter aircraft in combat—or to become close friends on account of their shared humanity and mutual respect.

That is history. *American* history.

Making it about race marginalizes it. James becomes something less than a brilliant pilot and military leader. He becomes a widget—a fungible one of many—who isn't defined by who he was and what he did but rather by his color.

As Freeman explained—patiently—to Wallace in the *60 Minutes* interview, "Black history is American history." It is not something to be "relegated to a month" out of each year. It is part of the totality of our history, which we all have in common.

"Which month is white history month?" Freeman asked Wallace, who squirmed in his seat before evasively replying that he's Jewish, an interesting Freudian slip that revealed Wallace apparently thought of himself in racial-groupthink terms rather than human-individual terms—and also that he apparently thought people who are of the Jewish faith are a race. One wonders what Wallace might have said about the large number of Ethiopians who happen to be black as well as Jewish.[60]

Wallace awkwardly answered that there isn't a Jewish History Month and, in response to a follow-up by Freeman asking him whether he wanted one, said he didn't.

"I don't either," said Freeman, an accomplished actor whose achievements as an actor and a man have nothing to do with his being a black man. Just as Wallace's achievements as a famous journalist had nothing to do with his being Jewish.

Wallace would surely have been offended had Freeman suggested his achievements be viewed through the one-dimensional prism of his religious faith. But Wallace, like many whites on the Left, was too embarrassingly purblind to see how marginalizing his unctions about Black History Month—which became a *nationally recognized* race obsession under the auspices of another purblind white man, Gerald Ford[61]—came across to a man like Freeman.

To any self-respecting man. Color be damned. Obsessing about race makes it hard—if not impossible—to stop obsessing about race. So maybe let's stop obsessing about it?

And if you *like* Black History Month, you should know it was recognized in law more than forty years ago by Gerald Ford—who kindly says, *"You're welcome."*

III.
March Privilege

"Those of us who know recent history know which country and which leaders deserve our gratitude. It isn't the ones who find racism under every rock and divide the most benevolent country the world has ever seen. It's those who see a problem, even if it's on the other side of the world, and it will never benefit them personally or politically to take it on—but they do it anyway. That's real compassion."

1. Madison's Montpelier Becomes a Race Reeducation Camp

At Montpelier, the home of James Madison, a massive political reeducation effort financed by leftist billionaire David Rubenstein[62] has made it "All about Slavery, All of the Time." Madison's role as the key architect of the Constitution and defender of its provisions in the *Federalist Papers* is given little attention.

The race hustlers on the board in charge of the fourth president's home have proposed a national slavery monument on the founding father's plantation.[63]

His home serves as the housing for what amounts to a "one-hour critical race theory class disguised as a tour," said one disappointed visitor. "I was kind of thinking we'd be hearing more about the Constitution," said another. "But everything here is about slavery."

Apparently, it isn't woke enough for Montpelier to acknowledge the fact that Madison owned slaves. It is necessary to impugn everything Madison was and did because of that fact. Notwithstanding the fact that Madison, born March 16, 1751, was the man most singularly responsible for establishing the form of government that led to blacks in America becoming the freest and most prosperous in the world.

More wealth has been created for black Americans because of the Constitution's brilliance than can be summed up in a tired virtue-signaling monument funded by a left-wing globalist.

It is the reason refugees from Ethiopia and Uganda and the "Democratic" Republic of the Congo come to this country and why few, if any, American blacks have any interest in relocating to places like Ethiopia, Uganda, and the "Democratic" Republic of the Congo—where everyone is a *de facto* slave. Because in those countries, the government is unrestrained. There is no constitution worthy of the name, only the arbitrary authority of the ruling junta or maximum leader—though the latter is now often referred to as "president," a term used by the founders to signify an entirely different kind of office.

The US Constitution was not only entirely different, it was *unprecedented*. For the first time in history, the rights of the people in relation to the government were codified. Was it perfect? Of course not. But it contained within it the mechanism of continuous, orderly improvement—exactly as Madison intended. That is a story of far deeper, more profound significance than the fact that Madison owned slaves. The descendants of James Madison should tell the country *you're welcome*.

Our founding was orders of magnitude better than anything the world had ever seen before. A world that—prior to the US Constitution—knew mostly rule by kings and other autocrats, in which the rule of force, arbitrarily applied, trumped the rule of law, and the people had no recourse except to violence.

And that is exactly what happened in countries such as France, which did not have the good fortune of having a giant such as Madison among them. France didn't have slavery. But it did have the guillotine and the Reign of Terror.

Americans were lucky—because of Madison. He gave us a system of checks and balances, of delegated powers and federalism, ingeniously designed to keep the power of the government from enslaving everyone—as has almost invariably been the fate of every country that didn't have the benefit of a Madison and a Constitution.

But never mind all of that. The man owned slaves. It must be obsessed over, hammered into the heads of all who visit Montpelier, so as to assure they leave the place thinking that's all there was to the man, who must be made despicable so that the Constitution can be rendered disreputable.

"The home of the Constitution should be the place that recognizes the contributions of the enslaved communities across America," says one of the new trustees of Montpelier, Rev. Larry Walker. "We want to make this a national monument to the 'Invisible Founders,'" whom Walker believes are the ones truly responsible for the Constitution and all that followed from it.

Having such a man as a trustee of Montpelier is not unlike putting Ralph Nader in charge of the Corvette Museum, in Bowling Green, Kentucky.

Thus, rather than putting up exhibits explaining Madison's role as America's preeminent political scientist—the man who put into practice the noble sentiments expressed by his mentor, Thomas Jefferson—visitors to Montpelier are shepherded from one race-grievance diorama to the next. These include "The Mere Distinction of Color," "Slavery and the Constitution," and an interactive "Slavery and the Presidency" display.[64] Push the button to see which ones owned slaves. Never mind what they did to free us all.

The wokeness even extends to the bookstore, where such titles as *Antiracist Baby* and *She Persisted*—by Chelsea Clinton, no less!—are on display. What either title has to do with Madison, Montpelier, or the Constitution is hard to divine.

But that is just the point: to get people who visit Madison's home to forget about the Constitution by refusing to teach them anything about it, to favor feeling guilty about it via the imputed, intergenerational guilt of the men who were responsible for it.

The object is to accuse them of responsibility for everything wrong done to black people while giving them no credit for anything they accomplished that was great—such as the country that has produced more freedom than any people have ever enjoyed, anywhere, ever.

"These people are doing what any totalitarian regime would do," said Douglas MacKinnon, author of *The 56*, which chronicles the lives of the signers of the Declaration of Independence.[65] "They want to create a whole new narrative not based on reality. As they say, the victor gets to write the history and now our history is being rewritten right before our very eyes."

And what of the history of the man behind the remaking of Montpelier into a shrine to latter-day wokeness? What is David Rubenstein's history as chairman of the Carlyle Group, one of the largest private equity funds in the world, with an estimated $376 billion in assets under management? Among other things, Carlyle functions as a kind of plantation owner for mobile homes, accused of rent-gouging the low-income residents who live there, so as to profit from their suffering.

According to a 2021 story in *The New Yorker*, Carlyle "began buying mobile-home parks, first in Florida and later in California, focusing on areas where technology companies had pushed up the cost of living."[66] This, in turn, drove up the rent on the land the mobile homes occupied. Many of the residents could not afford the higher rent—or "chattel loans"—needed to remain there. Nor could they handle the expense of moving their trailers elsewhere. So, they were moved into homelessness by billionaire equity king David Rubenstein, who never wrote a constitution, never defended the rights it enshrined so eloquently, and never served in public office, let alone two terms as president of the United States.

Rubenstein hopes, though, that the $10 million grant he gave to remake Montpelier will make people forget all about that—by making them obsess about something else.

2. I Won't Be Irishx for St. Patrick's Day

How about Saint Patrix Day for a change? No? Well, maybe we could just go with "Paxxy," as that could go either way. It would certainly be more gender-neutral—and inclusive—than the patriarchal and "gendered" form.

But then, the Irish, like myself, might object, since it's objectionable to deny objective reality—and even worse to insist that others do too.

An October 2022 poll of people of Spanish and Latin ancestry object to being told they must "identify" as "Latinx"—a neutered malapropism that subsumes them all into the same androgynous set.[67]

Cue Boy George's hit "Karma Chameleon" from the '80s[68]—one of the first attempts to get people to think in such terms.

Or rather, to get them *not* to think.

There are men, and there are women. This is sex. This is biology. The sexes aren't interchangeable, regardless how a person of a given sex elects to "identify" or dress.

Just as St. Patrick was a man.

Similarly, there are people who are Spanish or Mexican. Or South or Central American. Of both sexes too. There is no such *country* as "Latin America" and therefore no such thing as a "Latinx" person. Anyone who understands the diversity of the region knows that it encompasses a rainbow of different people and cultures—though once again, just the same two sexes.

That's why it's insulting as well as ungrammatical to refer to these different people generically—and androgynously.

But never mind that. It's OK to insult "people of color" when it suits the agenda of the radical Left—that being to collectivize people by making them fungible. Just the same as making objective reality—male and female—a fungible thing.

The good news is that the people being insulted aren't having it.

In 2022, WPA Intelligence and Visto Media conducted two polls of people of Hispanic, Latin, and Central and South American origin and asked them—as opposed to the leftist elites *telling them*—how they prefer to identify themselves. Barely 1 percent indicated they would like to be identified as "Latinx"—which, of course, is no identity at all, being nonspecific as well as androgynous. It is impossible to discern from that term whether the person is male or female—or what his or her ethnic background might be.

This is precisely the point of using such terms, of foisting such terms on people who never asked to be so identified. The arrogance and condescension of it all is halting. It is like naming a pet. Except we are talking about *people*. It's unclear whether the Left understands the difference.

The other 99 percent polled said they'd like to be identified as Hispanic or Latino or—*gasp!—American*.

Better get out the smelling salts. A few dozen leftists just hit the floor.

"This is pretty much consistent with everything we've seen from Gallup and from other polls that show most Hispanics want to be called Hispanic," said Giancarlo Sopo, a media strategist associated with the pollsters.

The malapropism "Latinx" is "not very popular in our community," he added.

Unsurprisingly, people on the Left (many of whom are white) attack Latinos and Hispanics—many of whom consider themselves Americans—for not "embracing" the malapropism and being good little doggies. An article in the Daily Wire had Democrats screeching that "machismo culture" is to blame. Also "too much homophobia and transphobia" among Hispanics and Latinos and Americans generally.

The demeaning framing is of a piece with everything the Left does—to those who do not agree with the Left or simply fail to obey.

Well, thank God for "machismo culture," then.

The Daily Wire in 2022 pointed out the obvious: Latinos and Hispanics have more pressing things to worry about, such as the surge in violent crime ruining their neighborhoods, the inflation that's eating away their wealth, and the porous border. More Hispanics and Latinos are worried about that than the Left wants you to think are worried about paying homage to the latest leftist pieties.

A clear majority of those polled at the time—56 percent—said they believe that the country is headed in the wrong direction.[69] In the 2020 presidential election, Donald Trump increased his share of the Hispanic/Latino vote. The same pattern seemed to be forming again in the aftermath of the 2022 midterm elections.

Something that truly worries the Left is that Hispanics and Latinos—people from Central and South America, generally—are fundamentally family oriented and traditionally minded. In other words, they are not reliably reflexive leftists. They do not believe that "topics such as gender identity and sexual orientation should be discussed with kids," Sopo said.

Except at home and with their parents.

And they are catching on to the Left's semantic games.

"I think Hispanic voters are incredibly smart and nuanced," Sopo said. They are "sophisticated enough to decipher fact from fiction." Like the fact that a man isn't a woman because he "identifies" as one. And that to identify as "Latinx" is to lose one's identity in a miasma malapropism invented by leftists to trivialize the diverse range of people who are Hispanic, Latino, Mexican, Honduran, Bolivian, Salvadoran—and American.

3. A Letter to George W. Bush from a Young Man in Africa

Dear President Bush,

You have never met me and likely never will. You are a former two-term president of the United States. I am from the streets of Gaborone, Botswana, in Africa.

Though our paths have never crossed, I want to thank you for something you did, something you fought for, and for which only now are you being applauded by the same media who spent decades hating you.

They hated you for the Iraq war. They hated you for being an oil man. They hated you for being from Texas. Most of all, they hated you for the shallowest reason of all: because you are a Republican politician.

Now, they praise you. From NBC News:

> President George W. Bush's reputation
> may have been forever complicated by
> 9/11 and war, but a proposal he made
> in his 2003 State of the Union address
> became a historic humanitarian success,
> one that resulted in 25 million lives saved
> from AIDS, 20 million people with HIV
> provided antiretroviral treatment and
> 5.5 million babies born to HIV-positive
> mothers but free of the virus themselves.[70]

Even National Public Radio regards you as something
of a hero now, long after you've left office.[71] I read
once these same people made films about you being
assassinated?[72]

Outside of the United States, we sometimes marvel
that your media there has its right to speak freely and
fearlessly enshrined in your magnificent Constitution,
yet uses that sacred right not as a duty to truth and
justice but as a weapon for base lies and deception.
The rest of the world envies your media for its status
and at the same time wonders why it wastes so much
of its time and authority on nonsense.

This is why I say thank you. And if you could hear me,
you would likely reply with: "You're welcome." When
you were in office, you used your 2003 State of the
Union Address to keep me alive.

You didn't know my name. You didn't even know that
I existed. But at that time, Africa below the Sahara

was facing catastrophe. HIV, the virus that causes AIDS, was ravaging our towns, cities, and countries. Our families were being torn apart. In my country, Botswana, about one in five of us faced the prospect of contracting and dying of the disease.

Most other countries faced a similar cataclysm or worse: as many as one-third of adults carried HIV in some sub-Saharan African countries.

America has its own problems, you could have argued. You were under assault from terrorism, still reeling from the shock of the barbaric 9/11 attacks on your people. You had a rampant drug problem in your cities.

Chicago has often resembled a war zone. Your southern border is often overrun with chaos. You could have argued all of these things meant America could not afford to help Africa deal with the blight of AIDS.

But you didn't do that. In 2003, you stood up for Africa before the entire world. That night, you didn't just stand up for faceless millions. You stood up for me, a black boy on the other side of the world who had nothing—nothing of my own and nothing I could give back to you or to America.

You did it anyway. Your country and your Republican Party are often vilified, even by your own media, for being racist and callous. We hear it now, incessantly, from the "woke" activists and their Democratic Party allies—most of whom have never set foot in Africa and never will. They will never even leave their New York or Los Angeles neighborhoods or their ivory tower jobs to see the world for themselves. They say America is irredeemably racist and evil and must be dismantled. They even engage in rhetoric that we Africans have become all too familiar with, because it is based on a kind of tribal hate that leads to violence and even genocide.

Staying in their bubbles, they miss all the good that America does, both before your 2003 announcement and long after. In 2003, your questionable Dr. Anthony Fauci proposed spending $500 million American taxpayer money to fight AIDS in Africa. You, according to NBC, took him aside and told him you wanted to spend much more to save lives: much more.

Since your announcement, America has literally spent billions fighting AIDS on behalf of people like me.[73] Millions of us are still alive because of America's benevolence and generosity. You have given us the most precious gift of all, Mr. President: the gift of life itself. I am now a college graduate and engaged to be married, all because of you.

Twenty years later, your program PEPFAR is finally recognized as one of the most important in world history—by the same media who called you a butcher and a murderer.[74]

Can you imagine Putin's Russia or Xi's China doing such a thing? Of course not. Those autocratic nations are throwbacks to a pre-republican era. They are both waging wars of a kind against your country, which seems to have lost its way and its will to defend itself. Your current president talks a lot about equity, but he's presiding over rampant chaos that is allowing and fostering drug cartels and human traffickers. Where is the compassion in that?

This is terrible for the whole world. America was and remains the world's leader in human rights, dignity, and life. May this never change, ever.

As for me and millions of others just like me—we survived. No, that's not quite right. We did not merely survive. We *lived*. We *thrived*. We are here today to help Africa stand on its own feet and rise and take our place among the nations.

Those of us who know recent history know which country and which leaders deserve our gratitude. It isn't the ones who find racism under every rock and divide the most benevolent country the world has ever seen. It's those who see a problem, even if it's on the other side of the world, and it will never benefit them personally or politically to take it on—but they do it anyway. That's real compassion.

Sir, your detractors once said, "Bush lied, people died." Nothing could be further from the truth.

Thank you.

4. Conservatism's Black Superman: Vince Everett Ellison

The most significant things can start from the most ordinary moments.
    "This started from a trip my daughter and I had, and we stopped by McDonald's, and this lady [who was] going to a pro-abortion march asked my daughter to join her because she saw she was Black,

and she thought she was a liberal Democrat," Vince Everett Ellison recalls. "And my daughter very, very nicely said, 'Uh, ma'am, I'm a Christian, and I vote my values.'

"And that was just so interesting to me because I said, why don't more people say that? 'I'm a Christian, and I vote my values?'"

Fear? The fear of being shouted at. The fear of being ostracized. The fear of being canceled and losing one's career, friends, and social standing. The siren song of the woke herd mentality can be enticing.[75] But not to the Ellison family.

A former Gospel singer, the son of sharecroppers, and now a vocal black leader, Vince Everett Ellison lives by his strong values: his Christian faith, strong family, the value of every life, America's unique freedoms and opportunities. He also understands the reluctance to speak up but is having none of it, as he told Tucker Carlson on Fox News.[76] In his sensational new documentary, *Will You Go to Hell for Me?*, Ellison rips into the Democratic Party for promoting what he calls perversion and evil.[77]

"They want you to castrate little boys and cut off the breasts of little girls. And they're telling people they're not going to be held responsible for this? That is a lie. The Democratic Party is an evil institution. They are controlled by a cabal of perverts, liars, and psychopaths," said Ellison.

"Evil is anyone who intentionally harms a child," Ellison told Emerald Robinson on Lindell TV.[78] He noted that Democrats in Virginia recently blocked two laws related to harming children. One law would have required schools to call parents if their child is transitioning from one gender to another. Another would have required boys and girls to compete in sports aligned with their birth gender. Democrats blocked both, interfering with the parent-child relationship and opening the way for biological boys to compete in girls' sports, which is both unfair and unsafe given boys' inherent size and strength advantages.

Ellison's courage is remarkable and contagious. One of the few black leaders to speak out for America and against the gender confusion and anti-family policies the Democrats are pushing in their quest for power, Ellison calls that party what it is: evil. The Democrats seem determined to prove him right at every turn, from the local level on radicalized school boards that spy on parents all the way to the top to the president who ran as a moderate but is governing as a hard-core, anti-family leftist.

Forget the canary, Ellison is the Black Superman in the mineshaft warning that the Left is obsessed with the total annihilation of Judeo-Christian values. The proof has arrived in the form of a mentally ill trans-terrorist, likely high on the liberal media's pro-trans, anti-religious propaganda,[79] walking into a school outside Nashville to hunt down Christians and kill them.[80]

The Democrats have gone all-in on child gender transitions, with even the Biden-led Pentagon announcing it believes kids as young as seven years old should be allowed to make the choice to take on powerful medications and surgeries to attempt to change genders.[81] Kids that age can't vote, can't drive, and are still growing physically, mentally, and emotionally. They aren't allowed to make the most basic choices without parental approval—but Joe Biden and the entire Democratic Party want them to be able to sign on for a lifetime of drugs, medical procedures, and extensive psychological counseling while refusing to listen to the growing number of Americans who now say they regret their gender transitions. This, Ellison says, is evil.

The same party preaches that one's actions and statements can be severed from their faith, Ellison notes. It's a political game the Democrats have been playing for decades, ever since formerly staunch and vocal pro-life leaders such as Rev. Jesse Jackson switched to being "personally" pro-life but politically pro-choice to maintain their standing with the party. The Democrats have only gotten more radical and more demanding of Christians to essentially renounce core tenets of their faith ever since. New York now allows abortion nearly up to the moment of birth and celebrates itself for its radical law.[82]

Ellison told Carlson that this is evil, built on convenient lies that imperil millions of souls.

"If you want to know what evil is, I'll make it easy for you. Anybody that intentionally harms a child, even Jesus Christ, the greatest human being [who] ever walked this earth, said, 'If you harm one of these little ones, it is better that a millstone be tied around your neck and you be thrown into the sea.' Well, I hope some of these Democrats can swim," Ellison said.[83]

But harming children seems to have become a key plank of the Democratic platform.

The stakes are too high, Ellison says, and they're not limited to Democrats. As he makes clear in *Will You Go to Hell for Me?*, the choices we make now in this life will affect the ultimate fate of our souls in the next.[84]

"Romans 14 and 12 tells us we will stand in front of God and be held accountable for everything that we do in our lives," he notes, singling out the black church for supporting Democrats and their policies that destroy lives and families and have harmed black America for decades.

It's past time to choose wisely. Today's act of convenience or cowardice is a choice that will echo into the future and eternity. Vince Everett Ellison's voice is one all of America needs to hear and listen to very soon.

5. Republicans Want Affirmative Action for Your Money

When Republicans might as well be Democrats, what's the point of having Republicans? Or voting for them?

Well, *some* of them.

Take US Representative Patrick McHenry of North Carolina, for instance. In 2023, he became the chairman of the House Financial

Services Committee, which you'd think would be concerned with *financial services*. Instead, McHenry is very concerned about diversity, inclusion, and equity—neatly acronymized as DIE. Which is precisely what will happen to the Republican Party if its representatives don't stop working overtime to show how very much they agree with everything the left wing of the Democratic Party is pushing.

For example, the sort of nonsense another Republican who might as well be a Democrat—Rep. Ann Wagner of Missouri—says the Subcommittee on Capital Markets would focus on under her "leadership."

That being what she calls the "best practices and policies that continue to strengthen diversity and inclusion in the capital markets industry." Meaning, rather than leave the market for capital free to decide the best uses of capital according to whether there is a market—and a good prospect for a return on the investment of that capital—the government ought to interfere with the market and allocate capital according to racial and other considerations having nothing to do with whether it makes sound financial sense.

Basically, affirmative action for money.

The premise is that it's unfair that some have it while others do not—and the *not-having* is due to "institutional racism" rather than institutional investors putting their money where it's perceived as likely to earn more of it.

Banks lend to people whom they deem likely to be capable of paying it back—based upon metrics such as having an income adequate to make payments and a track record of having made payments in the past.

This is called *having good credit*—but that is probably "racist" now too.

Clearly, more *inclusionary* policies are needed—such as requiring institutional lenders to "invest" in diversity. That being defined as people and ventures that aren't likely to generate money. It may not make a profit, but what matters—apparently—is making Democrats happy.

Of course, they never are. It doesn't matter how many Republicans-in-name-only roll over and beg to be kicked by them. And never mind that the Republican Congress just elected was not elected to push Democrat policies. The Republican National Committee seems to understand this, even if some Republicans do not. The RNC stated—*accurately*—that "Democrats prioritize wokeness over solving real problems."[85]

Like inflation that's costing Americans of all colors 8 to 12 percent more to maintain the same standard of living as two years ago. Like violent crime soaring 50 percent and higher, with almost all of that in "diverse neighborhoods." Talk about "disparate impact"!

But never mind all that. The Left—and some Republicans, who serve the agenda of the Left—only seems to care about preening before the perpetually aggrieved in the hope that they will be patted on the head for signaling their virtue.

It's what makes Republicans-in-name-only such as Mitt Romney so popular with Democrats. Yet Democrats never vote for him. They're awfully happy to help Romney repel Republican voters who might otherwise have bothered to vote—when there is something worth voting for.

It's how we ended up with Barack Obama, who bequeathed Joe Biden to America.

Another member of this club is Rep. Bill Huizenga of Michigan, a man who is doing his very best impression of his woke left-wing governor, Gretchen Whitmer, if she happened to be the chairman of the Subcommittee on Oversight and Investigations. That's the committee that should be investigating the actions and activities of Democrats, which is what Republicans were *voted into Congress to do*. But Huizenga is about making sure there is "agency" and what he calls a "programmatic commitment" to *diversity and inclusion policies*.

What either of those things has to do with oversight and investigation is hard to divine.

Much easier to understand is how badly some Republicans want to be seen as good Democrats, because Washington is a Democrat-controlled town, even if Republicans happen to control the House of Representatives. Bad Republicans—i.e., those who *don't* roll over for Democrats—aren't invited to the good parties. And of course, the legacy media is almost entirely under the sway of the Woke Left—and only well-trained "house" Republicans such as what the Washington Free Beacon cheekily labeled the Diversity Triumvirate are allowed within (and on air).[86]

It only took McHenry a couple of weeks to get the message.

Shortly after his appointment to head the Financial Services Committee, he was talking about how "Democrats wasted the valuable and limited time and resources of our committee to push burdensome mandates on American job creators" and that he would see to it that there would be "aggressive oversight" of the Biden administration. He even dissolved the Subcommittee on Diversity and Inclusion established by Maxine Waters, who doesn't identify as a Republican.

Fast forward just three weeks and it's time to DIE—which is precisely what will happen to the Republican Party if it doesn't stop groveling for the favor of the Democratic Party and the Democratic establishment in Washington that also controls the legacy media.

Companies that have gone woke have gone broke. The GOP will go away, too, if it doesn't wake up.

IV.

April Privilege

"America's founders set the radical principles of individual freedom and the ability to perfect a union based on the power of the people in motion, and this land became the land where a young black man named Michael could have white, Hispanic, black, Asian, and all kinds of other kids wanting to 'be like Mike.'"

1. Legendary Basketball Coach Phil Jackson Dunks on NBA Knuckleheads

In many new cars, a caution prompt appears on the touchscreen when you put the transmission in reverse. "Check for Safety," it urges.

One never sees him.

Or maybe it's *her*?

Phil Jackson, the former New York Knicks power forward (and later, president of the organization) might get the joke, having gotten into trouble for telling a similar one about NBA players wearing their causes rather than their names on their jerseys while playing "in the bubble" during the height of the COVID-19 pandemic.

"They went into the lockout year, and they did something that was kind of wanky," he began. "They did a bubble down in Orlando, and all the teams that could qualify went down there and stayed down there," he said on an episode of Rick Rubin's *Tetragrammaton* show. "And they had things on their back like, 'Justice.' They made a funny thing like, 'Justice just went to the basket and Equal Opportunity just knocked him down.' My grandkids thought that was pretty funny to play up those names."[87]

"I couldn't watch that," Jackson added. He explained that it seemed to him as though the league was "trying to cater to an audience or trying to bring a certain audience into play, and they didn't know that it was turning other people off."

And then the punch line, the one the woke didn't get: "People wanted to see sports as non-political."

As in, fans just want to watch the game and don't care about the players' politics. More to the point, they don't want to pay to see those politics on the court. Just the same as NFL fans wanted to see Colin Kaepernick play rather than take a knee.

Oh, the humanity!

More accurately, oh, the *pretended injury*.

The Woke Left doesn't like to argue, because it often can't, most of its demands being irrational and emotional—like a child stamping its feet because it didn't get what it wants *right now*. In lieu of an argument, the woke feign being insulted. This plays on the good-naturedness of most normal people, who strive not to offend people and are inclined to apologize when they are told they have.

And so, the woke pretended they were *offended*.

Jackson stands accused of having hurt the feelings of the woke players who wore their feelings on their jerseys.

"That's just what I was bringing up to the kids," Jackson told Rubin. "Visually, this is kind of humorous. I had nothing against BLM or the cause that was behind it. The humorous nature of going completely woke by the NBA really was like, it's pretty hard to watch."

Cue the wailing and gnashing of teeth.

Also the implication that Jackson, who is white, does not like blacks. Because obviously, any white man who makes a joke about anything woke must be a *racist*.

Predictably, NBA commentator Jalen Rose erupted just like a toddler who didn't get what he wants *right now* after Jackson remarked on "Justice" making a run for the basket.

"You're sitting there watching games with your grandkids and y'all think it's *funny* when 'Justice' passes the ball to 'Equal Opportunity'?"

Well, yeah—because it's *funny*.

But like most of the woke, Rose has no sense of humor. Everything must be sonorously political and politically correct. One does not make jokes about Stalin—or his political heirs.

Jackson must be excommunicated from the sport. "When somebody shows you who they are, believe them," Rose demands.

Well, how does "someone" transform into "Justice"? Isn't that a bit like looking for "Safety" when you put your car in reverse?

But Rose wasn't laughing.

Instead, he fumed that Jackson and everyone else who *does* think it's funny to see "Justice" vying with "Equal Opportunity" should "stop watching [pro basketball games] forever."

What's even funnier is the way Rose went on to frame Jackson, who as coach won eleven NBA championships, as a kind of *massa* and the black athletes who played for him as field hands: "The same Phil Jackson that won championships with some of the greatest black athletes in the history of the game—Michael Jordan, Scottie Pippen, Shaquille O'Neal, Kobe Bryant [and who] made millions on their backs and off their sweat equity," he said.[88]

Except those players also made millions—*hundreds of millions*, in the case of Shaquille O'Neal[89] and Kobe Bryant—and vastly more than Jackson ever did.

If anything, maybe it's *Jackson* who should be whining about "equity" and "oppression." Though of course, he didn't. Because he knew that would not be funny.

"You can't make this up," said Rose.

On that score, he's absolutely right.

2. Foreign-Born NBA Players See Privilege Where Natives Do Not

A couple of years ago, the National Basketball Association seemed to forget which nation invented the sport and keeps its existence possible. When Hong Kongers took to the streets to fight for their freedom against communist China, then Houston Rockets general manager Daryl Morey tweeted to support them. Morey is now the general manager of the Philadelphia 76ers.

The incensed, freedom-hating ChiComs went straight for the jugular and threatened to cut the entire NBA off from their market.[90] Faced with the choice of defending freedom or making bank, the NBA chose to make bank. It took fifteen months for China to resume doing business with the Rockets after cutting the franchise out of the country.[91]

Despite clear evidence that China is currently, as in *right now*, engaged in systemic and brutal human rights violations, including running racist concentration camps, the NBA's LeBron James refused to say a word about any of it. He'll trash America every chance he gets, anytime some thug forces a cop into an impossible split-second choice, even posting a threat to a police officer before deleting it,[92] but he's silent about China's abuses. Why? Has he been bought?

The NBA, which has a red-white-and-blue white guy for its logo,[93] went full woke after George Floyd and never once stepped up for law and order as city after city burned in the riots that summer. These are cities where the NBA has franchises and depends on cops for security at every game. Houston Mavericks owner Mark Cuban even canceled playing the National Anthem at home games and then had to backtrack.

One player who tried to stand up for America, foreign-born Enes Kanter, changed his name to Enes Freedom and expressed gratitude for the opportunities America has given him. He got traded to the Rockets, who immediately cut him, and he hasn't played in the NBA since. Both Freedom and the Chinese media knew why the twenty-nine-year-old had been summarily dismissed.

If you haven't noticed, that's *two* teams in deep-red Texas that didn't stand up for America. Just what does the NBA really stand for?

While the NBA shuns players who speak out against China[94] and seems to encourage the big dummies like LeBron and Kevin Durant, who consistently rip America, a curious thing has happened. Foreign-born players have gotten to work and now dominate the league.

Milwaukee's Giannis Antetokounmpo started the trend. The Greek-born star is one of just a handful to win back-to-back MVP awards, in 2018–19 and 2019–20. His true-life tale of going from poor, undocumented immigrant in Greece, being helped by people (white men) to get onto basketball teams and eventually the NBA, reads like a storybook.[95] White men at the Milwaukee Bucks take a flyer on him in the draft, and he's suddenly among the world's richest people. Giannis is the MVP of humility and heartfelt gratitude too.[96] While other players born in American freedom and privilege can offer nothing but criticism, Giannis put his head down, worked hard to be the best, and in 2021, led the Bucks to their first title in fifty years.

Nikola Jokic has picked up where Giannis left off. The Serbian-born Denver Nuggets center has won back-to-back MVP awards in 2020–21 and 2021–22. He has led the Nuggets into the playoffs since his arrival in the NBA and may yet bag a title in Denver. It would be their first ever.

Just behind these two is the Philadelphia 76ers' superstar, big man Joel Embiid. He has finished runner-up to Jokic two seasons in a row, and ESPN made the early case for him to win the MVP race in the 2022–23 season.[97] He did. Born in Cameroon, a country known more for soccer than basketball, Embiid is a seven-foot center who can dominate games with his physicality and smarts. Not only did he not beat up on America, Embiid became a full-fledged American in September 2022.[98]

"I've been here for a long time," Embiid told the Associated Press. "My son is American. I felt like, I'm living here, and it's a blessing to be an American. So I said, why not?"

"It's a blessing to be American." Isn't that *refreshing* to hear? For some reason, SB Nation left out the blessing part of Embiid's quote in its story about his new citizenship.[99] Who cut it, the reporter or the editors?

Embiid, Jokic, and Antetokounmpo come from different countries and backgrounds and play for different teams in the NBA. But they all have quite a bit in common. They're strong on family, deep on gratitude, and happy to be in the land of freedom and opportunity. Ask most NBA fans to list their favorite players, and at least one of these three makes that list because of their character, their drive, and their positive outlook.

While American-born NBA stars rant about "white privilege" and even threaten the cops who keep all of us safe—from their mansions and while surrounded by their paid armed security—the NBA and its fans are privileged to admire humble winners like these foreign-born ballers.

3. Stephen A. Smith: America's Last Honest Sports Pundit?

ESPN's Stephen A. Smith is a brave man.

Years ago, his network went woke. ESPN, which Disney owns, began injecting race into just about every discussion of every sport, pushing gun control, pushing the Left's agenda where it clearly doesn't and never will belong. Game highlights and analysis took a back seat to political pontificating.

Smith didn't publicly resist that, but he didn't really go along either. He's never really seemed interested in wokeness. He has frequently appeared on Fox News with Sean Hannity and Jesse Watters, which is usually two strikes against anyone who wants to avoid being canceled.

Lately, Smith has been flirting with a third strike.

Once Donald Trump decided to run for president in 2015, all of the media turned on him. The host and star of the most successful reality show ever, *The Apprentice*, the man behind the global brand of resorts, Miss USA and Miss Universe, and the man who had built an entire football league around Heisman Trophy winner Herschel Walker, was suddenly branded a "racist." Trump had been controversial for decades but had never been branded with the R-word throughout his career in real estate and everything else he's done. Democrats and their media stenographers brand any threat to their power as "racist," and the speed with which they slapped that ignominious title on Trump showed just how much they feared him. Many of Trump's oldest friends and associates turned on him—all to either make a buck for themselves or stay in good graces with the dishonest media.

But not Stephen A. Smith.

While Trump is called every insult in the book, including the dreaded R-word, Smith isn't having it. Appearing at the Semafor Media Summit, Smith refused to advance the narrative that Donald Trump is a racist.[100] No Trump apologist, Smith said he would never vote for The Donald—but also said flatly that he is no racist.

"I knew Trump before he ran for the presidency," Smith said during the event. "I thoroughly enjoyed talking to him. He was a huge sports fan."[101]

"He used to throw a lot of events at—you know—at his casinos and stuff like that, and I genuinely liked him," Smith said.

"I think he's changed, but I will tell you this: I think when people call him racist and stuff like that, I've never thought of Trump that way," Smith insisted.

"He's not against black people," Smith said, adding that he has never seen Trump show any animosity toward black people.

Smith's candor comes with no small amount of risk at his woke network. Sage Steele's promising career at the same ESPN has been chopped after she voiced her opinion on a podcast on COVID mandates and Barack Obama's decision to identify only as black despite having a white mother. Steele is mixed race and identifies as such, honoring both of her parents—not ignoring or seeming to exclude either one, as Obama does.

For that, Steele was relegated to lesser appearances, and ESPN forced her to apologize. She sued Disney,[102] which is one of the world's most woke, least tolerant corporations, for violation of her free speech.

Over at NBC, NFL sideline mainstay Michele Tafoya says she was told clearly to keep her conservative political opinions to herself.[103] Despite more than a decade at the highest level of sports broadcasting, four-time Emmy winner Tafoya knew she had to leave in order to "come out" as skeptical of the Left's hardline positions that dominate the media. There's no room at America's largest sports networks for anything but hard-left opinions.

Perhaps Smith can survive at ESPN without pouring hate on Trump, as everyone else seems required to do. Perhaps sports media is still so sexist that it only penalizes women for expressing genuine opinions that stray from the Left's orthodoxy. We may find out. But at this point, Smith has earned credit for stepping outside the Left's shadow and being his own—honest—man.

4. Celebrating the Great Emancipator of America's Pastime

Major League Baseball celebrates Jackie Robinson Day every year around April 15. But there should be another celebration in the MLB: Branch Rickey Day.

It was Rickey who emancipated Major League Baseball. Children should study him the way they used to study Lincoln before critical race theory showed up.

The particular man in question, Jackie Robinson, happened to be black. What mattered to Rickey—who happened to be white—was that Robinson was a superlative baseball player. So good, showing so much potential, that Rickey risked his career in baseball to recruit Robinson, who became the first black man to play in the Big Leagues, which the two men thus opened up to every man who could play the game at that level.

When Rickey became president and general manager of the Brooklyn Dodgers in 1942, all of the social legal pressure was against allowing men like Robinson to play Major League Baseball, no matter how well they played it. Robinson's talent was languishing in the segregated leagues, where he was playing for the Kansas City Monarchs. Rickey thought it absurd that anyone who had the talent Robinson obviously had should be kept out of what was, at the time, touted as the league for the best of the best.

He saw that Major League Baseball was in fact no such thing if it refused to let men like Robinson play.

Just as it would have made a mockery of boxing if Joe Louis hadn't been allowed to box Max Schmeling in 1936 and again in 1938. The first time, Schmeling won an upset victory over Louis by carefully studying Louis's moves prior to the fight and noticing a habit he had of dropping his left hand after a jab—reminiscent of Sylvester Stallone's Rocky character switching from left to right to beat Mr. T's Clubber Lang character in *Rocky III*. The Brown Bomber—as Louis was affectionately known to his fans—came back (like Rocky) and beat Schmeling in the '38 rematch.

The two men became friends after the fight and remained so for the rest of their lives, with Schmeling serving as one of his pallbearers when Louis died in 1981.[104]

Like Rickey and Robinson, Louis and Schmeling saw each other as equals and respected one another as men. That one was black and the other white was as relevant to them as the color of good spaghetti sauce is to a blind man.

But that was not an easy thing for Branch Rickey to act on in the early '40s, when there seemed to be very little payoff in letting the best man play—and much to be gained by preventing him from playing.

It was the actual Jim Crow era when segregation was both practiced and (in many places) the law. The content of a man's character didn't matter as much as the color of his skin—and the same was true of his ability. Major League Baseball was all-white because only whites were allowed to play. Men who weren't couldn't even try out. It was as silly as refusing to let the best doctor operate because he wasn't the right color—but that's the way it was.

And there was enormous pressure to keep it that way.

Some white MLB executives feared baseball fans would not be fans of baseball players who weren't white, no matter how well they played. This included the management of the Boston Red Sox, which gave Robinson a staged "tryout" where he had no chance of being inducted but was subjected to abuse on account of his race.

Rickey faced the same, as recounted in the excellent Ken Burns PBS documentary, *Baseball*.[105] In it, legendary sports announcer Red Barber tells of Rickey's determination to break down the color barrier, out of idealism and business sense—because it made no sense not to promote the best.

He wanted a meritocracy based on skills, not skin.

And so he risked everything—not just his career in baseball, as a prominent executive—by recruiting Robinson and integrating him into MLB, first via the Montreal Royals, the Dodger's "international" farm team—and from there to first base with the Dodgers proper— where he became Rookie of the Year in 1947 and went on to become an All Star player for six consecutive seasons (1949–1954), won the National League's MVP Award in 1949, played in six World Series— and became a national icon.

And something more. A legend.

Every year on April 15th, MLB celebrates Jackie Robinson Day.[106] Every player, black, white, Latin, or Asian, wears Robinson's number 42 to commemorate the day Jackie made his Major League debut.

Robinson set the example that another man would talk about years after his baseball career was over. That man was Martin Luther King Jr., who rejected the idea that a man ought to be judged by his looks rather than who he is—and what he does.

And it was another man who agreed with them both, who happened to be a white man. A man who didn't patronize any man but saw, respected—and promoted—talent when he saw it.

Even if it might have cost him everything, professionally and personally.

And that makes him a Major Leaguer too.

5. Colin Kaepernick Runs Over His White Parents

Former NFL quarterback Colin Kaepernick apparently isn't satisfied with his achievements. The forgettable virtue-signal caller has already trashed Betsy Ross and turned the NFL into a woke disgrace. He poisoned race relations among the 330-odd million Americans, and Nike rewarded him with a massive contract.

None of that is enough. Now, he's trashing the white parents who adopted him and raised him from birth.

Kaepernick, in an interview with CBS News, criticized the generous couple who took him home as their son after his birth mother gave him up. He told the liberal network that they were "problematic" due to some comments they made about his hair.[107]

Kid Kaepernick wanted to have his hair in cornrows like his basketball hero, Allen Iverson. This author wanted that hairstyle in 1999 too. His mom said it looked "unprofessional" and that he looked "like a little thug." As a former little white thug, I once had a haircut that caused my mom to suggest I looked like a bank robber, a Mohawk Indian, and then a cast member of *Queer Eye for the Straight Guy*.

Iverson had his own issues.[108] But since when don't parents get to have an opinion about their child's hair, or actions, or clothes, or anything else without being slammed with the charge of being racist or "problematic"?

Parents have always done this. It's called *parenting*. It has nothing to do with race. In Kaepernick's case, his two white parents say they brought him home and loved him like a son from day one. They haven't commented on his latest accusation, probably because they're heartbroken. They spent the best years of their lives making sure the biracial boy who was not biologically their son knew that they loved and cared for him as if he had been.

For all their love and effort, for all their striving and worrying over him, he's calling them out over what amounts to the microaggressions of parenting.

Contrast Kaepernick's comments with those of home run king Aaron Judge.[109] Like Kaepernick, Judge is an adopted biracial star athlete. The Yankee who won Rookie of the Year and has smashed Roger Maris's single-season home run record doesn't run around looking for slights to call out. He runs a Christian foundation off the diamond called All Rise that quietly helps kids.

Practically identical upbringing situations have produced very different outlooks. Where Kaepernick looks for slights to his sensitivities, Judge sees the hand of the Almighty: "God was the one who matched us together," he told the *New York Post* in 2015. The superior athlete of the two, if one goes by their achievements on the field of play, Judge also has the superior attitude. He doesn't trash his country or divide Major League Baseball. He's never trashed the parents who pulled him into their hearts and raised him as their own son.

Kaepernick's woke comments run the risk of hurting lots of black kids.[110]

There are likely young parents-to-be out there right now who, for whatever reason, are looking to adopt. They don't care about the race of the kids who are available, nor should they. They have hearts filled with love, with a baby-shaped hole that needs filling.

But thanks to a has-been quarterback who can't stop running his mouth for profit, those prospective parents may wonder in the back of their minds if, after decades of love and sacrifice, their kid might be fortunate enough to become famous and then use race against them somehow.

You're welcome, not welcome.

Colin Kaepernick has paved the way for that. His comments may hurt untold numbers of black and biracial kids out there who desperately need loving parents today. Does he ever think about that? Does

Colin Kaepernick ever stop to think about the real damage he does with each new accusation he lobs at his innocent targets?

6. All Rise for Aaron Judge's Parents

Everyone knows who Colin Kaepernick is—not so much for his feats on the field (he's now retired from the NFL) but rather because of his politics on the field. There's another player, still on the field, whose off-field work and background Americans should know more about.

They don't—because he doesn't make an issue of it.

He is Aaron Judge, the New York Yankees player who was the American League's runner-up for MVP during the 2017 season when he was just a rookie outfielder. Judge is also known for being physically impressive, standing six feet, seven inches tall and weighing some 270 pounds. That's big enough to play in the NFL.

When he was just thirty years old, Judge was already considered one of the most successful professional baseball players in the history of the sport. If he retired today, he'd be famous forever. Rookie of the Year. Silver Slugger. MLB All-Star after only seven seasons as a pro. The Yankees' vice president of scouting called him the "super package."

But those are just stats.

What's more important, arguably, is what Judge does off the field and out of the glare of the press. Judge is a Christian who founded the All Rise Foundation, whose mission statement is to "inspire children and youth to become responsible citizens and encourage them to reach unlimited possibilities."[111]

As he did. As he was given the opportunity to do—by the white couple who adopted him the day after he was born and raised him to become the man—and player—he now is.[112]

Clearly, this is evidence of oppression.

Judge, who is biracial, does not see it that way, of course. Nor do his parents, Patty and Wayne Judge, who were in the stands for the second game of a double-header against the Rangers in Arlington, Texas, where they watched their son hit his sixty-second home run and, in doing so, break Roger Maris's long-standing American League regular-season home run record.[113] As far as I'm concerned, he basically broke the MLB record, too, because you can throw the juice brothers Barry Bonds, Sammy Sosa, and Mark McGwire in the trash can full of asterisks.

Judge tied Maris's record on October 4, 2022, in Toronto—where Maris's son Roger (who is also white and so clearly an oppressor) attended New York's 8–3 victory over the Blue Jays to cheer the mixed-race man who did it. "Congratulations to Aaron Judge and his family on Aaron's historic home run number," Maris said. "It has definitely been a baseball season to remember. You are all class and someone who should be revered."

And not just for feats on the field.

"For the majority of the fans, we can now celebrate a new clean home run king," he posted.[114]

What he meant by that is that Judge is a natural. His athletic achievements don't come from a syringe or pills.

But his achievements aren't one-dimensional. Neither are those of his parents. Judge told the *New York Post* in 2015 that he believed "God was the one who matched us together."[115] Also matched together in the same family is Judge's older brother, John, who was also adopted.

He is Korean.

More evidence of the privileged oppressive nature of white people like Patty and Wayne Judge, both of whom worked as school teachers in Linden, California.

Aaron Judge should be the poster child not only for adoption but for the pro-life movement generally. Yankees fans should thank God Planned Parenthood was nowhere near his biological mother, and although she gave the baby up to a caring couple, she, too, should be commended. Everyone involved in bringing number 99 to the base-ball diamond should say, "You're welcome."

When, as a child, Judge noticed that he wasn't the same skin color as his parents, he asked them about it. "They told me I was adopted and answered all of my questions and that was that," he told the *Post*. "I was fine with it. It really didn't bother me because that's the only parents I've known."

Pretty good parents, it looks like.

"I know I would not be a New York Yankee if it wasn't for my mom," he told MLB.com in an interview. "The guidance she gave me as a kid growing up, knowing the difference between right and wrong, how to treat people and how to go the extra mile and put in the extra work, all that kind of stuff. She's molded me into the person I am today."

Judge doesn't "take a knee." He breaks records. He doesn't use his fame to shame those he might disagree with politically, including his fellow Yankees. In this he is unlike Kaepernick, whose "knee taking" put pressure on those who didn't—who could then be characterized as being in the wrong.

This is how the Left works. Not by uplifting and persuading but by beating down those who disagree with them.

Judge was raised better than that, by parents who loved him from the day they first saw him. They didn't see the color of their son's skin as something lesser. They just brought out the best in him and allowed him to flourish.

"My parents are amazing. They've taught me so many lessons. I honestly can't thank them enough for what they've done for me. I'm blessed."

And so are the fans of America's pastime.

7. Air Shows the Sneaker That Brought Racial Harmony to America

"A shoe is just a shoe until someone steps into it." If there's a quote that defines the Ben Affleck-Matt Damon movie *Air*, that's it.

Set in 1984, *Air* tells the story of how Nike basketball shoe head Sonny Vaccaro (Damon) sees a diamond in a young NCAA champion and risks it all to sign that winner to his company. At the time, Nike had virtually no presence in basketball shoes.

Let that sink in.

Company founder Phil Knight (Affleck) had built Nike by selling running shoes from the trunk of his car and on nearly insufferable Buddhist bromides. Having taken Nike public, Knight has come to focus more and more on keeping the board happy and only going for "knowable outcomes."

Vaccaro reminds Knight that there was nothing knowable in those early days. Nike's origins were all about innovation, superior design, and taking risks—three things our founding fathers used to create the Bill of Rights.

Risk is staring Vaccaro in the face in 1984. His mission at Nike is to sign major NBA talent. But the board doesn't believe anyone will wear a basketball shoe anyplace other than on an actual basketball court. This lack of foresight would keep Nike firmly confined to the running shoe business and out of what Vaccaro believes is the future—basketball.

A longtime student of the game, Vaccaro sees an eighteen-year-old guard from North Carolina as the future of the game, the future of shoes, and the future of everything in his world. But he has one problem:

Nike won't fund signing the young talent.

He has a total budget of $250,000—nowhere near enough to sign the young but as yet unproven pro talent and other NBA targets Nike has in mind.

"All in" comes from poker and is when a player decides to put all their chips in on one hand. Against the advice of Knight, his second-man Rob Strasser (Jason Bateman, who steals just about every scene he's in), Chris Tucker's Howard White, and even the young talent's agent, Vaccaro goes all in on the young guard he believes will be the greatest talent basketball and American sports have ever seen.

He bet the house on a young man from Wilmington, North Carolina, named Michael Jeffrey Jordan.

The threads and themes through *Air* are all about following your gut, owning it, taking risks, and competing against the best. In 1984, Nike is in a distant third in its competition with Adidas and Converse, both of which have basketball endorsement contract budgets dwarfing Nike's.

Those behemoths already have the likes of Magic Johnson[116] and Larry Bird on their rosters; capturing this young new talent should be a cinch for either of them and all but impossible for running shoe-focused Nike.

Vaccaro devises a whole new strategy. He enlists legendary Nike shoe designer Peter Moore (Matthew Maher), who comes up with a lighter, better-looking basketball shoe. And he creates the brand that will put the new player's name at the forefront, even ahead of Nike itself.

Everything about Vaccaro's plan is radical.

The shoe has more red on it than NBA rules allow, so Nike decides it will pay any fines the player incurs for wearing them—$5,000 per game. The branding is radical. The logo—of a man in flight with a basketball in his hand[117]—is radical. The financial arrangements that the player's mother (played to perfection by Viola Davis) negotiates are so radical, they threaten to upend the entire sports shoe and endorsement industries.

But the radical plan tied to a serious vision pays off. Vaccaro lands his target. Jordan signs with Nike, and basketball shoes move well beyond the court. What was a few million-dollar industry surpasses $4 billion—at Nike alone. Air Jordan will be a major brand forever, as it is decades after Jordan's retirement following his glittering career.

The risk was real.[118] Had Jordan signed with another company, Vaccaro would have lost his job and probably been forgotten.

In the same way that a shoe is just a shoe until the likes of Michael Jordan step into them, a land is just land until people step onto it and shape it to their principles and vision.

America's founders set the radical principles of individual freedom and the ability to perfect a union based on the power of the people in motion, and this land became the land where a young black man named Michael could have white, Hispanic, black, Asian, and all kinds of other kids wanting to "be like Mike."

When I think about the state of race relations in America today, I recollect all the false promises driven by the media and the culture. The election of Barack Obama was supposed to bring about a post-racial America.[119] It didn't happen.

In fact, far from it.

Obama midwifed both the Black Lives Matter movement and the media's "mostly peaceful" canard as the country burned.

In some future reality, someone might gender- and race-swap everyone in *Air* and remake it as an ode to wokeness. Ironically, the Affleck-Damon storytelling in *Air* is anything but woke.

It's an ode to America, to free enterprise, to striving to be the best and risking everything to get there. Most importantly, it made millions of white kids, including this author, want to be a black man who could fly.

V.

May Privilege

"Socialist politicians...view everything through a collective lens. It is beside the point whether an individual white person—living or dead—imposed harm on a specific black person, living or dead. The point, insofar as...advocates of financial Sippenhaft *see it, is that all whites are collectively guilty for the sins of all whites and, by dint of those collective sins, owe a collective debt."*

1. A College Commencement Address by President Joseph Robinette Biden to the Troubled Youth of America

Thank you, Madame Dean or Mister or whatever you are today, distinguished guests, and graduates.

As you step forward to accept your degree in underwater midget basket weaving today and ponder the debt you have amassed and hope you never have to pay off, you also step forward into the future. But before you do that, we must address the past. The grievous, terrible past, and why white people made it so awful. This includes me.

As you may have heard, I recently told another group of graduates and their families that racism is a grave threat to the country.[120] So terrible, in fact, that it is even more of a threat to the American way of life than nuclear-armed Communist China, Vladimir Putin's Russia, Islamic terrorism, Iran and North Korea's dictatorships, any pandemic scourge, and even the inflation I unleashed on you that's making it impossible to buy a house or a car.

China is no threat, and if you say it is, you're a racist. You hate Asians. I'll just tell you that straight up, Jack. Putin is a threat despite not being able to conquer a country smaller than several of our states. Pandemics, like most crises, are more useful than threatening. Iran and North Korea? C'mon man! They're not even white!

As for the inflation I'm allowing to tear through the economy and make everything unaffordable, well, I did that for a reason.

Owning your home, being able to freely move and live wherever you want…that's the so-called American dream. But it's no dream, graduates. It's a threat. The American dream is a nightmare for the environment and for indigenous people from whom we stole this land after they engaged in human sacrifice and fought each other for millennia and over which they didn't even assert ownership.

So, despite no one voting for me to kill off that dream for you while I stumble into my eighties, I did it anyway—for your own good.

The American dream is one of many terrible things invented and promoted by white people. And that's what I'm really here to speak to you about today. The scourge of white people and why they are the worst.

Well, I guess I should say "we." Because despite claiming at various times to be somewhat Puerto Rican or even mildly black, I am a white man. My skin color is a stain on America and a threat to the whole world. There is no whiter or less masculine name in the world than "Robinette." I am white, and I am sorry. I am the problem.

You see, it was a white man who first wrote down the ideas that we know today as capitalism. His name was Adam Smith, and he wrote a book in 1776—I'll get to the terribleness of that year in a moment—about the "Wealth of Nations." It was all about how the division of labor opens the possibility of prosperity, personal freedom as the foundation of national strength, the newfound ability for you to choose your line of work and how you might live your life. These truly toxic ideas, about how nations can unleash creativity so their populations can prosper and wars over resources might become a thing of the past, published just a few months before America's terrible founding, set Europe and most of the world on a course toward capitalist economics.

You've been in college for six years now, so I don't have to tell you how disastrous capitalism is. Your professors have seen to that, making sure you don't fall for the trap of thinking that capitalism has lifted humanity out of poverty and extended our lives, even making the two brain surgeries I have undergone possible. I thank your professors, who have never had to bother with real work like most of you soon will (if you can find a job in my economy) and who promote ideas of communal ownership of everything and total government power. Federal taxpayer dollars well-spent, I say.

Capitalism gave rise to industrialism, which gave rise to more discoveries. The discovery of fossil fuels, made by white people, has led to the ruination of our entire world. Look around you. Don't you see the oceans rising? Don't you hear the planet crying out? No? Maybe my doctors need to medicate you like they medicate me.

Now some may say that capitalism led to political freedom, and they would point to the most momentous event of 1776: America's Declaration of Independence from Great Britain. What kind of freedom was it, though, when only white men were allowed to write the Constitution, with its troublesome separation of powers? What has it all really led to? Freedom? Not according to my socialist friend Bernie Sanders. Are you truly free today?

No! The freedom America sells is nothing but an illusion invented by white people. After you graduate from this place, you have to go out and get a job! You have to earn money. You have to make a living and maybe support a family. White people are the reason you have to do all that. That is not freedom.

The age of industrialization and fossil fuels—driven by white people—has led to the age of invention. Now, that sounds great. But it's not!

A white man invented the telescope. Great, you say? No! The telescope made us want to understand the moon and the stars and go to new places. White supremacy in space, folks! White people invented airplanes. That's right. Two white men from a white nuclear family in a former Confederate state that once allowed slavery set about to defy nature and fly. And they succeeded!

Some of you may think this is a good thing. I'm here to tell you that it's not. Sure, today aviation moves goods to market and connects people who live in different cities and even on different continents. I flew here to depress you about the past and your future today, because thanks to white people, you have no future. Air travel is a multibillion-dollar industry, and industry is bad because people have to work in it. Flying also puts pollutants into the air. It depends on the dirty business of drawing oil out of the ground and using big refineries to make it burn. White people did that.

White people also invented cars to go places faster. You probably own one or more than one. And that's bad.

Sure, with your car you were able to get here today. You're able to have dinner with your family and friends after this ceremony. Your car will carry you to your job, and your family to your home, and whatever you order from Amazon to your house.

All of that is bad. Amazon was started by a white man, and thanks to capitalism, he created thousands of jobs and brings millions of products to our homes every day. His fleet of vans and your cars depend on fossil fuels—even if they're electric—to move. They pollute the air. They create the illusion of freedom that is so dangerous. White people did this.

White people really are the worst. They have done all this and so much more.

We have too many people in the world today. Do you know who's responsible for that? White people. They invented penicillin, which defeated infections and kept millions of (mostly white) people alive. They invented the printing press, which allowed the spread of dangerous thoughts. They invented television and the internet, which makes those dangerous insurrectionist thoughts move around the world at the speed of light. Which is really fast!

They invented the scientific method. They dreamed up the Magna Carta, which limited what people in power can do. They even invented the ability to launch rockets into space, so we can just go ahead and pollute the whole universe too.

White people did all that. That's why we are the absolute worst.

Except for my son, Hunter. He's the smartest guy I know.

2. Jim Brown, MAGA's Legendary Running Back, Says Goodbye

The sports world and American culture lost a legend on May 18, 2023.[121] Jim Brown just played a few seasons in the National Football

League, but he carved out a legacy that was unmatched at the time and still stands as one of the greatest careers in the game.

Brown brought speed, size, and power to the position. He could make opposing defenders miss, but he could also run right over them or through them. Brown could dodge you or punish you, and the uncertainty he created in the minds of opponents was just one of the weapons in his incredible arsenal.

Through nine seasons, Brown was one of the best, with over 2,300 carries, more than 12,000 yards, and 106 touchdowns. Brown retired from the game in 1966, but he's still the NFL's eleventh all-time leading rusher. His touchdown record stood for decades, until Dallas Cowboys legend Emmitt Smith broke it, and he's still number six for rushing touchdowns in the history of the league.

All of which is to say, Jim Brown's greatness on the gridiron is undisputed.

Brown didn't stop being a public figure once he retired from football. He became one of America's premier social activists, taking on political causes with the same power and conviction with which he carried the pigskin. He was just as fearless and unpredictable as an activist as well, never letting anyone own his mind or opinion.

So, it should not have shocked the world when Brown announced his support for another legendary figure several years ago: Donald Trump.

The Democrat-owned media has tried to paint Trump as some kind of incorrigible racist, but Brown was never bamboozled by any of that. In 2018, as Trump was mired in the phony Russia scandal made up by Hillary Clinton and pushed relentlessly by MSNBC, the *New York Times*, and CNN, Brown could have stayed on the sidelines. But that was never his style.

Brown suited up and got in the game.

"I should be criticizing Trump on every level because he does certain things that call for criticism," he told the *JT the Brick Show* on Fox

Sports Radio.[122] "But when I look at television, I see all these announcers become experts and they're pointing the fingers and they're not doing a doggone thing but pointing their fingers, I find myself really pulling for the president."

That took courage in the age of hyperpartisanship and cancel culture. But Brown wasn't finished.

"Now, that would make me very unpopular in the black community, very unpopular with a lot of Americans…but I think that there are certain good things that are coming out of this presidency because we've never seen anything like it," Brown said.

At the time, remember, Trump was already leading the US economy to its strongest point since Reagan. Black unemployment, in particular, hit historic lows during Trump's administration.

Trump acknowledged Brown's courage and support when the football giant passed away: "Legendary NFL running back Jim Brown, a man who, in his later years, became a friend of mine, died today at 87. He was tough and strong, but always trying to help people in need. That's how I got to know him. What an athlete, what a man. He will be greatly missed!!!" Trump said in a statement.

The two men probably didn't agree on everything. But they shared a vision for a stronger America in which the black community would be lifted up, not told it has always been oppressed and never stood a chance, as Joe Biden and his party constantly say.

Game recognizes game. Trump and Brown could have a man-to-man conversation about what success really looks like, how it helps more than just the individual who succeeds, and how America enables and fosters success when individuals are encouraged and allowed to give their all. Both men understood the real meaning of hope and how it can carry you forward when all else seems to be against you.

Jim Brown was a one-of-a-kind champion and a man of great strength and conviction. He will be missed for his prowess on the field and for his daring and audacity off the field.

3. The Wokes in the Machine

Amazon has given us a glimpse of our tech-tyrannical future. If you have Amazon's so-called "smart" devices or any other similar products in your home, be warned by Brandon Jackson's experience. Those devices can be operated from Amazon headquarters and turned against you.

I'm not making that up. Jackson, in May 2023, wrote about a weeklong ordeal in which the tech giant locked him out of devices he owns. Not rents—*owns*.

But those devices don't answer to him. They aren't under Jackson's control. They answer to their ultimate master.

In an account Jackson published on Medium.com, he explained how he finally regained control of the "smart devices" he had installed throughout his home.[123] But why did he have to recapture them at all?

His ordeal began when an Amazon driver delivered an order to his door. "The sequence of events that led to this digital exile began innocuously enough," Jackson wrote. "A package was delivered to my house on Wednesday, May 24, and everything seemed fine. The following day, however, I found that my Echo Show had signed out, and I was unable to interact with my smart home devices."

Jackson contacted Amazon and finally reached an executive. That's when he learned the company turned off his devices on purpose.

"When I connected with the executive, they asked if I knew why my account had been locked. When I answered I was unsure, their tone turned somewhat accusatory. I was told that the driver who had delivered my package reported receiving racist remarks from my 'Ring doorbell' (it's actually a Eufy, but I'll let it slide)."

Jackson says he never said anything racist. The driver misunderstood him. The driver reported him. And Amazon cut him off from devices.

Whether Jackson said anything foul is irrelevant. He owns those devices. Amazon has no right to cut him off and certainly no right to convict and punish him unilaterally. No right. That's not the corporation's job. Amazon's job is to sell things and make money. Period. It is not a digital justice system.

But I'm thankful that Amazon unmasked itself and, thereby, potentially other tech giants. The more digital we go in our everyday lives, the more control we surrender to faceless corporations dominated by woke, punitive, radical politics that allow for no dissent or mercy.

This future is here right now. The push to force Americans to switch to electric vehicles is certainly a piece of it. The freedom of movement is fundamental. But it's threatened by technology. Teslas, for instance, frequently receive over-the-air software updates. Could an update be used as a "kill switch" to lock you out of your car if some oversensitive person like the Amazon driver took offense to something you may or may not have said?

It isn't just Tesla. Pretty soon all of the other car manufacturers will be pushing EVs on us, because Joe Biden and the Democrats are mandating them. Every single thing those cars do and everywhere they go is digitally recorded. Every mile they drive, every charge they take, *everything*. They have internal microphones, which Tesla says are not recording anything.[124] But we've heard that from other tech giants in the past, yet it's been proven that some smart TVs that weren't supposed to be listening were (Samsung),[125] and some social media sites that weren't supposed to be listening were and still do. There is no reason to take Big Tech at its word about anything. Blatant political censorship ruled pre-Elon Musk Twitter and still plagues Facebook. They don't play nice.

Brandon Jackson wrote how it took some wrangling with Amazon across several days to regain control of the devices he thought belonged to him. Interestingly, Amazon never denied cutting him off.

The behemoth told Fox News, "We work hard to provide customers with a great experience while also ensuring drivers who deliver Amazon packages feel safe."[126]

Amazon didn't make the customer feel safe at all, and his experience was not great in any way. The company behaved tyrannically. It punished Jackson arbitrarily without allowing him any defense and accused him when he tried to find out what happened. He had to prove himself innocent with video from his doorbell camera. That's not how it's supposed to work, but, then again, Amazon isn't a court. It assumed the role of digital jailer.

Jackson said he might junk those traitorous little "smart" devices. Smart move! It's looking more and more like a dumb move to fill your house with "smart" devices and hit the road in a "smart" electric car. I'm hanging onto my gas cars as long as I can. The tech tyrants are waiting, probably licking their chops, thinking about all the control we will be forced to give them very soon.

4. The Return of "Welfare Queens"

Few things are more insincere than apologizing for what someone else did—especially when they didn't even do it. But that's just what California's Reparations Task Force for the descendants of slaves tried to do—by demanding the state of California apologize for what Ronald Reagan *didn't* do.

Or *say*.

"As California Governor (1967–1975), Ronald Reagan coined the term 'welfare queen' as racist coding to promote his philosophy preferring a limited government," according to the task force.[127] "This terminology conjures stereotypes of single Black women as hypersexualized, aggressive, and dependent on government income with frivolous spending habits," the latter a psychologically interesting malaprop in that frivolous spending habits define government.

Especially when it comes to what is styled "welfare" and other government wealth-transfer programs that have access to unlimited funding, the latter being provided by the wealth of the taxpayers forced to hand it over for redistribution, without even the compensation of accountability—which was a big part of what Reagan actually said.

"Despite that," the task force continues, "the majority of welfare recipients are white, this racist label blamed African American women for shortfalls in the United States' social safety net and suggested they were more responsible for their poverty than others. Then-Governor Reagan has also been reported to have made racist remarks regarding African delegates to the United Nations."

Never mind that it's not true.

Nor that Reagan can't apologize for what he didn't "coin"—because he's been dead for almost two decades, having died in 2004.

So who did "coin" the term Reagan is accused of using?

The Chicago Tribune.

It did so in a 1976 news story about Reagan, recounting a campaign speech he gave earlier that year during his first presidential run, describing a woman named Linda Taylor who apparently had managed to transfer about $150,000 of other people's wealth into her own pockets via the "social safety net."

Here is part of what Reagan actually said: "In Chicago, they found a woman who…used 80 names, 30 addresses, 15 telephone numbers to collect food stamps, Social Security, veterans' benefits for four non-existent deceased veteran husbands, as well as welfare. Her tax-free cash income alone has been running $150,000 a year."

And what Reagan said was essentially correct.

Taylor owned a new Cadillac, jewelry, and fur coats, paid for by taxpayers who could not afford such luxuries themselves—having been forced to "help" Taylor buy them.

Taylor was eventually charged with fraud, including the use of multiple aliases to obtain benefits far beyond what she was entitled to. She was eventually convicted and served time in prison.

Reagan was right. And the committee has it all wrong.

The truth was detailed in a 2013 *Slate* article about the controversy, which described Taylor's "brazen pilfering from public coffers."[128] When caught, Taylor "remained impassive, an unrepentant defendant bedecked in expensive clothes and oversize hats."

But never mind that.

Reagan is white and dead and male—and so must be guilty of being "racist." He is certainly *guilty* as far as the task force is concerned. Because it is necessary to conjure guilt when looking for someone to blame when the one who did the thing in question isn't a politically convenient one.

The *Tribune* doesn't quite have the target appeal of Reagan, who is the father of modern American conservatism and high up on the enemies list of the Woke Left, even though he's been dead for almost twenty years.

Reagan's name must be dragged through the mud for more than just what he didn't "coin." In addition, the task force demanded that the state of California's apology tour "must also include a censure of the gravest barbarities carried out on behalf of the State by its representative officers, governing bodies, and the people."

Meaning, of course, Reagan. And not just him either. Anyone who opposes the agenda of racial victimology and the profits (and power) to be mined by blaming people as a class for what they didn't do—and then making them pay for it.

The task force's indictment includes "suppression of the Black Panther Party in the 1960s and 1970s"—and never mind any *mea culpas* to the victims of the murderous activities of the Black Panthers during that time, which include the two Oakland police officers shot during an ambush organized by the Panthers' "minister of informa-tion," Eldridge Cleaver, in 1968.

Reagan and those who supported him are also apparently "guilty" of "terminating affirmative action programs in public employment," because it's "racist" to advocate the color-blind hiring of people based on qualifications rather than their skin color, as Reagan and those who supported him did.

A particularly idiotic assertion is that Reagan (and the state) were involved in "developing oil and gas projects and building hazardous waste plants near majority-black neighborhoods," with the implication being that was the point of the thing rather than incidental. There are no "oil and gas projects" or "hazardous waste plants" in Nancy Pelosi's neighborhood for a reason that has nothing to do with the color of her skin but a lot to do with the color of her money.

The committee also bemoans "racial disparities in the child wel-fare system, law enforcement, the prison population, jury service, health care, the number of black physicians and licensed attorneys," all of it to be apologized for on behalf of the man who didn't do any of it because Reagan had nothing to do with preventing anyone who was qualified to become a physician or an attorney from becoming one.

Because who would do that?

None of these facts matter when you need someone to blame in order to make those who didn't do it pay for it, which is what this "reparations" business is ultimately all about.

Someone alive today is to be blamed for what someone else—who has been dead for more than 150 years—may have done to some other person, also long dead, with the money going to some other person who didn't have it done to them, paid for by people who had nothing to do with what was supposedly done.

Interestingly, the committee demands handouts—whoops, "rep-arations"—equivalent to just about what Linda Taylor was pulling down each year in Chicago, back in the '70s: just shy of $150,000 each.

It's a good thing the Gipper is no longer around to see what the state he governed is doing these days.

Then again, if he were, he might do something about it.

5. Gavin Newsom and the Skin Color Marxists

The German National Socialists had a policy called *Sippenhaft*,[129] which they used to punish the relatives of people who'd done something the government of national socialist Germany disapproved of.

The idea was to instill fear—and guilt—in everyone. If you did something, your wife and children would pay for it.

Heinrich Himmler, the head of the notorious SS that was the main enforcement arm of national socialist policies, explained: "This man has committed treason; his blood is bad; there is traitor's blood in him; that must be wiped out. And in the blood feud, the entire clan was wiped out down to the last member. And so, too, will the enemies of national socialist Germany be wiped out down to the last member."

The socialist governor of California, Gavin Newsom, is in favor of enacting a similar policy[130] that involves a payout of $569 *billion*[131]— one that goes even further than punishing merely the relatives of people who affronted the government.

Newsom wants to make anyone who happens to be white "help" pay out about a quarter-million dollars each in reparations to anyone who happens to be black—even if the white person's ancestors had nothing to do with what was done to the ancestors of those black people.

What about Asians and Hispanics in California? Are they white adjacent? Time for them to pay up, too, for zero reason whatsoever?

"We are looking at reparations on a scale that is the largest since Reconstruction," said Jovan Scott Lewis,[132] a professor of African Diaspora Studies at the University of California, Berkeley.

According to an article in the *New York Post*, the payment of these reparations will "shrink the wealth gap between white and black Californians."[133]

Which, of course, it would—just the same as robbing Peter to pay Paul increases the net worth of Paul. But it also decreases the net worth of Peter. Wouldn't that oblige Paul's descendants to pay reparations to Peter's descendants, to make them whole? This is madness.

It is not exculpatory that a white person living in California today didn't have ancestors in California—or the United States—when the ancestors of black people living in California today were enslaved or otherwise oppressed.

And which black people, exactly?

Does dummy Newsom not know that California fought on the side of the Union in the Civil War?[134]

A great deal of genealogical divining would need to be done to establish a viable claim under the usual rules of evidence; how to divine whether a white person living today had an ancestor who oppressed black people in the past?

And how much did the white person's ancestor oppress the black person's ancestor?

No worries.

Any person with white skin will do, even if that person's white ancestors had nothing to do with slavery or any other form of oppressing the descendants of slaves.

Because socialist politicians such as Newsom view everything through a collective lens. It is beside the point whether an individual white person—living or dead—imposed harm on a specific black person, living or dead. The point, insofar as Newsom and other advocates of financial *Sippenhaft* see it, is that all whites are collectively guilty for the sins of all whites and, by dint of those collective sins, owe a collective debt.

Thus, California's Reparations Task Force—which Newsom tasked with imposing a latter-day version of *Sippenhaft* upon all whites for what was done to some blacks, particularly as regards to "discriminatory housing practices" during the period between 1933 and 1977.

According to the task force, black people living in California during that time were defrauded of about $5,000 annually in the form of lost equity in homes that were taken by the state through eminent domain to make way for roads or nicer homes—though it does not appear to have occurred to the task force that it wasn't "white people" who did this so much as the government.

Individual people—white or black—do not have the legal power to eminent domain anyone's home. Only the government has the power to do that. Nor do they have the power to incarcerate anyone, another one of the sins putatively laid at the feet of yesterday's white people—along with the "devaluation" of black health care and other such affronts.

But it won't be the government that's paying out the reparations to make amends for all of that. It will be the people of California who are forced to pay the government of California the taxes that the government then uses to pay reparations—and take the credit for having paid out.

Naturally, there will be no exemption from these taxes for black California taxpayers, whose tax money will be redistributed to other black people in direct cash payments or payments in kind (e.g., free tuition, housing grants, and so on) as "reparations" for the collective sins of white people.

In other words, it's no skin off Newsom's nose.

Besides, how many of these black people voted for Newsom instead of African American Republican Larry Elder? When they feel the pain, I suppose Gavin can say, "You're welcome."

Let's set aside the fact that Newsom is white. Let's not forget how much he oppressed Californians of all colors by forcing them to close their businesses while he went about his business, and often without wearing the mask he forced others—black and white—to wear.

What about reparations for them?

The people actually—demonstrably and specifically—oppressed by a very specific, readily identifiable person?

Socialists aren't interested in that.

What they are interested in is power—over everyone, black and white.

Newsom has established himself as excelling at that.

VI.
June Privilege

"If any entity in the United States deserves to have a reckoning with its ghastly history, it's the Democratic Party. The Democratic Party deserves cancellation."

1. Juneteenth? You're Welcome! Sincerely, the Grand Old Party

Juneteenth, otherwise known as Emancipation Day, is the day we celebrate the final end of slavery in the United States. On June 19, 1865, word reached black Americans in Galveston, Texas, that the Civil War had ended in a Union victory, and slavery had been abolished.[135] Former slaves were free.

The date began to be celebrated in Texas communities the following year as the Republicans worked to reconstruct the Union that the Democrats had worked so hard to divide and destroy since 1861. In 1980, Texas became the first state to make Juneteenth a holiday, paving the way for it to become a federal holiday in 2020.

When America's founders spoke of creating a "more perfect union," the abolition of slavery was one of the things they were getting at. The world they grew up in was one in which involuntary servitude of all kinds, including slavery, was common. Kings could take your land and home on a whim and have you executed. Royals believed they ruled by divine right, that their blood was better than yours.

The founders rejected all that, but the world wasn't quite ready for the radical ideas they had in mind, which included full equality under the law no matter what your name was or what color your skin happened to be.

Fast forward a few score and a handful of years, and the Republican Party came into being. The Republican Party was explicitly founded by people whose goal was the abolition of slavery in the United States. The opposition party, then and now called the Democratic Party, stood on the principle that slavery was not only legally and morally acceptable, it should spread to new territories and states as the country grew from its East Coast colonies toward the Pacific.

The Republican Party's first leader and eventual president, Abraham Lincoln, detested slavery and noted in one of his most famous speeches that "a house divided against itself [over the question of whether people can own other people] cannot stand."

The Democrats put that notion to the test, putting America through its most severe crisis, when they seceded from the Union explicitly on the question of whether states or the federal government could prohibit slavery.

The Democrats' shameful legacy on the question of slavery and race would only get worse from there. After fighting and losing the Civil War, some decided to fight on in guerilla terrorist action. The outlaw bandit Jesse James was one such terrorist. The Ku Klux Klan was founded to be the Democrats' terrorist wing by defeated Confederate officers—all Democrats by party.

During the terrible war, Democrats sought to undermine Lincoln at every turn. The press of the day coined a term for these Democrats—"Copperheads"—because like the venomous snake, they hid and waited for any chance they might take to undermine the Union's cause. One Copperhead had been Lincoln's top general early in the war. The incompetent George McClellan refused to fight as much as possible, and in the midst of the war (and after Lincoln had justifiably fired him), McClellan challenged Lincoln in 1864 as a Democrat. While claiming that he supported the Union cause, McClellan ran an explicitly racist campaign against Lincoln. A McClellan campaign broadside gave away the game.[136] It accused Lincoln of favoring "Negro equality," (which he did) and pledged that McClellan would oppose equality.

After the war, and after a Democrat actor named John Wilkes Booth murdered Lincoln, President Ulysses S. Grant did a remarkable but largely forgotten thing. As he worked to restore the Union and "bind up its wounds" as Lincoln had called for, Grant desegregated the federal workforce and conferred full civil rights on black Americans in 1866. During his tenure, Grant championed the Fourteenth Amendment, which granted birthright citizenship and empowered the US

Department of Justice to prosecute racist attacks on black Americans. He also cracked down on the Klan, all but stamping it out by the time he left office.

A Republican president led these real achievements for black Americans. They're largely forgotten now because our Democratic Party-aligned, union-controlled schools no longer teach real history and because the Democrats eventually undid Grant's laudable progress.

President Woodrow Wilson, a Democrat and a "progressive," is remembered mostly for leading America into World War I and for spearheading the establishment of the League of Nations—the first of which was unnecessary, and the second of which was a flop largely due to Wilson's blind partisanship, poor leadership, and, ultimately, his suffering a debilitating stroke. But Wilson should be remembered for his racism.

Today, if you look up the progress of civil rights in America—including desegregating the federal workforce and the military—you'll find that Roosevelt and Truman, both Democrats, led those efforts. That's true, but why? Because Wilson, another Democrat, had undone Republican Grant's efforts. Wilson resegregated the federal workforce and even breathed new life into the Ku Klux Klan.

How? In 1915, Wilson screened the infamous movie *The Birth of a Nation* at the White House. This ode to the Klan inspired William Joseph Simmons to resuscitate the racist terror group that Grant had destroyed. Wilson was an academic—the former president of Princeton, in fact—and an ardent segregationist. He even wrote a college textbook praising the Klan. As president of the United States, he rolled back practically all of the hard-won racial progress of the post-Civil War years and Reconstruction. So, when FDR and Truman ended various aspects of segregation later, they were killing off Wilson's toxic and un-American policies.

Fast forward to the Civil Rights Act of 1964. Democrats claim credit for that law because Lyndon Baines Johnson signed it into existence. But it's worth noting that even though Democrats controlled both houses of Congress at the time, Republicans actually voted for the law in greater numbers.

In addition to fighting for slavery and establishing segregation after they lost the Civil War, Democrats also brought about and supported a horrid institution that still exists: Planned Parenthood. Democrats, including Hillary Clinton, lavish praise on the organization that aborts more black children than any other by far. What they don't acknowledge is that Planned Parenthood was founded explicitly to kill minorities.

That's not a myth, and it's not even up for debate. Planned Parenthood founder Margaret Sanger was a socialist, a eugenicist (a rancid racial philosophy that counted Adolf Hitler among its adherents), and a virulent hate-filled racist. Sanger in 1938 spoke to an official Ku Klux Klan group. The organization she founded makes most of its millions today from abortions in clinics that happen to be located predominantly in minority neighborhoods and from funds it receives from Democrat politicians who, in turn, accept its praise, awards, and activist support.

Planned Parenthood's intent from its founding was to suppress the growth of nonwhite populations. Democrats, who accept socialists such as Bernie Sanders and Margaret Sanger for support, fund Planned Parenthood with your tax dollars. Democrats never really let go of their racist roots and have moved much closer to socialism despite its bloody history. They've just traded in their support of slavery in the nineteenth century for segregation in the twentieth century and for aborting black babies in the twenty-first century.

If any entity in the United States deserves to have a reckoning with its ghastly history, it's the Democratic Party. The Democratic Party deserves cancellation.

As for the other party, the one the media routinely smears as racist, Republicans have fought against all of the Democrats' racial evil and machinations and for that more perfect union the founders spoke of since the party began in 1854.[137] They have no ties to slavery, except for ending it, and no ties to segregation, except for voting to end that too. Democrats fund the abortion of black babies by the millions, while the Republican position is akin to the party's origins on slavery: abolition.

Juneteenth is a truly American holiday, all about the fight for freedom for all. Republicans deserve an honored place in the holiday's history.

2. The Summer Wind, Came Blowin' In, Black and Queer

White Fragility and *Gender Queer* will replace John Steinbeck and Ernest Hemingway on the summer reading list.

There is a reason why preadolescent children are being taught about masturbation, oral sex, and gay sex in government schools— and thereby *encouraged* to have sex years before it is normal for kids to begin thinking about sex.

And to be confused about their sex, on top of all that.

It is because they *are* being taught to think about it by teachers who are *encouraged* to obsess about it.

The National Education Association, which is the largest union representing government school teachers, recommends that the people who will be teaching your kids every fall spend their summer vacations paging through *Gender Queer*, which is a "book" in much the same way that *Penthouse* is a "magazine." The difference is, *Penthouse* used to be kept behind the store counter and was understood to be for adults only.

Gender Queer is meant for kids as a teaching aid.

It was written by someone named Maia Kobabe. *Someones*, actually.

It is difficult to ascertain who or how many persons we're dealing with here, as Kobabe uses the made-up pronouns "e/em/eir." In saner times, we would have identified "e/em/eir" as mentally ill.

Of course, we find ourselves living in very different times precisely because mental illness has been normalized. It is now considered normal for individuals to "identify" as *individuals*—plural—and to believe that biological sex is "just a construct" that can be changed by changing your beliefs about it. Just like your pronouns, which can change on a whim and everyone else is supposed to go along, no questions asked.

That, of course, is merely deranged—as would be obvious if anyone were to insist that they are in fact a Klingon and demanded to be addressed as such.

But peddling sex to underage children is *sick*.

And that is what the NEA recommends government teachers do, by urging them to spend their taxpayer-financed summer off reading *all* about it, so they'll be ready to tell your kids all about it when school resumes in the fall.

The book, which is mostly graphics with explicit bubble captions, follows the multiple-personality "journey" of "e/em/eir" as they "grapple" with "how to come out to family and society, bonding with friends over erotic gay fanfiction, and facing the trauma and *fundamental violation* of pap smears."

Only in the world of the woking dead could health screening for women to detect potential cancer before it spreads be styled a "fundamental violation" at the same time that genitally mutilating underage girls is styled "gender affirming care."

"E/em/eir" relates their joy at discovering their first sex toy: a "$10 bullet vibrator." They then go on to explain in detail the joy of their first orgasm: "It is still one of my most vivid, lovely experiences." "Lovely" is also the not-safe-for-work (but OK for school) explicit description—along with a very explicit graphic depiction—of the act of fellatio.

This is the kind of thing government schoolteachers are encouraged to read—and thereby encouraged to *impart to kids*, whose parents are forced to *finance* this rot through the taxes they're compelled to pay to "support" the local government schools and the teachers who work there.

Or is it *woke* there?

The woke cry "book ban!" and make clumsy comparisons to Nazi Germany when parents of underage kids object to such materials being available in the government schools they're forced to finance. And of course, parents are "hateful" when they question permanently physically altering children who are too young to legally buy or smoke cigarettes.

Gender Queer isn't the only grossly inappropriate title on the NEA's suggested summer reading list. *All Boys Aren't Blue* is all about the tyranny of the sex you're conceived and born with. Sex is a matter of belief, "assigned at birth," that can be changed later, and it's wrong for other people (such as doctors and nurses) to identify infants as "boys" or "girls."

The *New York Times* naturally effuses that *All Boys Aren't Blue* is "an exuberant, unapologetic memoir infused with a deep but clear-eyed love for its subjects." The book specifically targets "black kids who need guidance and resources."

Predictably, *All Boys Aren't Blue* author George M. Johnson "identifies" as "they."

And if you had any doubt that the recommended reading—and subsequent instruction—above *isn't* for kids, consider what the NEA recommends for students specifically. For example, there's *Milo and Marcos at the End of the World*, which is described as a "gay romance" about a boy hiding his same-sex interests from his "deeply religious parents." There's also *'Twas the Night Before Pride*, a "glittering celebration of queer families" that "puts Pride gently in perspective," and is modeled after *'Twas the Night Before Christmas*.

The entire NEA list—which may be found online[138]—is fundamentally about what woke government schoolteachers want your kids to become, before they even have a chance to understand who they are.

And who they aren't.

3. William Wokespeare and the Dogs of Virtue

In one of the best-known lines of dialogue from one of Shakespeare's best-known plays, *The Merchant of Venice*, the character Shylock—who is Jewish—asks:

> Hath not a Jew eyes? Hath not a Jew hands, organs, dimensions, senses, affections, passions; fed with the same food, hurt with the same weapons, subject to the same diseases, healed by the same means, warmed and cooled by the same winter and summer as a Christian is? If you prick us do we not bleed? If you tickle us, do we not laugh? If you poison us, do we not die? And if you wrong us, shall we not revenge?[139]

Shakespeare—through the character Shylock—is pointing out our common humanity. This is a common thread running through all of Shakespeare's work, which happened to be written by a white man for all men—for all time. Full stop. Billy Shakespeare says, "You're welcome."

And for women, too.

For what else is *Romeo and Juliet* about—if not the love of a man for a woman and a woman for a man?

But woke "scholarship" sees something else. Well, it sees one thing. Always—obsessively—the same thing.

"Shakespeare's work," says Daniel Pollack-Pelzner in an article for *The Atlantic*, "was central to the construction of whiteness as a racial category during the Renaissance, and white people, in turn, have used

Shakespeare to regulate social hierarchies ever since."[140] This is probably news to the people—of all races—who have read Shakespeare and seen the plays. It would also be news to every liberal actor who has adapted the Bard at his most moving, from Orson Welles[141] to Kenneth Branagh.[142]

Pollack-Pelzner writes approvingly of an essay collection called "White People in Shakespeare," that is "cannily" edited by a UCLA professor of Shakespeare and race....

Of course. It's as predictable as the lead editorial in *Pravda* during the Brezhnev era, for those who remember.

It is also almost like the kid in the classic Bruce Willis movie, *The Sixth Sense*—except instead of seeing dead people everywhere, people like Pollack-Pelzner see racism everywhere. Including, apparently, in *Othello*[143]—a play about a black man who isn't a slave or subordinate but who (like Shylock) is riven by the same passions and plagued by the same doubts—and devils—as often beset other men.

All men.

The "green-eyed monster" of jealousy, for instance.

It is not a weakness of some men, according to the color of their skin. It is a weakness with which all men must wrestle, as Othello does: "No, Iago," he says to his scheming subordinate, who is trying to make his master suspect his wife Desdemona of being unfaithful to him. "I'll see before I doubt; when I doubt, prove. And on the proof there is no more but this...away at once with love or jealousy," as he wrestles with himself over whom—and what—to believe.

In the end, Othello gives in to his doubts, is overwhelmed by jealousy, and kills his faithful wife—which is a tragedy that all men can understand and hence the appeal of this play, which is as powerful today as it was when it was written more than four hundred years ago because it is about people, not race.

The fact that Othello's character is black is as incidental as the fact that the man who wrote the play was white. But not to a race-obsessed man like Pollack-Pelzner, who sees "hierarchies" being constructed by the Bard, in order to "define whiteness."

Never mind that Othello does not "define" himself thusly.

"Shakespeare's work," Pollack-Pelzner nevertheless continues, "was central to the construction of whiteness as a racial category during the Renaissance."

What Pollack-Pelzner seems to be saying here is that because most of the people who lived in Europe four hundred years ago happened to be white, they were deliberately "constructing whiteness as a racial category"—as a pyramid scheme of white privilege.

If so, then—by the same logic—the people living in Africa four hundred years ago were also "constructing blackness as a racial category"—when, in fact, they were, like the Europeans of the time, relating stories about their experiences as people.

That they happened to be black was a superficiality.

There was no conspiracy—of either whiteness or blackness. Yet leftists of the Pollack-Pelzner school are determined to make everything about whiteness or blackness,[144] perhaps because they have lost sight of what Shakespeare's plays are all about. Which has as much to do with race as a NASCAR race, though Pollack-Pelzner probably sees "racism" in that too.

"What's beautiful in Shakespeare—or what Shakespeare's speakers take as beautiful," he writes, "is often cast in racial terms."

Well, where, exactly? Is Juliet described in racial terms? Can he cite even one example of such? None are adduced. Instead, he imputes race and race-obsession where it does not exist, so as to construct the race-based narrative he wishes to advance.

"On historical grounds, there's a lot of evidence to suggest that even if people in the 16th and 17th centuries didn't use racial categories in quite the same ways we might, they were wrestling with the construction of social hierarchies based on emerging categories of race that went on to shape our world."

"Oy vey," Shylock might have said.

As Shakespeare is probably saying, right now—as he views the stage upon which the "poor player struts and frets his hour...and then is heard no more. It is a tale told by an idiot, full of sound and fury, signifying nothing."

4. Mind-Boggling Emoji Bean Counting

Wokeism now extends to emojis[145]—because it's not enough to obsess about skin color (and other external attributes) in the real world. The virtual world must also be corrupted by the same sick obsession with race—by people who claim to be "fighting racism."

People like NPR writer Alejandra Marquez Janse, who believes that figuring out which emoji is racially correct for each application is "more complex than you think."

Which of course, it is, because of people like Janse and her co-author, Asma Khalid. A simple cartoon image of a thumbs-up or down must now be shaded exactly to match the skin color of the sender. This is part of a "conversation about race and identity" that people like Janse and Khalid seem unable to stop conversing about.

Perhaps because if they did, they'd have nothing else to converse about. And that silence would be as deadly to the writing careers of people like Janse and Khalid as the Cuomo brothers have been to CNN's ratings.

"In 2015, five skin tone options became available for hand gesture emojis," the pair carefully explain. "Choosing one can be a simple texting shortcut for some but for others it opens a complex conversation about race and identity."

Yikes! This is some wacko stuff.

Is there—could there possibly be—anything less "complex" than a cartoon thumbs-up image?

I like this. How hard is that?

Traditionally rendered in cartoon yellow—to convey the sentiment without the additional race freight. Which freight must be added—so that there is a need for "conversation."

The pair quote Andrew McGill of *The Atlantic*, who found that "some white people may stick with the yellow emoji because they don't want to assert their privilege by adding a light-skinned emoji...."

As opposed to just wanting to send a thumbs-up text—and that's all there is to it.

If Janse and Khalid were genuinely interested in a "conversation" not based on race, they might have written an article in praise of the racially neutral Simpsons' yellow thumbs-up symbol, which says the same thing in every language and regardless of the color of the sender's skin.

But Janse and Khalid want emojis to say other things. Or believe they do, *sub rosa*.

So do some texting wokesters quoted in the NPR piece, including Sarai Cole who "identifies" as "black and an American descendant of slavery." She told Janse and Khalid that she is "confused" when friends who aren't black or American descendants of slavery text her using the brown emoji thumbs-up—which they are apparently not supposed to use.

Janse and Khalid do not ask Cole why her friends should not be able to "identify" as whatever they wish—a cardinal tenet of identity theory. Or, for that matter, why she—a black American descendant of slavery—uses the brown emoji.

Isn't that...*cultural appropriation*?

Then again, if Rachel Dolezal, the white former chapter head at the NAACP, can "identify" as black (so as to advance her career at the expense of actual black people),[146] then how can Cole object to her brown friends "identifying" as whatever color they like—and emoji'ing accordingly?

That would make things simpler. Let people use whatever color emoji they like, for whatever reasons they like. Some people like green. Or red. It doesn't need to mean anything more than that.

But, unsurprisingly, Cole sees something sinister in that.

"I think it would be nice if it is their default," she explained to Janse and Khalid. "But if they're just using it with me or other brown people I would want to look into that deeper and know why they're doing that."

Of course. There must always be a *why*. And it must always be some deep-seated, pathologically poisonous, racially invidious reason. It can't just be a cartoon image of a thumbs-up.

It's why Jennifer Epperson, who also "identifies" as black (though she could be brown or white or perhaps even candy-cane red and green) told Janse and Khalid that "she changed her approach [to picking emoji colors] depending on who she was talking to," defined as follows:

"I use the default emoji—the yellow-toned one—for professional settings and then I use the dark brown emoji for friends and family," explaining that she doesn't "have the emotional capacity to unpack race relations in the professional setting."

Which "unpacking" is a necessity of her own creation—or a figment of her imagination.

Most people don't see race when they see an emoji. They see a symbol of a sentiment, a convenient shorthand for expression. According to the logic of Epperson, Cole, and the race wokesters of NPR, we'll need black, brown, and every other conceivable shade of the rainbow for heart symbols too. Not just *red*, because that leaves out everyone except American Indians.

Whoops! Sorry: Native Americans and other *indigenous peoples*.

It's arguably just as "confusing" for people who don't fall into either of those two racial boxes to use red hearts to convey the sentiment, I love you, as it is for people who aren't brown to use black thumbs-up emojis when they ought to be using a less "confusing" emoji.

Actually, it's just *insane*—a simpler way to understand (and dismiss) this whole sorry race-obsessed business.

People who can't just send a thumbs-up—or an I love you—without "unpacking race relations" might stop to consider that if this is all that's left of "racism" in America, it might be time to start "unpacking" something else.

Beginning with themselves.

VII.
July Privilege

"It isn't that liberals hate walls exactly. They have no problem walling off their high-rent enclaves to keep themselves safe from fellow Americans *they consider undesirable. Oftentimes, the walls are invisible, so they can pretend they don't exist. They can pretend they're virtuous while they're at it."*

1. Walter White Fights His Privilege

Losers tend to find other losers.

The last time anyone heard from Chris Wallace, he was leaving Fox News—the top cable news network in the world—for CNN.

Actually, it was CNN+, which died before it could even get off the ground. CNN itself is still floundering, barely qualifying as an also-ran in cable news.

Wallace emerged and spoke with *Breaking Bad* star Bryan Cranston as part of Max's *Who's Talking to Chris Wallace.* The actor, who is also known for playing a dentist on *Seinfeld,* straight-up drilled American history. He claimed that a phrase as innocuous as "Make America Great Again" might be racist.

"I…when I see the Make America Great Again, my comment is, do you, do you…Do you accept that that could possibly be construed as a racist remark? And most people, a lot of people go, how could that be racist [to] make America great again? I said, so just ask yourself from, from an African American experience, when was it ever great in America for the African American? When was it great? So if you're making it great again, it's not including them."

Life in America for black people is actually great right now. They live in the freest country in the world. It's getting worse in our cities for black America and everyone else, but that's not a mark against our country's greatness. It's a mark against the foolish Democrats who defunded the police and unleashed crime on the streets.

Ask any black person in South Africa or Zimbabwe if they would trade places with any black American. You'd get *a lot* of takers. After all, Wakanda is not a real place.[147]

Life was actually great for African Americans under Donald Trump, author of the phrase "Make America Great Again." Blacks enjoyed great employment and greater opportunities than ever before.

Black America had historically low unemployment under Trump, a fact you almost never hear anyone in the media bring up.

Trump's policies proved the American idea that a rising economic tide lifts everyone.

Life was also great for African Americans under Ronald Reagan. America stood astride the world, rebuilding its economy to heights not seen for years afterward, while facing down and ultimately defeating the Soviet Union with its evil empire.

Cranston's point is that because slavery existed, America isn't, and never was, great. Because there was oppression, America was never great. He even compared America to Germany, arguing that we have a history similar to its Nazi past.

But if you talk to most black Americans, they'll disagree with that. It's the radicals who build their careers on trashing America who agree with it.

Cranston only listens to them.

The man known to many as Walter White forgets—or probably never knew—that the American founding he decries set in motion the engine of freedom that eventually freed the slaves and recognized civil rights for all. It's no accident that it happened in America.

The founders designed the Constitution and its philosophical foundation, the Declaration of Independence, to do just that.

America didn't exist until July 4, 1776, and American slavery was ended by Lincoln's emancipation proclamation on January 1, 1863. That's eighty-seven years of American slavery. Not one hundred, not four hundred, not five hundred. *You're welcome.*

It took eighty-seven years for America to declare war on itself and end an abomination brought to North America by the Dutch, French, English, Spanish, Portuguese, and others.

Frederick Douglass, who was black and had escaped slavery himself, noted this fact in 1852, when he mused over the purpose of the Constitution and the Fourth of July in light of the existence of slavery.

"American slavery is inconsistent with America's founding principles and with Christianity; it is terrible for the nation and endangers the Union; you should get rid of it," Douglass said, and he was right.

"The Constitution isn't a pro-slavery document," Douglass continued, and he was right again.

The escaped slave declared: "In that instrument I hold there is neither warrant, license, nor sanction of the hateful thing; but, interpreted as it ought to be interpreted, the Constitution is a GLORIOUS LIBERTY DOCUMENT. Read its preamble, consider its purposes. Is slavery among them?"[148]

Against the law, white people took it up themselves to teach Douglass the English alphabet. Thank God they did.

The Constitution was written and agreed upon by the framers that people like Cranston consistently denounce. Slavery was not there. It could have been. But the evil of it nagged at the conscience.

The founders compromised because they had to in the midst of a dangerous war with the superpower of the time. They still put in place the machine that would, one day, crush slavery under its wheels. And so it did.

America did not invent slavery. She inherited it from Europe's colonial powers and from deep human history in which slavery has existed for thousands of years (and still does in places).

But America's gift to the world is the idea that all men—all—are created equal, and no government can be allowed to deprive us of our natural rights. Such a government is illegitimate and should be done away with. This was a breathtakingly radical idea at the time.

Douglass read the Constitution and understood what it would do a decade or so hence. Why can't Cranston, who has the benefit of hindsight, do the same now?

He can but chooses not to. Like so many Hollywood hypocrites, Cranston is happy to enjoy the wealth Americans have given him while bashing everything that makes it possible and valuable.

It's fashionable to hate America in Hollywood and the media. It's practically mandatory.

That doesn't make it right.

They want to dismantle a system that makes their very ability to criticize it without fear of harm possible. The question is, with what would they replace America? What other system is purposely designed to spread freedom? China's? Russia's? Of course not.

Cranston likes to discuss white privilege, but the truth is he's blind to his own. He is privileged to pretend to be other people and build wealth far in excess of what the vast majority of humanity can even comprehend.

He's not alone in that. Black America has billionaires, a secretary of defense, revered writers, actors, musicians, church leaders, a former president, and everyday people who—like all Americans—are blessed with the fortune of where and when we were born.

2. Wakanda Is a Make-Believe Place, But America Has Real Black Heroes

Black Panther: Wakanda Forever racked up critical praise and an Oscar nomination for its positive portrayal of a mythical African country from which superheroes rise.[149] If it were real, Wakanda would be an incredible place: forward-thinking in technology yet still holding fast to its rich traditions.

The Left hates both of these things, however, when applied to the United States. Our technology gets trashed as destroying the planet. Our traditions are smeared by people steeped in Marxist critical race theory, our heroes denigrated, and our statues and monuments pulled down or vandalized.

The sad fact is the same hate-filled Left is busy not just tearing down America but ignoring the real present-day achievements and courage of great black Americans. These Americans refuse to be victims. They refuse to be bullied. But they also refuse to be penned up in the Left and its false, anti-American narratives.

Winsome Sears came to the United States from Jamaica at the age of six. To the American Left's way of thinking, she ought to be an intersectional champion—a woman (when they choose to define the term), an immigrant, and black.

True, she's a legal immigrant, so that's a strike against her if you're on the Left.

Sears has never been anyone's victim. She worked hard, excelled in school, and joined the United States Marines, where she served as an electrician. Her life of public service also includes running a shelter for the Salvation Army. When she entered politics, Sears started shattering walls immediately. She upset a career Democratic politician and became the first female, black, naturalized citizen to serve in the Virginia House. Today, Winsome Sears is Virginia's first female, black, naturalized citizen to serve as the commonwealth's lieutenant governor.[150]

You'd think all this would have made Sears the toast of every network and print newsroom in the country. The problem with Sears is she's a conservative Republican. Those two words erase all of her intersectional wins and all of her real achievements for the Left. So they pretend she doesn't exist.

The Left and the corporate media do the same, and have for decades, with Supreme Court Justice Clarence Thomas. In fact, they tried to destroy Thomas before his career on America's highest court ever started. Then Senator Joe Biden led that racist charge, attempting to tie Thomas to spurious sexual harassment charges. That was rich, given the fact that the white Biden was acting as a henchman for the white Senator Ted Kennedy, who had left a young woman to drown to save his own career and who had built up a legendary career of sexcapades himself.

Biden's shameless smearing of Thomas failed to keep him from becoming just the second black man to serve on the Supreme Court, where he has built up a career noted for its independence and fearlessness as a consistent champion of American constitutional government.

Like Winsome Sears, Thomas would be one of the most celebrated black men of all time but for the fact that he's a conservative Republican.

Dave Chappelle isn't a conservative Republican at all, but he's still a hero. Why? Because he believes in the bedrock American principle of free speech and fearlessly defends it with his life. That's no exaggeration: After one of his Netflix comedy specials outraged the Left, a man attacked Chappelle on stage with a handgun that also had a knife blade.[151] Such an attack tends to be classified as attempted murder. The culprit got less than a year in jail for the crime, which he said was triggered by the jokes Chappelle and another comedian told. Jokes that work well are often said to "kill," but only in our snowflake age may they get the comedian who tells them killed.

Chappelle has faced more than that one attack. His comedy specials spare no one from his laser-sharp humor, including the trans community, which has tried to force an ideological dictatorship on the world over the past few years (with help from the feeble-minded but opportunistic Joe Biden). Chappelle doesn't hate trans people; he's made that clear, but he despises psychological and ideological oppression. He's made that clear too. He's faced numerous attempts to cancel him, and that actual physical attack, for his courage.

The Left doesn't celebrate this real black American hero. It wants his career ended and his Netflix contract ripped up. To its credit, Netflix stands by Chappelle and is maybe the last bastion for real free speech in the United States.

America isn't short of black heroes who live real lives in our real, amazing country. Senator Tim Scott of South Carolina is the first black man to serve as a senator from the South since Reconstruction.[152] Michael Williams was a successful energy industry regulator in Texas years ago,[153] where Wallace Jefferson served as chief justice of the state Supreme Court.[154] Leo Terrell is one of the most successful civil rights litigators in the United States.[155] Denzel Washington, of course, is one of the most successful actors in Hollywood. All of these and many more black Americans succeed every day, living by their principles, never tearing America down, always showing gratitude for living in (what was and should be again) the freest and greatest country the world has ever known.

None of them are celebrated as the bona fide real-life heroes they are. Americans of all backgrounds should celebrate our real heroes and take a small break from the vibranium-rich mythical land of make-believe.

3. Justice Clarence Thomas Lops Off the Head of Affirmative Action

How far have we *not* come?

How about a sitting Supreme Court justice—a black woman, no less!—denouncing "colorblindness for all"?[156]

Those were the words—of abuse—penned by Justice Ketanji Brown Jackson in her dissent from the court's landmark 6–3 decision in *Students for Fair Admissions v. Harvard* and *SFFA v. University of North Carolina*, which bars colleges and universities from excluding applicants on the basis of race.

The court's July 2023 decision seemed like a measure of just how far America has progressed in race relations. At last, the people generally accept that it is wrong to deny a qualified applicant admission (and implicitly, a job or any other such thing) on the basis of their race.

And yet, it's also a measure of something else to find a member of the highest court *disagreeing* with that proposition.

Is it 1953 or 2023?

In Justice Jackson's opinion, it would be "worse" for black people to be considered according to their merit rather than their color because "race still matters." And so it does to a few people who apparently think it *is* 1953.

For Jackson, it is *right* to legalize racial exclusion on account of what she styles the "lived experiences of *all Americans* in innumerable ways."

Because she does not, in fact, favor "all Americans." She favors taking *action, affirmatively,* against those who do not fall into the racial (and implicitly, other) categories she considers undeserving, regardless of their merit and on the basis of their color. She believes people of *some* colors should be denied entry to colleges and universities whose standards they otherwise meet—solely because of their race.

That was the question at issue in *SFFS v. Harvard*, which was brought on behalf of students who didn't get into Harvard (as well as the University of North Carolina, a party to the case) because they had been "de-selected" on account of their race.

The admissions process at Harvard and UNC included a racial bean-counting system that sought to ensure there would not be a "dramatic drop-off" in admissions of students who are not white, relative to the prior year's admission. In practice, this meant that if there were *too many* qualified white applicants relative to qualified black applicants, the white applicants were denied admission to make space for less-qualified applicants who happened to have the right melanin levels.

This part of the process is called the "lop."

As in *lopping off.* The "lop list" evaluates candidates on the basis of four criteria: legacy status, recruited athlete status, financial aid eligibility, and race.

Race is a "determinative tip" in the admissions process.

Well, it *was.*

Writing for the majority, Chief Justice John Roberts said—without using the exact word—that Harvard's "lopping" of qualified people from the list on the basis of race violated Title VI of the Civil

Rights Act and that similar practices by the University of North Carolina violated the Equal Protection Clause of the Fourteenth Amendment. "Eliminating racial discrimination means eliminating *all* of it," Roberts wrote.

Roberts may be faulted for many things, including his bizarre view that it is "constitutional" to force people to buy the services of private, for-profit health insurance providers provided the mandate is characterized as a "tax." But his reasoning that using race to deny people admission to college is *racist* is unassailable.

Because it is racist by definition.

The Woke Left, of which Ketanji Brown Jackson appears to be a member in good standing, has a much different definition. It believes that racism is legitimate when it is practiced against white people, who have supposedly benefitted from "institutional racism," which affords whites all kinds of unfair advantages at the expense of all blacks and other "people of color."

So, it's payback time. It doesn't matter if you haven't engaged in discrimination personally, let alone had the power to discriminate unlawfully or otherwise.

Here's the problem with Justice Jackson's tone-deaf dissent: it presumes sameness based upon superficialities, when in fact there are substantive differences far more relevant than color.

Consider the white kid who grew up in a single-wide trailer and got by on food stamps who maybe lost his place at Harvard to one of Barack Obama's privileged daughters. A majority of the court ruled that white kid deserves the same shot at a Harvard education that Obama's kids got. At the heart of the court's decision is that it is no less cruel to turn away a poor white kid in favor of the children of rich and connected black people today than it was to turn away a poor black kid on the same basis, so long ago.

A black kid like Thurgood Marshall, for instance.

The first black Supreme Court Justice attended "historically black" Howard University because schools such as Harvard and UNC took pains to exclude people of Marshall's color once upon a time. It is why there had to be "historically black" colleges and universities in the first place.

But that was more than fifty years ago.

Over the years, the idea that anyone ought to be "kept in their place" based on their race has been shunted to the periphery of moral sensibility for the simple reason that the practice is so obviously *wrong*. It does not take an Oliver Wendell Holmes to understand this.

But it *does* take an epic dummy like Ketanji Brown Jackson to style the court's decision as "let them eat cake obliviousness."

She objected to thwarting what she called the "crucial work" of rewarding—and necessarily punishing—people on the basis of their race. That is how we get to a fair and equitable society—somehow, eventually—in Justice Jackson's purblind view.

This is what happens when a president nominates and the Senate confirms a judge who couldn't even define what a woman is because she is "not a biologist."

Thankfully, there are still at least six other justices gifted with common sense—among them Justice Clarence Thomas, who did not mince words in calling Justice Jackson's dissent "racist."

"Rather than focus on individuals as individuals," Justice Thomas wrote in his concurring opinion, Justice Jackson preferred "invoking statistical racial gaps to argue in favor of defining and categorizing individuals by their race." While racism is an ugly reality of our past, he went on, the core issue is that "*the law* must disregard all racial distinctions" *today*.

In other words, it's 2023, not 1953.

Boom! Justice Thomas mic drop.

4. A Practical Guide to Hunting White People in South Africa

It's *very* "racist," according to people like Justice Ketanji Brown Jackson, to support the Supreme Court's landmark 2023 decision repudiating race-based college admission policies.[157] But it *isn't* racist to sing a song that urges the *mass slaughter* of whites, according to many of the same people.

It's just a "struggle" song, says Julius Malema, the Marxist leader of the South African Economic Freedom Fighters.

Right.

And the "Horst Wessel Song"—the anthem of Nazi Germany—was also just a "struggle" song.[158] The National Socialists said *exactly* that. The leader of National Socialism titled his book, *Mein Kampf*—*My Struggle*.

Neither had *anything* to do with racism....

See how far that gets you with a leftist?

Of course, leftists have their own special (fungible) standards and definitions. For a leftist, the meaning of a word is whatever he says it means, neither more nor less (per Humpty Dumpty). Thus, when a leftist "asks" to "have a conversation" about how much of your money they intend to *take*, they aren't *asking* you anything. They are *telling* you.

So much for "conversation"—which is also always only within the boundaries of what leftists say is permissible to converse about. Anything else is "hate" speech. As for example, wanting to have a *conversation* about how a boy can "transition" into a girl.

Pointing out that a boy is a boy—no matter how he dresses or acts—is an act of "misgendering."

To state that a *man* cannot bear children is "misinformation."

The allowable form is *birthing people*.

Of a piece, leftists don't disallow the singing of a hate-filled song when it is sung by a black leftist—even when the song demands the blood of white people. Even when the leftist who sung it at a political rally for leftists affirmed the threat by responding with a *specific* threat directed at Elon Musk—for doing what white leftists used to do when confronted by racists:

He called out the *racism*.

"They are openly pushing for the genocide of white people in South Africa," said Musk, who was born in South Africa, is white, and is *not* a racist. "Why do you do nothing?" he asked South Africa's president, Cyril Ramaphosa, who is black.

Cue crickets.

And this, from Malema: "I will sing this song...when I feel like [it]. It's not my song. It's a *struggle* song. Why must I educate Elon Musk? He looks like an illiterate." The latter being an interesting insult given the words of the "struggle" song, which literally urge the killing of the "boer," which means just one thing: a white South African. It has no other meaning. That is what a boer is, by definition.

But that means nothing to a leftist.

The effrontery is astounding. But the threat is even more alarming—as well as the silence of the Left, which indicates approval of the threat.

Malema went on to say that "the only thing that protects [Elon Musk] is his white skin."

Protects him? From what, exactly?

Everyone understands what Malema meant, without having to parse what he meant. South Africa has an extremely ugly history of racial violence, including racial violence by blacks against blacks during the apartheid era—when blacks who were considered to have collaborated with the white-run government were regularly "necklaced"—i.e., they had a truck tire placed over them, doused with gasoline, and set afire.[159]

Is Malema rekindling those flames?

"You must never be scared to kill. A revolution demands that at some point there must be killing because the killing is part of a revolutionary act," he told an assembled mob of ninety thousand in Johannesburg on July 29, 2023.[160]

It looked a lot like a colorized version of a Nuremberg rally, circa 1936.[161]

Die Fahne hoch…the lead words of the "Horst Wessel Song," which goes on to describe *killing people* (the opponents of National Socialism).

The song sung by Malema and his followers is eerily similar in its *message*. It also dates back to the apartheid era, which was of course the apotheosis of actually racist—which the Left once pretended to oppose (just as it once pretended to favor free speech). Black South Africans were not allowed to participate in South African politics and had about the same legal standing as cattle.

Understandably, many South African blacks were not happy about this. The African National Congress—led by Nelson Mandela—worked to change this. And did. South Africa became a country in which blacks and whites have *equal* rights.

That, of course, is *extremely* "racist"—to leftists such as Malema and those who follow him. Just as it is "racist"—to American leftists—to call Ketanji Brown Jackson out for defending college admissions policies that specifically *exclude* certain races (while favoring others).

Like Brown Jackson, Malema seems to want to recreate apartheid—just in reverse, this time. If you're wondering how that isn't racist, you'll have to ask a leftist.

But don't expect a straight answer.

Instead, expect that you'll be called a "racist" for asking the question.

5. Whitesplaining Is Super Fun! Everyone Should Try It!

The real problem everyone has with "whitesplaining" is the tragic fact that it is undeniably rooted in objective truth. Hence it gets a cute nickname.

But what *is* "whitesplaining"? What does it mean exactly?

It depends on who you ask.

If you ask woke leftists obsessed with race, it is anything that questions the woke racism of the Left, including questioners who *aren't* white. Even if she is *also* woke.

Take the black and female former director of diversity, equity, and inclusion at Apple Computer co-founder Steve Wozniak's alma mater, De Anza College in San Jose, California.

She was apparently not "black" enough, at least when it came to her thinking.

Dr. Tabia Lee in March 2023 was accused of "whitesplaining" for—get this—raising questions about Black Lives Matter co-founder Alicia Garza,[162] who leads a very lavish lifestyle apparently funded by the contributions of people who thought they were helping people who *don't* live in a $6 million, 6,500-square-foot house with a dozen bedrooms, several fireplaces, and parking for twenty cars.[163]

It is unacceptable—it is *racist*—to ask whether Garza might have misappropriated those funds because that would undermine the Black Lives Matter movement.

Like Hunter Biden, Garza enjoys a particular kind of *privilege* that transcends her race (and his). What they have in common isn't the color of their skin but rather the content of their ideology. And the solidarity that attends being on the right side of a privileged and powerful ideology that doesn't care about truth or logic or fair play.

It cares only about *power*—and doing whatever is necessary to get it, hold onto it, and expand it.

Which naturally entails destroying anyone who dares to question it.

Lee also got into trouble for her *inclusive* attitude—toward Jewish people—and because she questioned being pressured to join a socialist network. Above all, her crime was raising questions about keeping black people in their place by insisting they ask no questions and do as they are told.

Such questioning isn't merely "disrespectful" (as one De Anza College trustee put it), but it is also evidence that Lee is secretly a "right-wing extremist," her DEI *bona fides* notwithstanding.

The incident calls to mind the old Charlie Daniels song, "Uneasy Rider,"[164] about a "long-hair"—this was back in the hippie days—who finds himself in a dive bar in the deep South, surrounded by unfriendly good old boys. Everyone's white, including him. But he's not one with them.

He thinks fast and tells them that one of *them* isn't who they think he is—that there's an undercover FBI agent in their midst, sent there to infiltrate the Ku Klux Klan.

The ruse works. In the ensuing fratricidal melee, our long-haired hero makes his escape.

Lee, on the other hand, got fired after she was denied tenure.

The college said it parted ways with Lee because she was "difficult to work with" and couldn't take "constructive criticism." Lee says she was pressured to support what she calls "third-wave anti-racism ideology." This ideology places the highest value on lockstep obedience to ideology, which can be as racist (and sexist) as a midnight Klan rally.

Consider Justice Ketanji Brown Jackson's dissenting opinion in *Students for Fair Admissions v. Harvard*.[165] Four months after Lee's firing from De Anza College, the court ruled 6–3 that it is unconstitutional to exclude candidates for college admission on the basis of race. Jackson railed *against* that "anti-racist" idea. She did so because it conflicts with the agenda of the Woke Left, which increasingly no longer even pretends to be outraged by racism, except when there isn't any in evidence.

So Tabia Lee asked some questions about BLM and Alicia Garza and lost her job. Lee didn't call Garza the "N" word. She was, however, "guilty" of not saying the *right* words. Words like "Latinx" and "Filipinx." Words that academics invent and foist on the public, like Kwanzaa, the made-up holiday that blacks don't celebrate but many woke whites insist be *respected* as "authentic."

Lee also failed to use people's prescribed pronouns—an offense that certain countries without a First Amendment want to make an honest-to-goodness crime—and wondered out loud why her colleagues capitalized "Black" while keeping "white" lowercase. She looked askance at the woke notion that concepts such as "timeliness" and "objective thinking" are manifestations of "white supremacy."

"To me, white supremacy is associated with White Nationalism, the KKK, and Neo-Nazi organizations," she said. But when you run out of those, you have run out of excuses.

Time for some whitesplaining!

Two weeks after the Supreme Court's landmark affirmative action decision, Lee sued De Anza College with help from the Foundation Against Intolerance and Racism. She accused the college of violating her First Amendment rights and said she was made a target for not being "the right kind of black person." The trouble is, Lee herself was part of the problem that ultimately became *her* problem. It is hard to complain about being struggle-sessioned out of a job when your job was *director of diversity, equity, and inclusion.*

Yet she professed to be shocked that "diversity, equity, and inclusion programs on college campuses are being turned on their heads" and that even she, as "someone who some may assume would be on the side of so-called social justice warriors," was "too heterodox" in her thinking.[166]

She shouldn't be. Piranhas tend to eat their own.

6. Liberal Whites and Their Walls of Virtue

Many people may, at first glance, think this book is some kind of jaw-boning of left-wing people of color. But if you are really paying attention, you will realize this book is really about whites.

Liberal whites. The modern slave drivers of cultural Marxist tyranny.

You see, the Left hates Trump in part because he tried to wall off America from Mexico so as to keep America from *becoming* Mexico through the influx of millions of Mexicans, along with millions of Central and South Americans.

It isn't that liberals hate walls exactly. They have no problem walling off their high-rent enclaves to keep themselves safe from fellow *Americans* they consider undesirable. Oftentimes, the walls are invisible, so they can pretend they don't exist. They can pretend they're virtuous while they're at it.

Nevertheless, *zoning laws* serve the same functional purpose as physical walls. They keep people out of places. A story in the July 2023 issue of *The Atlantic* detailed how it's done.[167] Richard D. Kahlenberg, who wrote a book on "how snob zoning, NIMBYism, and class bias build the walls we don't see," visited Scarsdale, one of the most affluent suburbs of New York City and bluer than cobalt. Its residents voted for Joe Biden in 2020 by a three to one margin—an astounding outcome in what was otherwise a very close election.

Yet the residents of Scarsdale don't support the policies of the Biden regime, at least when it comes to *their* neighborhoods—not unlike John Kerry, Biden's "climate" envoy—and another Scarsdale favorite—who doesn't fly coach. That's for the rest of us, the folks who can't afford to fly private.

And most of us can't afford to live in liberal enclaves such as Scarsdale—assuming anyone who isn't woke *wanted* to live there. But, assuming they did, they'd need to be able to pony up the *$1.8 million* a typical home sells for there.[168] Many homes sell for a great deal more than that. And the relevant point is there aren't many alternatives to those pricey homes because Scarsdale's zoning laws effectively outlaw the construction of *affordable housing*, to use a term regularly ululated by leftists who pretend to be concerned about its lack.

Much the same as they regularly express "concern" about affordable health care—like Obamacare—that they themselves opt out of.

And just as they opt their kids out of the horrendously underperforming government schools they insist people who cannot afford to send their kids to private schools send *their* kids to—and pay increasingly exorbitant property taxes to finance, rendering them even less able to afford the private schools the kids of the "elite" attend. Those kids will go on to Ivy League schools like Harvard and Yale, where they will train for six- and seven-figure jobs that will put them in position to eventually afford a $1.2 million home in a place like Scarsdale or San Francisco or Washington, DC.

The sorts of places, in other words, that are walled off invisibly from the low-income masses that liberal elites pretend to love but do everything in their power to avoid.

The Atlantic, being as blue as the people who read it, treats this hypocrisy with tender-loving indulgence. It refers to "good white liberals"—i.e., the people who are keeping out the browns and blacks—as well-intentioned people who own anti-racist tracts such as *White Fragility* and are *appalled* by the Supreme Court decision that tore down the wall of race-based exclusionary admissions practices at Harvard and elsewhere.

We are supposed to believe these "good white liberals" simply had *no idea* that exclusionary zoning laws exclude certain kinds of people.

Doesn't *everyone* live in a $1.2 million-dollar single-family home?

There may actually be some truth to this Marie Antoinette-like naïveté. Rich liberals don't spend a lot of time in the company of working-class Americans. They tend to assume everyone else is just like them. This explains, in part, why these same people cannot imagine that *anyone* could support any elected Republicans. It is also why they don't cringe when Biden's transportation secretary, Pete Buttigieg, urges people who are worried about the cost of gas to buy a $50,000 electric car.

Doesn't *everyone* own one?

In Scarsdale, many do. It is the ideal accessory for a $1.2 million home.

Of course, average people cannot afford a $50,000 EV, or a $1.2 million home, or the property taxes and upkeep of a home. They could afford a duplex apartment or maybe even a modest townhouse for a fraction of that sum, but zoning ordinances in places such as Scarsdale have made it all but impossible for developers to build such *affordable housing* there.

If the woke elitists who enjoy a comfortable suburban life really cared about affordable housing, they'd tear down the walls that prevent it from being built and that keep the people they don't want around out.

That's about as likely to happen, of course, as Scarsdale voting two-thirds for the GOP in the next election.

7. White Crackhead Privilege, Revisited

How much blow could Abe Lincoln smuggle into the White House inside that stovepipe hat of his? Of course, we will never know because it's a ridiculous question.

Maybe Hunter Biden could borrow a *line* (so to speak) from notorious '80s-era Washington, DC, mayor Marion Barry. When caught on video buying crack cocaine, His Dishonor insisted that he didn't actually *smoke* it. No, no! He just liked the way it *smelled*. Crack is the new potpourri, you see.

Nobody doubts Hunter Biden smoked crack.[169] He recorded himself doing it. The video turned up on his notorious, abandoned laptop computer—the truthful contents of which were dismissed as Russian "disinformation" by the same Big Tech/Big Media truth suppressors that endlessly promoted falsehoods about Donald Trump.

"You know what, I actually smoked crack with Marion Barry, I swear to f---ing god," Hunter bragged to a friend.

How long before he brags to a friend about leaving something white behind at his dad's office?

Coke fiends tend not to have the best judgment or discretion. It's why they take videos of themselves committing crimes and then leave the evidence for anyone to find.

But some of them have the very best of luck.

Or rather, *pull.*

They have white crackhead privilege.

Hunter Biden is probably the only American who got slapped with *misdemeanors* for failing to report to the IRS several *million* dollars earned trading on his name[170]—or, rather, his father's influence. A rich friend ended up paying Hunter's taxes on his behalf. But months later, the Justice Department has been oddly reluctant to ask hard questions about Hunter's income. (A federal judge in August 2023 rejected a deal that would have let the president's son plead guilty to the tax charges and skate on a felony gun charge.)

We still know next to nothing about the $83,000 per month Hunter was paid to sit on the board of the sketchy Ukrainian energy company, Burisma. It is the kind of gig you get when you have something sketchy to offer in lieu of relevant expertise.

If Hunter Nobodyinski had not paid taxes on millions of dollars' worth of unreported income, the dude would absolutely be going to federal prison. That might not be so bad for Hunter, given all of the drugs available there.

Hunter Biden's misadventures bring to mind Tony Montana, the lead character in Brian De Palma's 1983 crime classic, *Scarface.* Tony was all about pushing it to the limit.[171] So is Hunter.

But there are some key differences.

The obvious one is that Tony actually *worked* for a living—with his hands, with his wits, and occasionally with a chainsaw.

Tony came up the hard way. He arrived in Florida as a refugee from Fidel Castro's Cuba with nothing to his name and the tropical print shirt on his back.

Hunter came up the easy way, with a name that opens doors—and wallets. It's also a name that closes down investigations.

Tony worked his way up the underworld food chain and, after much difficulty, ultimately became the boss.

Hunter was born at the near-apex of the political elite, the son of a Big Guy who made sure Hunter never had any difficulties, no matter how much trouble he may have gotten himself into.

Think about that felony gun charge he faced after investigators learned he lied on a federal firearm application. Federal law prohibits illegal drug users from owning a gun. (The 5th US Circuit Court of Appeals in August 2023 struck down the law, setting up a possible Supreme Court challenge.) Once again, video evidence exists of Hunter *waving around a gun* while smoking crack, which apparently isn't even the firearm he lied to get. Instead of jail time—or even a felony conviction that would render him legally ineligible to possess a gun ever again—federal prosecutors wanted Hunter to enter a diversion program and promised to expunge his record if he completed two years of probation.

Tony Montana would never have been so lucky.

Neither would have the hundreds of thousands of ordinary people who have been convicted of felonies—and spent time in prison—for the sorts of crimes Hunter clearly committed, crimes his father insisted other people should be prosecuted and punished for.

As a US senator in 1994, Joe Biden wrote the law that resulted in harsher penalties for drug offenses[172]—for people whose last name isn't "Biden," anyway, especially black and brown people. People like

Tony Montana. Yes, the character is fictitious, but the reality is count-less thousands of Hispanic people got more than a diversion when they were caught doing the same—or less—than the president's son was caught *on video* doing.

When Congress passed the crime bill in 1994, Joe Biden boasted that "the liberal wing of the Democratic Party" was now in favor of "60 new death penalties," "70 enhanced penalties," "100,000 cops," and "125,000 new state prison cells"—one of which should have Hunter's name on it.

But maybe, just maybe, Hunter's luck will finally run out. In the movie, it happened when Tony pushed his luck beyond the limit. In real life, Hunter may have done exactly the same.

It's one thing to smoke crack in the bathroom of a DC bar with Marion Barry listening to rap songs by Future.[173] It's another to bring it into the White House. Do we know for certain that the cocaine the Secret Service discovered in July belonged to Hunter? No. But how about all those other times and all of those other things we *do* know about for certain?

The karma police eventually came calling for Tony Montana, who was at least man enough to stand up for himself,[174] as opposed to hav-ing another man stand in the way for him. But Hunter's man isn't as steady on his feet as he used to be.

If the son were to become a major liability, the father who enabled him and ran interference for him may be seen in the same light—just in time for 2024.

VIII.
August Privilege

*"You are a bad person—a 'Nazi'—
if you disagree with the Left.
On* everything.*"*

1. Addressing the "Very Fine People"

When the truth doesn't support the narrative of the Woke Left, the Woke Left pushes untruths to bury the truth.

It's why so many Americans continue to believe the "very fine people" lie about what Donald Trump did and *didn't* say in the wake of the mayhem at Charlottesville, Virginia, in August 2017.

Hundreds gathered to support and oppose the removal of a Confederate monument.

The narrative-lie is that Trump defended the indefensible actions of neo-Nazis—including one who drove his car into a crowd of protestors, killing thirty-two-year-old Heather Heyer.

But Trump did not laud the neo-Nazis as "very fine people." In fact, he did the *opposite*.

The president said, unequivocally, that he "totally condemned" the thugs, including the man who used his vehicle to kill one person and injure five others. (The driver was later found guilty of first-degree murder and sentenced to life in prison.)

The problem for the Woke Left was that Trump didn't condemn the people who had come to *peacefully protest* the removal of the Confederate monument.

For the Woke Left, the peaceful protesters were no different from the neo-Nazis. Trump's refusal to lump the peaceful together with the violent revealed him as a neo-Nazi himself.

What Trump, in fact, said was: "You had some very bad people in that group, but you also had people that were very fine people, *on both sides*."

Emphasis on the point the Woke Left has tried to stifle and delegitimize.

For the Woke Left, there was no other side. The only side that mattered, as far as they're concerned, was the side that supported removing the Confederate monument.

Everyone else was by definition a "Nazi"—including President Trump.

But what *really* aroused the fury of the Woke Left was Trump's refusal to admit he's a "Nazi" and apologize for it.

Trump would not kowtow to the Woke Left, which has for decades relied upon the desperate desire of its supposed adversaries to be *liked*.

It is why leftists tend to like milquetoast Republicans such as Senator Mitt Romney of Utah and former Speaker of the House Paul Ryan, who would contort themselves into pretzels to avoid offending the Left, even when they have done nothing wrong other than weakly oppose a left-wing or liberal policy preference.

The Left very much likes the idea of tearing down every monument to American history that displeases them. Well, President Trump doesn't like that. He wasn't about to apologize for it in 2017, and he won't apologize now. Nor will he stop defending people who aren't "Nazis" but who merely object to the kind of tactics used by Nazis to lie about the truth.

As Larry Elder, a black man who isn't a woke leftist, pointed out in "The Trump Charlottesville Lie Just Won't Die," Trump was very careful to separate the Nazis at Charlottesville from those who were merely *at* Charlottesville—both for and against removing the monument.[175]

"But not all of those people were neo-Nazis, believe me," Trump said. *"And I'm not talking about the neo-Nazis and the white nationalists*, because they should be condemned totally. But you had many people in that group *other than neo-Nazis and white nationalists*."

Emphasis added again in the interest of telling the truth.

Elder elaborates: "Critics ignored the 'and I'm not talking about' part and accused Trump of defending the attacker and violent protesters as 'very fine people on both sides.' That lie has become an article of faith for Trump haters."

Yes, it has. Which is why I had to use this book to mock the stooges.

It has also become a talking point for Joe Biden, who seems to be congenitally incapable of distinguishing truth from falsehood, especially when it comes to anything having to do with President Trump.

Throughout the 2020 election campaign, Biden said—and continues to insist—that Trump said "there are very good people on both sides" without qualification.

"I had no intention of running for president again," Biden said at a March 22 press conference, "until I saw those folks coming out of the fields in Virginia carrying torches and carrying Nazi banners and literally singing the same vile rhyme that they used in Germany in the early '20s or '30s."

For Biden and for the Woke Left, this encompasses *everyone* who was in Charlottesville that day who *wasn't* there to support removal of the Confederate monument and the effacing of American history.

Which, in reality, includes tens of millions of Americans.

For the Woke Left, any opposition is not only intolerable but also immoral.

You are a bad person—a "Nazi"—if you disagree with the Left.

On *everything*.

Donald Trump dared to question this, which is why he was and remains so hated by the Woke Left. They could not shut him up.

That their antics don't work on Trump is why the Woke Left goes berserk at the mere mention of his name—and why they desperately want his name off the ballot.

2. You're Welcome, Sheila! You Only Have Free Speech Because of Dead White Guys!

US Representative Sheila Jackson Lee went on a tear in 2023. At the outset of the session, the Texas Democrat filed a bill in the newly Republican-controlled House that would go after what she defines as "hate speech." The bill effectively would make this book a federal crime—and might make you criminally liable if you shared it with anyone who then went on to commit a crime.

Any infringements on free speech codified into law have long been a political minefield. One person's "hate speech" is another person's inconvenient truth. One person's reasonable objections can become targeted as harmful threats. For instance, during the darkest days of the COVID pandemic, you could be deplatformed from social media and lose your job for saying things that politicians found inconvenient but were in no way hateful or even harmful.

Speech codes that were once confined to left-wing university campuses have come to own newsrooms and dictate how pre-Musk Twitter crushed dissent from the Far Left's most intolerant and unreasonable orthodoxies—orthodoxies that change with the political winds by the hour.

Into all of this history steps Jackson Lee, one of life's backbenchers. The title of her bill gave her game away: Leading against White Supremacy Act of 2023.[176] Her bill would target millions of Americans' right to free speech based solely on their skin color. That's quite obviously racist in its own right.

Jackson Lee's bill is nothing but an attempt to weaponize the federal government to exact revenge on people she hates because of their genetics. Perhaps she should add "Mugabe" to the end of her name, after the dictator who stole property from white farmers and destroyed the country of Zimbabwe.[177]

Now, let's be clear about a couple of things. Sheila Jackson Lee doesn't know the top of her head from the surface of Mars. She once stated, from the well of Congress, that we have put humans on the Red Planet (we haven't). She once said there are two Vietnams (there aren't).[178] She said the Constitution is four hundred years old (it's not).

She's probably also totally unaware that she owes her office and the right of free speech to countless white men who made it happen. The right to free speech and the right to criticize your government simply was not a thing before the American Revolution. It had been argued for and written about in political treatises, and it had been fought over in wars, but the Declaration of Independence and the United States Constitution set forth the arguments for it and then made it the bedrock law of our land, respectively.

The Declaration and the Constitution were written and signed by white guys: Thomas Jefferson and James Madison, respectively, were their principal authors. Apologies to Franklin, Adams, Hamilton, and Jay (more white guys). They were paid for in blood by white men, under the command of a white man, George Washington, who leftists like Jackson Lee want to be written out of history.

Jackson Lee's bill is a targeted attack on Americans' right to speak out on very specific issues, including border security or criticizing positions held by someone who is a minority (such as Jackson Lee).[179] According to National File, "if federal investigators determine that the web postings of a third party had 'inspire[d]' someone else, even someone they don't know, to commit a federal hate crime, that person would be arrested, and federally charged with a hate crime of their own."[180]

Charged with a federal crime for a social media post? Yes. That is what the most hated boss in Washington and the most historically ignorant member of the legislative branch want to do.

Sheila Jackson Lee is a ridiculous clown, but her overt assault on free speech is far from funny. It's the kind of nightmare spawned in the hell of Stalin's Soviet Union or Maoist China. And just because her bill went nowhere in 2023 doesn't mean the idea is dead. It's very much alive and well among the woking dead.

3. The Ballad of Stanley Armour Dunham

Ladies and gentlemen, I want you to meet my friend Stanley. At first glance, Stanley was an average man who built a successful business selling furniture. But in the end, he was so much more than a furniture salesman. He had no idea that the little boy he chose to raise, when he expected to enjoy his retirement, would grow up to become one of the most famous men on the planet—and also one of the most insidious dividers of the American people the world has ever known.

Stanley was born average but hardscrabble. He wasn't born the oldest or youngest son in his family, and he wasn't born in one of the world's elite cosmopolitan centers. The dust bowl was his family's midwife. He was born in a small town in the American Midwest to an average, albeit literate, family.

Stanley's parents owned a humble little café to make ends meet. But tragedy struck him early in life when he discovered his mother's lifeless body. She died by her own hands. The shock of that day swiftly changed young Stanley's life. He went from living with his parents and siblings to being sent off to live with his grandparents. He drifted, married his high school sweetheart on prom night, and then drifted some more. His turbulent life with his own grandparents turned out to be a foreshadowing of the life Stanley would nurture in his own twilight years.

But before we get to that, we must discuss Stanley's service. When World War II broke out, Stanley rushed to defend America. Just a little over a month after Pearl Harbor, Stanley had raised his hand and volunteered to serve in the army. He was sent to France, where he saved civilization alongside millions of other Americans whose names you don't know. His young wife gave birth to a little girl called Ann. He returned home from the war, tried to go to school to get his degree, but ended up making a living managing furniture stores while his wife trailblazed her way into leading a bank.

Little Ann grew up and fancied herself a scholar. She met a man while she was overseas, they briefly married, and had a son.

Stanley got a good job opportunity, so he and the family, including Ann's son, moved from the American Midwest to Hawaii, while Ann pursued her studies with more vigor than she devoted to family life. When Ann returned from her overseas work, her son remained with his grandparents—not with either of his parents or stepfather, dubious other people that drifted in and out of his mother's orbit.

Years passed.

Stanley died a few years before seeing his grandson live up to his full potential. Three years after Stanley's death, the young man wrote a bestselling book about his upbringing, a book largely about his absent father and about his negligent mother, and mostly not about the loving, patriotic grandfather who worked his ass off to raise the boy.

The book was a runaway smash hit. It could have spawned a literary career, but instead, it launched a different career—a career in which Stanley has been forgotten.

We never hear about Stanley these days, a white descendant of American settlers at Plymouth Rock. We hear about his grandson all the time, mostly when he's accusing America of "systemic racism." But what about the racism of ignoring the people who raised you, because their race is inconvenient to your ambitions?

Stanley, of course, was Stanley Armour Dunham from Wichita, Kansas. A grandfather who never expected to raise a biracial grandson, Barry—better known as Barack Hussein Obama, the forty-fourth president of the United States and the first black man ever elected to the office—who has all but ignored the white grandparents who made his success possible. Nevertheless, Stanley says, "You're welcome." And now you know the rest of the story.

4. White Teachers Get Chopped First

It used to be just "affirmative action," the term used for race-based preferential hiring practices. The Minneapolis Public School District in 2022 went to the next level by adopting race-exclusionary hiring practices.[181]

If you're white, you need not apply. There is zero chance you'll be hired. Your résumé does not matter. Your color excludes you from consideration. Because racism—the real thing—is now institutional-ized in Minneapolis. No joke.

Once upon a time, racism was practiced by individuals who refused to hire or do business with people they didn't like on account of their race. This was a despicable practice but limited in its harm precisely because it *wasn't* institutionalized. It was practiced here and there, often covertly, by dint of the practitioners being regarded by most people as despicable.

That private sanction prevented systemic racism.

Government schools in Minneapolis—for that is what they are, since they are controlled by the government, and people are forced to pay for them by the government—codify racism. In effect, it is the law—and thus, institutionalized.

Put on your robe and hood before you read the following state-ment, which you might even call...*Protocols*[182]:

> To *remedy past discrimination*, Minneapolis Public Schools and the Minneapolis Federation of Teachers mutually agreed to contract language that *aims to support* the recruitment and retention of teachers from under-represented groups as compared to the labor market and to the community served by the school district. [Emphasis added.]

"To remedy past discrimination"...by *blackballing* (whoops!—trig-ger word) people who haven't "discriminated" against anyone. Because discriminating against them today is how you remedy past discrimi-nation. Makes sense!

"Aims to support"...when, in fact, the policy is specifically written to *exclude*. Here is the language of exclusion, *verbatim*, straight from the mouth of institutionalized racism:

> If excessing a teacher who is a member of a population underrepresented among licensed teachers in the

site, the district shall excess the next least senior teacher, who is not a member of an underrepresented population.[183]

Yes, they're treating "excessing" like a real word.

How does one "excess" an applicant for a job? As opposed to assessing him. Remember, the racist who wrote this is in the business of education.

As it turns out, the malapropism does have a meaning. It means firing—*the white teacher*. And not hiring any replacement teachers who are white.

Manhattan Institute senior fellow Christopher Rufo has described the Minneapolis policy as "the inevitable endpoint of 'equity,'" by which he means the institutionalization of the racism that "affirmative action" policies were (supposedly) meant to eradicate. It is no longer simply an attempt to look for qualified applicants who happen to be other than white and to encourage them to apply—assuming they are qualified. It is the deliberate exclusion from any consideration of people who are white, regardless of their qualifications or seniority.

The Minneapolis school system and its union partners in reverse Ku Kluxery insist that white teachers already working be the first ones to be fired—so as to replace them with non-white teachers, who (according to the compact protocols) cannot be laid off, irrespective of seniority or *performance*.

In other words, incompetent teachers—such as those who use "excessing" rather than assessing (or terminating)—are guaranteed their jobs, on the taxpayers' dime, whether they "perform" or not.

So long as they're of the right race.

"Students need educators who look like them and who they can relate to," say the latter-day Father Coughlins of the Minneapolis government school system and their union partners-in-racism. "This language gives us the ability to identify and address issues that contribute to disproportionately high turnover of educators of color."[184]

Fox News quoted attorney Harmeet Dhillon of the Center for American Liberty, which litigates attempts to institutionalize racism, as urging any teacher currently employed by the Minneapolis school system threatened with loss of job on account of his color to "call a lawyer."[185] Heritage Foundation education fellow Jonathan Butcher agrees, citing Title VII of the Civil Rights Act and the Equal Protection Clause of the Constitution.

But while the legal objections are sound, this is ultimately a moral question. How did it become moral to discriminate openly? More than that, when did it become OK for organs of the government like the Minneapolis school system to discriminate openly?

The world is truly turn'd upside-down—a reference to the tune played by British troops surrendering to the American army at Yorktown,[186] the decisive battle of the Revolutionary War—only if Americans of goodwill—of all races—surrender to this.

To this inversion of morality—and legality—being pushed by modern American racists, who does not agree with Martin Luther King's injunction that human beings should be judged and treated not according to their skin color but the content of their character—and their résumé?

5. Obama's "Dreams" of My Woke Nightmare

Barack Obama rode a wave of American goodwill—and, let's face it, liberal white guilt—all the way from obscurity to the presidency in part on the success of his book, *Dreams from My Father*.[187] *Dreams* was hailed as a literary masterpiece, "quite extraordinary" according to Toni Morrison, a work of real art unlike anything most presidents are able to achieve after their time in office, never mind when they're still climbing the dirty political ranks to the White House. It helped make the myth of Obama in much the same way Bill Clinton cast himself as the "Man from Hope" on his way to the White House more than a decade earlier.

Never mind Clinton wasn't from Hope, Arkansas. (He was really from the seedier tourist trap of Hot Springs.) The Hope myth stood and still stands taller than the nasty little man who shrunk the world's most powerful office with his uncontrolled physical urges and small-ball niche politics.

Like Clinton, Obama has never been known for a lack of ego or his fidelity to the truth. During his first presidential campaign, he sold voting for him as "the moment when the rise of the oceans began to slow and our planet began to heal." He must've flopped, else why are today's Democrats so strident about climate now?

Obama also pledged that America, then the fairest, strongest, and most influential nation the world had ever seen, would be "fundamentally transformed" if it put him into power. That was a breathtaking thing to say, and a claim in which he made himself America's moral king, but again, Obama was never one to shy away from hyperbole.

Myths, and those who make them, often require a dragon of some sort to be slain along the way on the hero's journey. But it seems to have been lost on Americans of 2008—and was hidden by the media that fawned over Obama then and still holds him up with the angels now—that Obama's dragon may have been America's place in the world.

Obama's is a myth that is still worth examining and deconstructing. He's still pulling the strings behind the Democratic Party and the president currently in the White House. The media-entertainment complex hands him millions of dollars every year. Joe Biden may be president, but Obama has his spindly hand up his former vice president's back and has almost the entire media ready to spread his message or cover for him.

In *Dreams from My Father*, Obama grants himself a special moral standing in American history at the intersection of race and history.

Lots of other Americans are biracial, millions in fact. But according to Obama, he alone had the proper epiphany and understood what it meant for America's atonement for its sins.

In his personal gospel tract, Obama cast an argument with his then girlfriend, Sheila Miyoshi Jager, as a turning point on his journey to self-discovery and the presidency. Jager was by his own account Obama's first love—he proposed marriage to her twice, and she shot him down both times. Instead of marrying a white mainstream liberal, Obama would eventually marry Michelle Robinson, who would later admit that the only thing that ever made her proud of America was its election of her husband to the presidency. Not, you know, liberating Europe from the Nazis or defeating communism during the Cold War. Not even kicking Saddam out of Kuwait, the unity that sprang up after the 9/11 attacks, or the invention of the iPhone.

According to Martin Luther King Jr. biographer David Garrow, author of *Rising Star: The Making of Barack Obama*, Obama and Jager tell opposite versions of the argument that led to their breakup and formed a pivotal point in Obama's political life.[188] In *Dreams*, Obama says they argued over his emerging identity as a black American upon seeing a play about race issues during his own struggle with his biracial nature. But in *Rising Star*, Jager says he refused to condemn clearly anti-Semitic statements made by Steve Cokely, who was then at the center of Chicago politics as a mayoral aide.[189]

The difference between the two accounts is stark and important.

In Obama's telling, he was waking up—"going woke," as we would say today—to truths about America and his own racial identity, truths that he could not ignore and which would inform his principles and priorities in politics for the rest of his life.

But in Jager's telling, Obama was a moral coward and not the brave man facing unpleasant truths and transforming himself by force of will so he could later drag his country into the light. Here, according to Jager, was the unpleasant truth of black racism against Jews. And

Obama lacked the courage to condemn it. He still needed Chicago and its Democratic political machine to get where he wanted to go.

The statements Obama should have condemned were a heinous blood libel. Chicago was then hosting an exhibit that Obama and Jager saw together on the ghastly Holocaust crimes of Adolf Eichmann. Cokely took the occasion to accuse Jewish doctors of infecting black babies with AIDS in Chicago to commit genocide against the black community. Cokely made the comments in lectures organized by notorious anti-Semite Louis Farrakhan. Condemning all this should have been a no-brainer for one as morally upright as Obama.

But no. Obama not only failed to condemn Cokely's statements at the time, but he has never condemned them, and, if Jager's telling in Garrow's book is correct, he has spun up a myth to hide the truth about himself. The truth is Obama is a weak man and a racist to his core. In place of the Eichmann exhibit, Obama substitutes a play in which the main character is radicalized by understanding his racial identity. A man transformed by a transcendent work of art is much more admirable than one who fails to see and call out even the most obvious moral failures in those around him.

This isn't a small moment in Obama's life by his own telling. And for what it's worth, Jager has gone on to a scholarly career in which she's known for her factual rigor. She has stayed out of politics mostly and doesn't spin myths. She doesn't *need* a myth. But Obama did and does and seems to have successfully built his political dreams upon a platform of fraud and deceit.

Obama may indeed have awakened to his own racial identity, but he became blinded by the woke.

This is where wokeness leads—to biased focus on one group's suffering in ways that minimize, distort, or even blot out the suffering of any other group. Every people has suffered and inflicted suffering. The Jews blood libeled by black radical Cokely had very recently suffered mass murder that was preceded by Nazi blood libels. Ukraine had suffered mass murder at the hands of Stalin before that. None of that was America's fault. The Spanish, long condemned for their treatment of the Aztecs during the Age of Exploration, had themselves been subjugated to centuries of brutal rule by the Muslim Moors, from which they only freed themselves in 1492.

Spain's interest in seeing Catholicism—not Islam or any other faith—spread in the New World has gone unexamined in light of the centuries of its own oppression before the Reconquista. Woke history isn't interested. The Aztecs themselves had subjected the people around them to bloody brutality, leading them to side with the Spanish aliens, as had the Maya before them subjugated others, as did the Inca, and so forth. Their barbaric oppression of other people enabled Spain to build alliances and defeat them.

None of that was America's fault. Woke history isn't interested in any of that.

Yet real history is replete with such horrors. African leaders played terrible roles in the slave trade and had also captured and enslaved white Europeans and even Americans in the decades before the American Civil War that ended slavery in the United States in a bloody conflagration. President Thomas Jefferson launched America's first overseas war against the Barbary pirates, who were enslaving Americans in North Africa. The US Marine Corps commemorates this in its hymn with the references to "the shores of Tripoli." Slavery still exists around the world long after America bled so fiercely to end it here.

Precisely none of this enters the thinking of the woke, or of one Barack Obama, self-proclaimed moral king. America is the world's greatest sinner in their telling, and must be—in their words—dismantled and fundamentally transformed into something else. Obama, his fellow travelers in the "Squad," and the leftists who dominate the media and academia mean business when they say it. They want the America that we know and love killed, taken apart, buried, and never mourned.

6. What's Black and White and Racist All Over?

The Left never means what you thought it said. You have to *deconstruct the meaning* behind what the Left says.

For example, when the Left says it is in favor of free speech, it means it is in favor of free speech *for leftists*. If you say something the Left doesn't like, your freedom to speak (or tweet) is not what the Left is in favor of.

When the Left says it is against racism, it does not mean it is for treating individuals equally, based on their merit rather than their race. It means it is for treating *white people* badly, on account of *their* race.

That's what the leftists who control the Gannett media chain—which owns *USA Today*, among other properties—has been doing to the white people who work for it, according to a class action lawsuit filed in August 2023 by current and former employees who say they were *kept in their place* by anti-white policies that caused them to be overlooked for promotions they deserved and were in some cases fired—so as to make room for less-qualified people who happened to be anything but white.[190]

The foundation of the lawsuit is a company policy announced in 2020 that stated it was the goal of Gannett to "expand the number of journalists focused on issues related to race and identity, social justice and equality"—which, per usual, when it comes to the Left has to be deconstructed in order to understand what that *actually* means.

Gannett's goal is to "expand the number of non-white journalists"—who (in the wacky world of woking dead *actual* racism) are the only ones who can understand and thus competently cover "issues related to race, social justice and equality." This is a core tenet of the postmodernism that is the rotten core of modern leftism.[191] It insists that what you look like (and what equipment you've got) determines not only who you are but also what you think.

Thus, only a "person of color" can understand "people of color"—excluding, of course, people of one color. They are biologically incapable of understanding "people of color." If you are half a preferred color and half a non-preferred color, I don't know what to tell you other than it is *racist* for them to say otherwise.

It goes without saying, of course, that journalism is no longer a matter of getting the facts straight. It is about filtering them—through the prism of postmodernism and of course race-based cultural Marxism. It is a prism of hostility toward people who happen to be one particular race—and it's become acceptable in certain circles to treat people who happen to be of that race as pariahs.

Somehow, that is *not* racist to the postmodern leftism.

Interestingly, this modern form of racism also subtly denigrates the favored races, who are not to be hired or promoted according to their merit but in accordance with their color, which causes their merit (if it exists) to be suspect. Yet that is the explicit object of polices such as Gannett's, which seek "newsrooms that reflect the demographics of the communities they cover by 2025."

Get more black people! *Any* black people! Just so long as they *are* black people! It's all a bit grotesque.

"Gannett," says the lawsuit, "executed their reverse race discrimination policy with a callous indifference toward civil rights laws [and] the welfare of workers and prospective workers, whose lives would be upended by it," the plaintiffs state. The action seeks monetary damages—including lost pay and benefits—as well as the elimination of the policy that *institutionalized racism* at Gannett.

Speaking of that…

The Supreme Court in July 2023 repudiated another form of institutionalized racism[192]—something the Left constantly accuses "society" of doing, but which only the institutions controlled by the Left, including colleges and universities as well as large corporations such as Gannet, Target, and Progressive Insurance,[193] have actually been imposing as policies.

Starbucks was recently obliged to pay $25.6 million to a white former manager, Shannon Phillips, who, the jury agreed, was fired because of her race in order to placate the racism of corporate policies meant to show just how *not-racist* (toward other races) Starbucks is.[194]

Major car companies such as General Motors and Ford have "diversity" officers at the highest levels. Take, for example, Telva McGruder, the chief diversity, equity, and inclusion manager at GM. Her counterpart at Ford is Lori Costew,[195] whose job is—ostensibly—to "foster a culture of belonging." Except for those who belong to a certain wrong category of people....

Practically every large—and woke—corporation has such *zampolits*, a Russian (Soviet) word that means *political officers*. Their job is to institutionalize racism—the "good" kind—that makes it more difficult to get promoted (or even hired in the first place) if you're a person of a certain color.

Or sex.

Well, any of them except the *male* sex. Especially if the person is also "of" the *wrong* color. And the wrong interests (i.e., heterosexual).

The Left, then, is not opposed to racism—when it suits the Left. When it serves the interests of the Left. "We will vigorously defend our practice of *ensuring equal opportunities* for all our valued employees against this meritless lawsuit," says Gannett's legal counsel, Polly Grunfeld Sack.

That being the same thing that race-fixated admissions officers said in the wake of the recent Supreme Court decision forbidding colleges and universities to discriminate against anyone on account of race—including the one race it's become OK to discriminate against.

It amounts to: We're going to discriminate against the people we don't like no matter what we have to say in *public*. We'll just do it quietly—and pretend we didn't, deny it when people notice it—and accuse *them* of "racism" when they say anything about it. Presto!

If it sounds a lot like Mississippi circa 1953 rather than what America should be in 2023, you're probably a racist.

7. The Life and Times of Kammy Abromowitz

The late, great Joan Rivers once wrote, "The girl was a tramp from the moment her mother's water broke. You think I'm kidding? When the doctor spanked her at birth, she cried for more!"

And since she might be the next president someday—possibly a president without an election—it would probably be a good idea to get to know who Kamala Harris is.

We know she's not a mother.

The vice president didn't get married to heavyweight entertainment lawyer Doug Emhoff until 2014, by which time she was already fifty. Many mothers are *grandparents* by then. We also know she liked to date men a lot older than fifty. Specifically, the real "Slick Willy," as former president Bill Clinton once called onetime San Francisco mayor and serial womanizer Willie Brown, who was *sixty* when the future vice president wasn't yet thirty (and Brown was married).

Isn't it one of the tenets of wokeism that women shouldn't tolerate womanizing men? Apparently, that only applies when it doesn't *help*. (Just ask Hillary Clinton.)

Young Kamala jumped to the proverbial head of the line in the political hierarchy of San Francisco with the help of her...um, *mentor*, who was old enough to be her father and just about ready to begin collecting Social Security, at an age when most twenty-nine-year-old women are getting married and having children.

But Kamala had something else.

The "constant companion" of Willie Brown was appointed to the California Medical Assistance Commission and the Unemployment Insurance Appeals Board while Brown was speaker of the California

State Assembly, a Democratic fief in which *favors* of all kinds are given—and received.

It was a modern transactional sugar daddy to sugar baby situation.

Harris apparently caught the real Slick Willy's eye a few years prior when she was working in the Alameda County District Attorney's Office.

A gifted BMW soon followed.

Followed by the $72,000-a-year gig at the California Medical Assistance Commission.[196] That was in the early 1990s. Adjusted for inflation, that job would pay more than $150,000 today.

It's nice work, if you're willing to do the kind of work necessary to get it.

But even that was chump change compared with the $97,088 (more than $200,000 today) Kamala was paid when Brown appointed her to the Unemployment Insurance Appeals Board.

"Speaker Willie Brown," noted an article in the *Los Angeles Times*, "has given high-paying appointments to his former law associate and former Alameda County prosecutor" Kamala Harris for the *unique skill set* she possessed. The paper didn't actually print the last part. It wasn't necessary to say it.

What else is there to say about a young woman who "dates" an old man?

What did people say about Anna Nicole Smith?[197] She "dated" an even *older* man. Both men had something to offer other than senior citizen discounts at the Golden Corral buffet.

Harris was eventually dumped very publicly by Slick Willy when the latter was inaugurated as mayor of San Francisco in the mid-'90s with his estranged wife Blanche (whom Brown wed in 1958, six years before Kamala Harris was born) rather than his "constant companion" by his side.

Love, as they say, hurts.

Sacramento Bee reporter James Richardson said Brown "stunned his friends by announcing that he was breaking up with Kamala." Perhaps this is the origin story of the infamous Kamala Cackle?

Despite Harris later publicly calling Brown an "albatross around her neck," he continued to extend her *every* courtesy, including a front-row seat (and just a few seats to the right of Brown's wife) at the 2014 dedication of the Willie L. Brown Jr. Bridge at Treasure Island.

Brown's wife emitted a cackle of her own, too, when a reporter asked her prior to the 2020 election what she thought of Harris being appointed to a cushy gig by another elder mentor, the president of the United States, who is just about the same distance in age from Harris as she was from Brown when they began their relationship.

"I'm sorry, I don't want to comment at all," Blanche said.

Perhaps the most interesting thing about this affair is what it tells us about the hypocrisy of left-wing ladies who use their unique attributes to climb the ladder ahead of people whose merit ought to have put them in those places.

Brown continued to pay for what he got, supporting Harris politically when she was elected San Francisco's first black (well, half-black; her mother is a Tamil Indian, considered Asian) district attorney in 2004.

But when Kamala set her sights on offices beyond Brown's patronage, he got a very public note from his ex-inamorata: "His [Brown's] career is over. I will be alive and kicking for the next 40 years. I do not owe him a thing," she said. And when her memoir, *The Truths We Hold*, came out in 2019, not a word about him was mentioned.

She did say, in a tweet back in 2020, that young women shouldn't "let anybody tell you who you are, you tell them who you are."[198]

It reminds me of something Heidi Abromowitz once told her friend Joan Rivers. "One good turn deserves another…and another…and another."

Willie Brown might have some insights about that.

But gentlemen never tell.

IX.

September Privilege

"First Asians, then Hispanics. What will be the next group to be liberated from the Left's oppressive racial groupthink?"

1. It's a Matter of Time until Hispanics Are "White Adjacent"

In today's leftist political lexicon, the white American who doesn't vote for Democrats is the worst thing a person can be. You're racist, they say, or at the very least, voting against your own interests. If you're a white woman voting Republican, you're less of a woman than the man-creature in a dress who interviewed Joe Biden at the White House.[199] You're all that's wrong with America and the world, you're a racist, and you will eventually be displaced by demographic destiny. You're also polluting the air and killing the planet that black, indigenous, and people of color (BIPOC) always lived on within perfect harmony.

It's inevitable, white America! Your days in the sun are fast coming to an end, and with it, your oppression. Not long after that, the America you know and love will transition into a permanent socialist future. This is what the Left has planned for us, for decades, using BIPOCs to achieve unchallenged power.

But some BIPOCs refuse to go along with the program.

The BIPOC-obsessed Left has been at work on a magic trick that even Criss Angel wouldn't dare attempt. They're trying to make millions of nonwhite people into white people without their consent.

The term for this trick is "white adjacent."[200] Google that and you'll find literally thousands of thumb-sucking essays, op-eds, and tweets on the topic.

This sleight of hand is already underway. Asian Americans are getting turned white by leftists. They're not actually white, they're just...*next* to white. Almost white. And that's bad. The race-obsessed Left finds the success of Asians in America confusing.[201] Some Asian Americans are already wondering if they're actually white.[202]

Kenny Xu has detailed how this comes out in critical race theory, the divisive race indoctrination that every human resources department in corporate America is forcing on everyone who has a job.[203]

Under critical race theory, everyone is either an oppressor or they are oppressed, and the lines are drawn according to explicit racial characteristics. "White" equals "oppressor." "BIPOC" equals "oppressed."

If that sounds simple-minded, that's because it is. If that sounds like it ignores eons of history in which all races have oppressed other races, and even their own race at some point, that's because it does. CRT is based on ignorance, imposes ignorance, and reinforces ignorance.

Xu notes that CRT has no idea what to do with Asians who've come to the United States either in the last one hundred years or the last one hundred seconds and gone on to succeed here. How can an oppressive, white supremacist society ever allow nonwhites such as Asians to succeed? Yet, succeed they have.

Robin DiAngelo, author of *White Fragility*, has found a solution.

"The closer you are to whiteness—the term often used is white-adjacent—you're still going to experience racism, but there are going to be some benefits due to your perceived proximity to whiteness. The further away you are, the more intense the oppression's going to be," DiAngelo declared.

Notice DiAngelo's formulation provides no room for individual agency. No room for taught and learned values. No room for the role of the family. No room for achievement of any kind. All of a sudden, the pro-choice Left stopped believing in choice. It's all about the skin color. No room for the human mind to have a single thought or make a single decision. You are the color of your epidermis and nothing else.

A generation ago, such thinking was so evil, it had to be stamped out. Now it's being weaponized and embedded into every nook and cranny of our society.

The Biden administration is dominated by this mindset. That's among the reasons it moved the goalposts from "equality" to "equity," and it's forcing the military through political indoctrination and building leftist political offices into all federal departments. Equality before the law was achieved; equity is now being forced despite clear majority opposition.

The Atlantic's Jemele Hill built her career on this ideology, and the once-thoughtful and august magazine has continued to publish and promote her even after she declared another BIPOC cohort is no longer "of color."

With Hispanics making a conscious choice to abandon the Democratic Party in large numbers, Hill said they are—surprise!—"white adjacent." Poof! Millions of Hispanics are practically white!

Even though Hispanics can be quite brown and have complex lineages that include doses of indigenous, African, and Asian blood, which the Left would define as "people of color" and members of the BIPOC brigades in good standing, they're now as white as Asians.

Hispanics seeing what's in front of their eyes and exercising their freedom of choice is a major problem for the progressive Left. Hispanic voters rejecting socialism threatens the Left's long-term utopian project.[204] Many of them (or their parents) escaped socialist dumps, after all. Hispanic voters were once seen as BIPOCS who would blaze the eventual and inevitable path through which the Democrats would achieve an unbreakable lock on power forever, granting white leftist socialists free reign to do to America whatever they want without fearing that elections would ever undo their work.

The Lone Star State is a perfect example. Texas has voted solidly red since the late 1990s. The Texas Democratic Party has spent every minute since it fell from grace selling itself to the hard left on policy, despite the state's individualist mentality, in the belief that Hispanics in that red state would eventually grow enough in numbers to overwhelm the state's white population and turn Texas forever blue. But don't take my word for it. The Texas Democratic Party has literally been saying this for decades. The national Democrats have banked on this and have openly said that Hispanics turning Texas blue would end the Republican Party and shift the entire country leftward. There was even a book about it: *The Emerging Democratic Majority* by John B. Judis and Ruy Teixeira.[205]

That majority should have emerged by now. (For what it's worth, Teixeira has since revised and updated the thesis—he is no longer quite certain of his predictions from twenty-one years ago.) Texas became what's called a majority-minority state years ago, meaning white Texans are no longer the majority. BIPOCs make up the majority of the state's population. Yet Texas is as Republican as ever. Texas Latinos flipped a district long held by Democrats to Republican Mayra Flores, the conservative Latina who is married to a Border Patrol agent who also happens to be Hispanic. The Border Patrol itself is heavily Hispanic despite its being an instrument of white oppression in the BIPOC lexicon.

Texas Hispanics also elected Tony Gonzales to Congress from his border district on a platform of conservative values and law and order.[206] Bush acolyte and former representative Will Hurd explicitly distanced himself from those values and was only able to hang onto that same district by a thread. Gonzales made the district deeper red, and other nearby districts appear set to follow in 2024 and beyond. Donald Trump made the case for border security, energy independence, and a strong economy, and once-blue counties in the deeply Hispanic Rio Grande Valley trended very red, very quickly.

To the BIPOC masters, this colors far outside their narrow lines. Critical race theory doesn't allow for choices or values, just skin color. Demographics are ironclad destiny.

The same trend is happening in Florida, where Governor Ron DeSantis picked up considerable support among the state's large Hispanic population in his 2022 reelection bid.

Reacting to a tweet that DeSantis was so popular among Florida Hispanics that he was set to win deep blue Miami-Dade County (in fact, he was the first Republican gubernatorial candidate to win there since 2002), Jemele Hill posted: "That proximity to whiteness is a real thing. Also reminds me of an adage I heard a long time ago about how the oppressed begin to take on the traits of the oppressor."[207]

Where did the impressionable Hill first hear this toxic "adage"? Where did it come from? Most likely from Ibram X. Kendi or one of his disciples. Robin DiAngelo, perhaps, taught Hill to hate white people and everyone else who doesn't think exactly the way she demands they think.

As Hispanics decide the Democrats are only delivering division, inflation, crime, chaos, and overt attacks on their faith and their families, they're making the sensible decision of their own free will to seek a different party that embraces their beliefs. Hill and her cohort demand that Hispanics think and vote a certain way or risk alienation. They're painting Hispanics white so they can pour scorn on them and shame them, as they pour hate on white Americans every single day.

The Atlantic is fully on board with forcing people of certain skin colors to all think and be the exact same leftist thing,[208] as is the *New York Times*, the *Washington Post*, the *Houston Chronicle*, and every other major leftist organ. So is Joe Biden's Democratic Party and the media culture generally. All of the major sports are on board, and so is academia, with Big Tech tightening the screws on opposing thought. Question the Left's narrative in any way, and you may find yourself denounced, fired, ostracized, deplatformed, and made digitally into a nonperson.

Who's the real oppressor here?

Hispanics will soon learn that being white in America comes with built-in disadvantages.

If you're looking for a silver lining in all this, maybe this is it. Pushing former BIPOCs out into the cold, white world gives them a kind of permission to think for themselves and vote however they want. More and more of them will wake up from the woke and choose their own destinies. Making former BIPOCs white actually erodes the racist construct that is the Left's political coalition, fracturing it, and shrinking it—pushing their socialist scheme farther over the horizon.

First Asians, then Hispanics. What will be the next group to be liberated from the Left's oppressive racial groupthink?

2. Be Thankful for Elizabeth II's White Privilege

"The Queen is dead. Long live the King." And so it goes when one English monarch passes and another steps up to the throne. They change England's national anthem from "God Save the Queen" to "God Save the King," and continuity is maintained. Queen Elizabeth II's passing on September 8, 2022, gave way to her son Charles, who took the royal moniker of Charles III.

Why he went with Charles and not the other royal names available to him—he could've been King Arthur II, for instance—is something only he can answer, given the records of previous kings named Charles. The first one got embroiled in England's devastating civil war and literally lost his head over it.[209] His son's accession only proved the pointlessness of that war and the necessity of getting one's civil rights codified in writing. America's founders took that lesson to heart a century later.

But enough about Charles III, whose reign is in its infancy.

The extreme haters on *The View* marked the end of the longest reign in English history by denouncing Elizabeth II and her country.[210]

"The monarchy…was built on the backs of black and brown people," said co-host Sunny Hostin, a woman incapable of reacting to anyone or anything white with anything other than undiluted hatred and contempt. "She wore a crown with pillaged stones from India and Africa, and now what you're seeing, at least in the black communities that I'm a part of, they want reparations."

Every monarchy has its moments of greatness and its crimes and misdemeanors. Americans threw off the yoke of England because

King George III was a tyrant. Charles I was so awful they did away with the monarchy entirely for a few years. Cast about the world for the records of pharaohs, caesars, czars, and kings, and you'll find plenty of despots, madmen, knaves, and fools, along with a few heroes here and there.

Elizabeth II was in a category of her own. Her long reign comprised class, grandeur, patriotism, and service. Maybe in Hostin's mind, the late queen's greatest crimes are, first, being born white, and second, being a stalwart friend of America. In today's woke, intolerant, and often racist media, both of those are cancelable offenses.

And so Hostin, who is so oppressed in America that she enjoys a multimillion-dollar life most Americans can only dream of and is enthroned on a media platform from which she can address the entire world, denounces someone whose crown Hostin would never be fit to hold. Hostin lacks judgment, discernment, self-control, and fairness.

The fact is, Elizabeth II was more than the queen of England. She was a symbol of stability in uncertain times and a fighter for freedom when the Nazis and then the communists imperiled it most. She provided a sense of youth and optimism in the postwar world when she was coronated. And she was one of the world's greatest philanthropists. *People* magazine researched and detailed all of the many charitable organizations to which the queen lent her authority, name, prestige, and finances.[211] The list stretches into the hundreds of groups and millions of lives touched and ought to be humbling to a hater such as Hostin, about whom nothing is and never ever will be "sunny."

The list of the queen's charities included works in hospitals, education and training, the environment, and museums. She worked to preserve traditional rural life in England. She worked to deliver world-class medical services to people who desperately need them in Africa and all over the world. She was a lover and preserver of history in England and around the globe. The head of the Charities Aid Foundation said Elizabeth "did more for charity in the last 60 years than probably any other monarch in history." That isn't just monarchs of England; that's *worldwide*.

Louis XIV, France's "Sun King," built himself the opulent estate at Versailles to demonstrate his wealth and power. The Saudi sheiks live on lakes of oil and make hundreds of millions of dollars per day, which they spend on who knows what. Vladimir Putin sits atop a throne of lies and blood, and also vast quantities of oil and gas, and is but the latest tyrant to become a billionaire by grand theft of his country's national resources.

Elizabeth II did more for the good of the world than any of them, with a lot less at her disposal.

For that, she deserves far more respect and honor than the likes of Hostin and the haters can ever grasp.

3. They Were Never Going to Stop with the Confederacy Statues

How long before the *White* House is considered "racist"? And will it have to be torn down too? The logic—or rather, the politics—trends unstoppably in that direction.

Statues of white men are being taken down on the same basis.

At first, just some statues—of certain white men—such as those who served in the army of the Confederacy, which attempted to do what the American colonies did successfully those four score and seven years prior. That is, they sought to separate from a union they believed ruled over them by force rather than—wait for it—the *consent of the governed*. The very thing Abraham Lincoln claimed he was defending by forcing the Southern states back into a union they clearly no longer consented to be part of.

The issue has been clouded by the slavery issue, of course. The statues of Confederates had to go because of the association of the Confederacy with slavery.

But George Washington wasn't a Confederate.

On the contrary, his excellency was the commanding general of the army that succeeded in achieving the separation of the thirteen American colonies from Great Britain—and won them a government they consented to. But Washington—and other colonial-era leaders such as Thomas Jefferson—*were* white men.

And *all* white men are "patriarchs" and "oppressors." They are "racists," whose statues in public spaces have got to go, for the sake of "reckoning with historical injustices that continue to haunt our cities," in the words of New York City Councilwoman Sandy Nurse of Brooklyn.[212] She is the author of a bill that would topple the statues of Washington and other dead white males, notwithstanding the fact that Washington *liberated* New York City from the British occupation on November 22, 1783.

Of course, that's just *history*. Remove a people's history, and you remove a people.

Also, there's the fact that Jefferson was the man who wrote the document that proclaimed "all men" to be "created equal" that established the moral underpinnings for the ending of slavery long before the war that ended it. No other man had ever proclaimed this. And no other country was ever founded on the idea of it.

Never mind.

It's the politics—of perpetual grievance—that matter.

President Trump understood this long before most began to realize that taking down *some* statues would lead, inevitably, to taking down more and—ultimately—all of them.

History would be replaced with something more in tune with politics. Washington's achievements—and Jefferson's significance—are to be disappeared along with their monuments, because the politics of perpetual grievance requires scorched earth repudiation that everything these men stood for was bad—and nothing they did was good.

"This week, it's Robert E. Lee," President Trump said—*in 2017.* "I notice Stonewall Jackson's coming down. I wonder, is it George

Washington next week and is it Thomas Jefferson the week after? You know, you really have to ask yourself, where does it stop?"

The answer is, it doesn't. Trumpadamus predicted it all.

There is reasoning with people who think in terms of black and white—and think everything that's black (or brown or red or some other hue) is always good, and anything that's white is always bad. They are *racist* to a degree that would make an Imperial Wizard blush.

And they are something much worse.

They are effacers of our *common* endowment, in italics to emphasize the fact that regardless of color, everyone who is a citizen of this country is an American—and by dint of that shares in our common endowment. This includes the good—and the bad. And the truth is that without the good—done by Washington, Jefferson, and other white guys—there would be no America and no common endowment for people of all colors.

If the effacers have their way, they'll eventually have to rename New York City itself—as the name derives from *York*, in England. And then they'll have to come up with a new name for their own Cultural Affairs Committee, also prefaced by New York City.

And if "New York" has got to go—along with the statues of dead white men such as Washington and Jefferson—how long before every statue (and place name) that *isn't* a tribute to someone who *wasn't* white has got to go? Can we—will we be allowed—to refer to America? After all, the name derives from a white explorer, Amerigo Vespucci,[213] who followed Columbus—another white explorer—to what Europeans (mostly white, again) referred to as the New World.

America takes its name from his.

Just as the District of Columbia is named after Columbus. That is as much a part of American history as Martin Luther King Jr.'s march on Washington. And King—like Washington (and Jefferson) also had his flaws. He serially cheated on his wife, for instance. And he apparently cheated on his doctoral dissertation by plagiarizing the work of others.[214] But these do not efface his message—or his impact. He is taken for the overall good he did—and not canceled for the bad things he did.

He is part of American history. At least for now.

As are Washington, Jefferson, and those Confederates too. We do not honor our history by effacing it. Nor by denying the good while harping only on the bad. History is more nuanced than that.

And America is better than that.

4. Ibram X. Kendi and the Grifting of White Dummies

Boston University may one day become a place of higher education again.

It took a step in that direction, at any rate, when officials decided to begin *deconstructing* the university's White Guilt Center—whoops, the Center for Antiracist Research[215]—which finds "racism" everywhere white people happen to be and then gets them to pay for it.

A whole *center*—and a staff of forty-five people—devoted to that project.

This is the multimillion-dollar grift of Ibram X. Kendi—a kind of second-generation Al Sharpton *sans* the iconic pompadour and track suit, who (like Reverend Al) makes money by making white people feel guilty. This causes them to hand over money for things like the Boston University Center for Antiracist Research—founded by Kendi and a kowtowing BU back in 2020, in the wake of the "mostly peaceful" Black Lives Matter protests.

As well as for Kendi's book, *Antiracist Baby*, which is more a graphic novel written to make white babies feel guilty for having been *born* "oppressors."[216] It has become a staple of critical race theory struggle sessions and a must-read for woke parents worried they might have passed that "racist" gene on to their progeny.

All of it has made Kendi—formerly Henry Rodgers—*very* wealthy, like the leadership of the Black Lives Matter rioters he lionizes in his graphic novel. He is reportedly worth somewhere in the neighborhood of $215 million.

A question Boston University might want to research is: How does an oppressed black man in his early forties earn that kind of money in a country that *systemically* keeps the black man down? Kendi doesn't answer. Perhaps because he knows the answer is to hurl accusations—which all too many have been afraid to question, out of fear they'll be called you-know-whats by Al the Younger and his ilk.

Fact is, Kendi has made more money in twenty years as a "doctor of race" pointing fingers at "racists"—including white babies!—than 99.9 percent of "privileged" white people will ever earn in their entire lives.

That is why *The White Privilege Album* had to chronicle this buffoon.

You can't make $215 million working in a steel mill or turning wrenches or being a cop. But you can make it by getting and then leveraging a PhD in African American studies (which of course *isn't* even a little bit racist in the way it would be if someone were to get a degree in white American studies) to get a high-paying job at a college endlessly belaboring race.

Because that's how you get people to stop seeing "racists" everywhere—kind of like that kid in the late '90s Bruce Willis flick, *The Sixth Sense*,[217] who saw dead people.

Except of course those were *real*.

Kendi's doctoral dissertation was titled, "The Black Campus Movement: An Afrocentric Narrative History of the Struggle to Diversify Higher Education, 1965–1972." Are you impressed?

The Klan could take a cue from this. Sheepskins are more effective as tools of shakedowns than burning crosses and robes.

Kendi really knows how to work it. He is a top-notch flimflam man.

The White Guilt Center—whoops, the Center for Antiracist Research, of which he is the director—has shaken loose an astounding $43 million in less than three years since its founding, according to records obtained by the *Daily Free Press*.[218] How much of this went into Kendi's very oppressed silk-lined pockets is not known. What is known is how much white guilt financed all of this—including a $10 million, no-strings-attached gift from Twitter's then CEO Jack Dorsey, as well as virtue-signaling check writing from woke corporations, including Stop & Shop, Deloitte, Peloton, and Deckers Outdoor Corporation.

But where did the money go, if not into Kendi's bank account?

Well, some of it went toward funding an "Antibigotry Convening" that "included many intersectionality themes," such as "ageism," anti-fat bigotry, and "transphobia." What these have to do with *race*—aside from the hustle—no one at the center has yet been able to explain.

Some of the cash did go toward financing an "Anti-Racist Curricula Team" at BU. The problem there, of course, is the absence of anything actually racist in BU's curricula. Unless you consider the insistence upon grammatically correct English and correct answers based on facts—as opposed to one's *feelings*—to be racist.

In the woke world of critical race theory, "facts" and "grammar" should have no place in a university because they are manifestations of "privilege," which is synonymous with "whiteness" and thus "racist."

How's *that* for shareholder value?

But Boston University—where one year of undergraduate study costs $63,000[219]—rightly questions the value of Kendi's obsession with making *everything* about race. Three years into Kendi's grift—whoops, tenure—university officials wondered where all the money went.[220]

Saida Grundy, a professor who worked at the center back in 2020–2021, described "a pattern of amassing grants without any commitment to producing the research" the money was supposed to fund.

Other former workers describe "mismanagement" and accuse Kendi of "mishandling" the manna[221]—whoops, the money granted by those seeking to assuage their guilt by financing the propagation of research into "microaggressions," so named because you have to look under a racist microscope to see them.

But don't dare ask Ibram X. Kendi for an accounting—lest you be accused of being a you-know-what.

5. Remember That Time Joe Biden Sprung Nelson Mandela from Jail?

Joe Biden can add great white Mandela fabulist to his résumé.

Never forget he once again told a whopper of a lie about his mundane political career to make himself seem greater than he is.

"I got stopped when I was a young senator trying to see Nelson Mandela in South Africa," Biden said unchallenged during a forum broadcast on *NowThis News*. "Afterward he heard, and when he got released, he came to see me in Washington, and he walked up to me [and] said, 'Thank you.'"[222]

None of that happened. None of it. Joe Biden made it all up. Again.

He has told this particular lie several times over the years, and it got so bad that even the *Washington Post*'s biased fact-checker ended up calling it "ridiculous" in 2020.[223] When Biden did visit South Africa in the 1970s, he was hundreds of miles from where Mandela was in prison. His own press secretary has admitted that he was separated from black politicians in a black-run country, not South Africa. Even CNN had to acknowledge Biden's "Mandela effect" lie.[224]

Biden was actually friendly with segregationists during the time he dishonestly claims to have been arrested looking for Mandela, and even NBC News has dismantled his history on this. "His legislative work against school integration advanced a more palatable version of the 'separate but equal' doctrine and undermined the nation's short-lived effort at educational equality, legislative and education history experts say," NBC News reported in 2019.[225]

Separate but equal? From the man who claims Nelson Mandela hunted for him in Washington just to thank him?

Joe Biden has a habit of lying without fear or principle. Remember when he ran for president as a moderate unifier, only to attack America's energy producers and foist divisive and counterproductive woke training on the US military as soon as he was safely in office? He has governed from the hard left and would use a narrow advantage in Congress to seize permanent power for Democrats if he could.

Remember when he trashed Georgia's election security law as "Jim Crow 2.0"? That law is less restrictive than the laws in his own state of Delaware, and turnout among black voters *increased* in the Peach State after the legislation took effect.[226] But Joe Biden doesn't care. The truth is little more than a slight inconvenience to him.

Biden's lie ended up taking jobs away from black businesses in Atlanta, which was supposed to host the Major League Baseball All-Star Game. Instead, MLB moved the game to lily-white Denver, Colorado. Biden didn't care.

As far back as the 1970s, Ronald Reagan had Biden pegged as a "smooth but pure demagogue." That means he could and would easily lie without conscience to gain political advantage as he thought it suited him. That's all he's ever done.

Here's some reality in South Africa that Joe Biden will never admit: it was a white South African leader who dismantled apartheid and freed Nelson Mandela. That man was President F. W. de Klerk. Elected to South Africa's presidency in 1989, de Klerk set about changing his country and righting wrongs. He lifted the ban on the African National Congress, of which Mandela was a leader, suspended executions, and the following year, he freed Mandela himself. While Joe Biden was lying, getting everything from wars to judges wrong, and generally being the luckiest untalented politician in history, de Klerk was actually making a real difference for his country and the world.

The reality is Joe Biden won a Senate seat from a tiny state and has used his hammerlock on it to amass influence he could peddle to make himself rich and win the presidency essentially by default. Add the world's heaviest dose of media bias. Add Zuckerberg's bucks donated to build Democratic vote machines in blue cities. With all of this, you could elect a reanimated corpse.

And they did.

Joe Biden has been a plagiarist and fabulist his entire political career. Most of the media ignore the fact that his 1988 presidential run—that's how long he's been in politics—flamed out once it was proven he'd swiped his autobiographical speech from the leader of the British Labour Party. Joe Biden has been a plagiarist and a thief going all the way back to his university career, the *New York Times* reported.[227] And he's even lied repeatedly about that university career.

Enabling Biden's self-dealing dishonesty across the decades only empowered and emboldened him. Over the years, he's repeated a lie about himself, South Africa, and Nelson Mandela, despite it being repeatedly proven to be a lie. He has plagiarized, smeared (he shamelessly told a black audience that Republicans—the party founded to end slavery and that voted to pass the 1964 Civil Rights Act by a greater percentage than the Democrats—would "put y'all back in chains"[228]), and divided America his entire political career, putting himself first and his party over country the whole time.

Joe Biden was one of the senators who poisoned the judicial nominations process for decades, in service of the far-left Democrats as far back as the 1980s. The media let him get away with it. He lies about inflation and its causes now. The media lets him get away with it. He lies about his drug-addled son's lucrative deals with Ukraine and even the Chinese communists, about which he dishonestly claims to know

THE WHITE PRIVILEGE ALBUM

nothing. CBS News only got around to reporting about that two years and a midterm election into Biden's destructive administration.[229]

These are serious lies that speak to Joe Biden's total lack of honesty and character. Selling out to the highest bidder, even when this includes our enemies, ought to be treated as the deeply serious national security issue that it is. America has not faced a threat as insidious as President Joe Biden, inveterate and shameless liar.

Virginia Woolf said, "If you do not tell the truth about yourself you cannot tell it about other people." Joe Biden can't tell the truth about anything, or anyone, at any time.

Always remember when you hear the grievance lobby screaming the words Mandela, apartheid, or white privilege, President F. W. de Klerk says, "You're welcome."

6. Michael Rapaport Apologizes to the Very Fine People

Even liberals like the actor Michael Rapaport are beginning to understand what the Left is up to—and realizing what's been done to Donald Trump.

And to *them*.

Like many liberals—and many Americans—Rapaport believed the news when he heard that Trump had defended neo-Nazis as "very fine people" in the aftermath of the melee in Charlottesville, Virginia, back in August 2017. If you recall, the focal point was a protest surrounding the pending removal of a statue of Confederate general and Mexican–American War veteran Robert E. Lee.

In fact, Trump said the opposite. And more.

Here's what he *really* said—the full quote in context:

> "Excuse me, they didn't put themselves down as neo-Nazis, and you had some very bad people in that group. *But you also had people that were very fine people*

on both sides. You had people in that group—excuse me, excuse me, I saw the same pictures you did. You had people in that group that were there to protest the taking down of, to them, a very, very important statue and the renaming of a park from Robert E. Lee to another name."[230]

Note the difference.

The corporate left-wing media left out the "both sides" part. They also left out how Trump specifically denounced the neo-Nazis at the melee as "very bad people," a clear statement of unambiguous condemnation. Because, of course, the Left meant to condemn Trump for what he never said, and then to lie to get the public (including Rapaport) to believe what they *claimed* Trump said.

Where you get your fake news determined the reality (or the left-wing figment of your imagination) of the Charlottesville incident.

It was not merely sloppy journalism, either. The "very fine people" portion was very deliberately amplified to create a false impression about what Trump said.

"I'm not talking about the neo-Nazis and white nationalists because they should be condemned totally...we condemn in the strongest possible terms this egregious display of hatred, bigotry, and violence."

Clear enough?

Well, no. Not if you listened to the "news." Not if you listened to Joe Biden, who endlessly repeated the "very fine people" lie during the run-up to the 2020 election. Biden *continues* to accuse Trump of praising neo-Nazis.

Politico reported that Biden "adamantly defended his assertions that President Donald Trump embraced white supremacists after a deadly demonstration in Charlottesville, Va., engaging in an animated exchange after his public remarks here."[231]

The story continues: "At the suggestion that Trump had condemned the actions of marching white supremacists, Biden grew adamant, wagging his finger" in his trademark manner. "No, he did not, he walked out and he said—let's get this straight—he said there were very fine people in both groups," Biden lectured.

Biden must know *by now* that this is false. Then again, Biden also thinks he knows that he drove an over-the-road truck for a living and doesn't know when his son Beau Biden died.

"I used to drive a tractor trailer," Biden told an audience in 2021, "so I know a little bit about driving big trucks."[232]

Except he never did. Biden may have hitched a ride in a tractor trailer as a senator,[233] back in 1973, but he never drove one.

Biden's memory is not very good. But neither is his integrity.

Of course, it is not just Biden. It is the thoroughly—and now openly—mendacious media that serially lies to the public, and so egregiously that even Hollywood liberals like Rapaport aren't buying the lies anymore.

The actor, who played a starring role in the Sylvester Stallone film *Cop Land* as well as in *Beautiful Girls* and many others, said as much on the Patrick Bet-David Podcast.[234]

"One thing that I really disdain in the mainstream media," he said, "is if the other side, or a president you don't like, does something good, it's never acknowledged."

The conversation then went on to the Charlottesville melee, and how the media straight-up lied about what Trump said afterward.

"That thing about Charlottesville," Rapaport said, "that I really ranted about," referring to his criticisms of Trump that were based on lies he'd heard and believed. "…I was wrong," the actor admitted.

That's something Joe Biden—something the Left—has never done. And never will. Because the Left isn't interested in the truth. It cares only about what serves its interests. The Left is interested in power obtained and held by any means necessary.

"When you see the full quote, that wasn't what [Trump] said and I ranted on him hard for that, hard…I was like, 'what are you talking about, man?'"

But "that wasn't what he said."

The way the media and the Left *continue* to lie about what Trump said has caused even liberals like Rapaport to become…well, if not quite full-on Trump supporters, then at least skeptical and remorseful about some long-held opinions and beliefs. Because they cannot in good conscience support the deliberate, serial lying of the Left. Or Joe Biden. Or whomever the Left might put in place of the obviously declining serial liar and grifter.

"I won't vote for them. That's not happening," Rapaport said.

Maybe the wheel is turning.

Other prominent liberals, such as the comedian Bill Maher, have also been publicly expressing their unease with the lying Left.[235] In Maher's case, he's angry about the lies the government and the press spread during the pandemic—especially the way the Left went after people who dared to tell the truth about masks and lockdowns, among other things.

It's all lies, ladies and gentlemen. It's time to *stop the spread*, as the Left likes to say.

And that is why the Very Fine People on Both Sides were the impetus for this book.

X.

October Privilege

"Baseball takes more than raw athleticism. It takes the patience and the skill that a father is most likely to help provide. The baseball diamonds in urban America aren't being used to learn the sport—they're filled with needles, not with kids playing catch with their fathers."

1. Black Lives Matter Loves Hamas

Ladies and gentlemen, stories like this are the reason I wrote this book.

Birds of a feather flock together—and that includes cowardly, violence-loving terrorists.

Black Lives Matter—which is an *organization* rather than a movement—has exactly that in common with Hamas, another organization that operates similarly. They both stage cowardly attacks on innocents on false pretexts—and then blame their victims for making them do it.

So it's no surprise to find that BLM supports Hamas.

The Chicago chapter of the latter organization posted an "I Stand with Palestine" graphic on Twitter (now X)[236]—hurriedly deleted in the wake of immediate backlash—that depicted a terrorist paraglider descending toward the Israeli Nova music festival—where on Oct. 7, 2023, terrorists proceeded to slaughter an estimated 270 defenseless civilians, raping and mutilating many of the women first.

They took *video* of their deeds and posted them online.

The Los Angeles chapter of BLM said, "*Resistance* must not be condemned, but *understood* as a desperate act of self-defense."

How much "resistance" did the women raped by the paragliding Hamas thugs who descended on the music festival put up? How about the babies that were beheaded (apparently, in front of their parents)?

And how are we supposed to "understand" people who commit such acts?

It takes a tough "freedom fighter" to pounce on and brutalize women and children attending a music festival. One of the reports coming out of the scene of the recent Hamas attacks tells of an elderly woman who was too frail to be marched out of her home, so the Hamas thugs locked her inside and then set fire to the house, which burned to the ground with the elderly woman inside.

To characterize such atrocities as "self-defense" is a metastasis of the way the BLM riots of 2020 were characterized by apologists for those as *mostly* "peaceful." And it is precisely such apologias that have egged on such atrocities and those who commit them. They are organized metastatic forms of the same thing that befell another apologist for violent thugs, the leftist agitator Josh Kruger—who was recently murdered by violent thugs.[237]

Sow the wind, reap the whirlwind.

"We, too, understand what it means to be surveilled, dehumanized, property seized, families separated, our people criminalized and slaughtered with impunity, locked up in droves and *when we resist*, they call us terrorist," said the LA chapter of Hamas.

Whoops, I mean BLM.

"When we resist." Language such as this is *almost* as vile as the actions being apologized for. And then temporized for.

Later, BLM Chicago posted: "Yesterday, we sent out msgs that we aren't proud of," referencing the post of the black-silhouetted terrorist paragliding toward the unsuspecting soon-to-be-victims at the music festival.

And then this—to take it all back: "We stand with Palestine & the people who will do what they must to live free." Which presumably includes murdering (and raping) women, beheading children in front of their parents, and burning elderly people to death.

"Our hearts are with the grieving mothers, those rescuing babies from rubble, who are in danger of being wiped out completely." BLM is not referring to the atrocities committed by Hamas terrorists. It is standing with terrorists who committed them. It is criticizing the Israeli government for *responding* to the terrorists' attacks.

But not everyone is having it.

One of them is Amar'e Stoudemire, former Arizona Suns Rookie of the Year in 2003 and, more recently, a player development assistant for the Brooklyn Nets. He's black (and Jewish)—and thinks *innocent lives matter*. He has publicly called out both Black Lives Matter and Hamas, calling them—correctly—"cowardly" for "kidnapping children, putting them in cages, killing women, killing the elderly."[238]

He's right, of course—because it's inarguably true. *Men*—who aren't cowards—don't "defend themselves" against children, women, or old people. And those who do *are* cowards and terrorists, by definition. The excuse doesn't change the nature of them—or what they do.

Stoudemire went on to address the poltroonery—and hypocrisy—of BLM supporters who refuse to condemn either BLM or Hamas by saying something to them that's probably not fit to print in a family newspaper: "To the people who say, 'Well, let me figure out exactly what's happening before saying anything,' F*** you.

"All you politicians who always have something to say on the contrary—I see you," he continued, followed by the same expletive, also deleted. "All you Black Lives Matter people who always have something to say and always supported everything else and you quiet now, [expletive deleted] you, too."

His exasperation—and disgust—are understandable.

Attacking women, children, and old people who can't defend themselves is bad enough. It is worse than burning down cities and looting businesses owned by people who did nothing to harm anyone. But much worse than both is pretending *you're* doing such things in "self-defense" and to "fight injustice."

"Take a good look, liberal Jews," Karol Markowicz, columnist for the *New York Post* and Fox News, remarked. "This is the sh-- you supported."[239]

Expletive deleted to that!

2. The Myth of "Systemic Racism" Ended Long Ago on the Supreme Court

Three Supreme Court justices have been black. All three of them were appointed by white men.

Clearly, this is evidence of "systemic racism."

Interestingly, the one black president—Barack Obama—didn't appoint a single black justice to the court. Instead, he appointed two whites, one of whom identifies as a "wise Latina."[240]

Obama even had a white heterosexual male ready to replace the late Justice Antonin Scalia,[241] but, alas, he was blocked by Senator Mitch McConnell and now spends his days raiding Melania Trump's unmentionables drawer and harassing grandmas who wandered the US Capitol on January 6.

A white male president's most recent appointment to the Supreme Court, Justice Ketanji Brown Jackson, heard arguments for the first time in October 2022. As it happened, she heard cases concerning the constitutionality of affirmative action.

Yet no affirmative action was necessary to get three black Americans on the court. Their race may have influenced their appointment as a matter of politics, but there is no legal requirement that a black lawyer must fill a vacancy on the court.

The nation's first black justice was, of course, Thurgood Marshall, appointed by President Lyndon Johnson (a white man) in 1967. Marshall served until 1991. He had been previously appointed to the US Court of Appeals for the Second Circuit by another avatar of the white male patriarchy, President John F. Kennedy.

Marshall would probably never have risen further than his practice as a small-town lawyer in the then backwater Baltimore of the 1950s had it not been for the "racism" practiced by two powerful white men. Kennedy and Johnson say, "You're welcome."

The nation's second black justice, Clarence Thomas, narrowly avoided not being confirmed after having been appointed by another white man, President George H. W. Bush, to replace Marshall.

Bush had reportedly given serious consideration to nominating Thomas as the replacement for Justice William Brennan when the latter retired just before Marshall. Brennan, of course, was white and male. Clearly, it is an example of systemic racism that Bush contemplated replacing a white justice with a black one.

Thomas eventually replaced Marshall but only after a partisan attempt to block him from the high court led by a black woman, Anita Hill, who infamously accused Thomas of sexually harassing her when she worked for him at the Equal Employment Opportunity Commission in the 1980s. Hill's allegations were first taken at face value—a kind of prequel to the #MeToo movement that insists accusations be treated as facts.

Thomas had this to say about Hill's claims:

> This is not an opportunity to talk about difficult matters privately or in a closed environment. This is a circus. It's a national disgrace. And from my standpoint as a black American, as far as I'm concerned it is a high-tech lynching for uppity blacks who in any way deign to think for themselves, to do for themselves, to have different ideas, and it is a message that unless you kowtow to an old order, this is what will happen to you. You will be lynched, destroyed, caricatured by a committee of the U.S. Senate rather than hung from a tree.[242]

Ultimately, Thomas was confirmed and has served with distinction.

Interestingly, Joe Biden—then a senator—presided over the Anita Hill hearings and said he believed Hill's allegations. "Oh, I thought she was telling the truth at the beginning," Biden said, according to the *Washington Post*. "I really did."[243]

When Biden decided to run for president, he expressed regret for not doing more to derail Thomas's nomination[244]—which he expressed during the reboot inquisition of Brett Kavanaugh, a fellow white male. Biden did all he could to prevent Kavanaugh from becoming a Supreme Court justice, urging (as former vice president in 2018) that the hearings be delayed for as long as necessary to accommodate the assertions made by Christine Blasey Ford about what the judge supposedly did to her as a high school student forty years ago.

Biden also initially refused to condemn the attempt made upon Kavanaugh's life after he became a justice.[245] You can imagine the reaction if an attempt had been made to take the life of a sitting black justice. Well, except perhaps Clarence Thomas's life. Being a conservative makes him an "Uncle Tom" in the eyes of leftists.

To be "black," you must agree, as Biden himself has lectured.

But Biden did at least do what America's only black president failed to do. Last year, he nominated Ketanji Brown Jackson to succeed white male Justice Stephen Breyer.

This, clearly, is another example of the "systemic racism" that pervades this country.

3. The "Patriarch" Who Put Americans in the Driver's Seat

An irony of history is that Henry Ford designed the first Volkswagen. It's just that he called his the "Model T." But it was the first car built for *the people*.

Before the introduction of the Model T on October 1, 1908, cars were for affluent people only—because only the affluent could afford to buy what were then largely hand-built, one at a time, and made-to-order automobiles. Ford's idea was to simplify and standardize. He wanted to use fewer parts, with each one made to fit every car that was made just like it. Instead of craftsmen hand-building cars one at a time, by 1914, a moving assembly line put out a brand-new Model T every ninety-three minutes.

These manufacturing efficiencies saved time, which saved money. A first-year Model T listed for $850. By 1924, the same car—and it was essentially the same car—cost only $250. The Model T was the only car that got cheaper with each new model year, because Ford was the only car company that lowered production costs and passed the savings on to buyers. Henry Ford knew there would be more of them—and ultimately more money for him—if more people could afford to buy his cars.

That included the people who built them.

That, in turn, included an unprecedented number of black Americans who migrated from the poverty of the rural South and found well-paying jobs at Ford plants in and around Detroit.[246] Some became skilled machinists and foremen, earning their way into the new American middle class. By the end of World War I, Ford was the largest employer of black workers in Detroit. Many of those black workers were driving a car, previously something only the privileged (and mostly white) could afford.

The Model T ended that privilege by making it general.

"I will build a car for the great multitude," Ford said. "It will be large enough for the family, but small enough for the individual to run and care for. It will be constructed of the best materials, by the best men to be hired, after the simplest designs that modern engineering can devise. But it will be low in price that no man making a good salary will be unable to own one and enjoy with his family the blessing of hours of pleasure in God's great open spaces."[247]

Ford put Americans on wheels. Their *own* wheels. It was peak individualism.

He made it possible for average Americans to go places most of them would never have otherwise seen because average Americans could now go practically anywhere they wanted to go, anytime they wanted to go there, in a Model T Ford. Previously, Americans were tethered by their proximity to a bus or a train line. Or limited by how far a horse could go before it needed a rest. Millions of Americans had never traveled farther than fifty miles away from the town they were born in prior to the introduction of the Model T.

Now it was possible for them to drive fifty miles in a couple of hours.

And they didn't need paved roads to get there either. The Model T was designed for dirt roads. For *bad* roads. And bad weather too. It rode high off the ground on deliberately skinny wheels designed to cut through mud and snow. Practically anything that went wrong on the road could be fixed by the side of the road too. The Model T's engine did not even have a fuel pump—because gravity rarely fails. It had a very low-compression engine, so it could burn almost any kind of fuel without risking damage to the engine. And if you could crank it, you could start it.

The T didn't even need a battery!

It wasn't just personal transportation that Ford revolutionized either. Farmers used modified Model T's to plow their fields. And when the crops were ready, they could be brought from farm to market much faster via a Model T flatbed truck than a horse pulling a cart.

Ford built essentially the same Model T, tweaked here and there, through 1927, by which time *more than fifteen million* of them had been sold. The only other car that matched Ford's number was, in fact, the Volkswagen. But it only managed that feat after a production run that lasted decades longer, from the late 1930s (with an interruption during the war years) through 2002, when the last one rolled off an assembly line in Mexico.

And remember: it was the Model T that inspired the Volkswagen—and every mass-produced car that has come since, including modern inheritors such as the Toyota Corolla and Honda Civic. They all owe a debt to Ford, who showed the world how to make a car for everyone, not just for the privileged few.

And that's not all. Ford used his own money to finance relief programs for down-on-their-luck Detroiters during the Great Depression, built community centers, fixed up schools and ran low-cost commissaries in what leftists today call "underserved" communities. This self-taught farm-boy engineer considered it his privilege to help others—with his own rather than other people's money.

And by putting Americans of all colors and walks of life on wheels. Even if the Model T itself was only available in *one* color.

4. Those African Kings Owe Me Some Paper

Who owes what to whom?

The supply line of history rarely lies, and CNN is trying to stick me for my papers.[248]

If the ancestors of people who enslaved people owe reparations to the ancestors of those who were enslaved, then perhaps it is time for a "conversation"—as the Left likes to put it—about paying reparations to the descendants of people who fought and died to help free enslaved people.

Someone should put the question to former CNN host Don Lemon, a man who even off the air lectures *endlessly* about the moral necessity of paying reparations to the descendants of the enslaved—even if the people who will be "asked" (i.e., *forced*) to pay them not only had nothing to do with enslaving *anyone* but had ancestors who fought and died to free the enslaved.

Thus was Don Lemon schooled by Hilary Fordwich,[249] an expert on the British royal family who appeared on CNN following the death of Queen Elizabeth II. She had come to discuss the royal succession. Lemon invited her there to gaslight her about "slavery."

But the gas lit up like a blowtorch—in *Lemon's face*.

"And then you have those who are asking for reparations," Lemon began. "For colonialism...and they're wondering, you know, a hundred billion dollars...twenty-four billion dollars"—Lemon was referring to the wealth attributed to the British royal family. "Some people want to be paid back...and members of the public"—Lemon was referring to himself—"are wondering, 'why are we suffering when you are, when you have all of this vast wealth?' Those are legitimate concerns...."

Fordwich would have none of it. "Where was the beginning of the [slave] supply chain?" she queried Lemon. And then she told him. "It was in Africa."

Yes, it's an inconvenient truth that black African royalty enslaved other black Africans, turning them over to Western middlemen in exchange for princely sums. Should the descendants of these kings be made to cough up reparations to the descendants of the people they enslaved? It would certainly be fairer than "asking" descendants of the people who fought and died to end slavery as an institution to hand over money to the descendants of the people they helped free.

Fordwich schooled Lemon on this point. "Two thousand naval men died on the high seas to stop slavery," she said, referring to the sailors of the British Navy who intercepted slave ships filled with "cargo" provided by African kings.

"Which was the first nation in the world that abolished slavery?"

That would be the British, who outlawed it in toto in 1833 and had outlawed the trade in 1807—several decades before hundreds of thousands of Americans fought and died to end slavery in the United States.

Maybe the descendants of those people are owed reparations too. Or at least, thanks. None such ever seems to be forthcoming from the likes of Don Lemon, for whom "slavery" is a cudgel to beat people who had nothing to do with it over the head with. And to make them pay for it too.

The schooling of Lemon continued.

"Well, I think you're right about reparations," Fordwich said. But, she added quickly, "If reparations need to be paid, we need to go right back to the beginning of that supply chain and say, 'Who was rounding up their own people and having them handcuffed in cages?'"

Once again, that would be *African royalty*, as Fordwich explained to an increasingly nonplussed Lemon. "They had them in cages, waiting on the beaches. No one was running into Africa to get them."

People with English, Welsh, Scottish, Irish, Canadian, and American blood all fought to end slavery in one form or another. So, it's time to pay!

These facts are true—and discomfiting to the agenda of leftist propagandists like Lemon, who identifies as a real journalist. The propaganda and guilt-shaming has become so blatant, aggressive, and historically ignorant that even liberals (who aren't leftists) like the comedian Bill Maher have had enough of it.

Not long before Fordwich's thorough dismantling of Don Lemon, Maher attempted to educate leftists about slavery by stating similar inconvenient truths about it. "Did Columbus commit atrocities? Of course! The people back then were generally atrocious."[250]

As in people of all colors, not just one color of them.

"Everyone who could afford one had a slave—including people of color," Maher told his *Real Time* audience on HBO. "The way people talk about slavery these days, you'd think it was a uniquely American phenomenon that was invented in 1619," referring to the year the first African slave supposedly landed in North America.

And never mind that native Americans—also "people of color"—regularly enslaved the peoples of other tribes.

Naturally, Maher's attempt to reason with the Left triggered an eruption of leftist outrage, with the Left predictably accusing Maher of defending "white supremacy." This is almost as ridiculous as "asking" the descendants of people who fought and died to end slavery on the high seas and the battlefields of the American Civil War to hand over "reparations" to the descendants of those they fought and died to help free.

It was nice to see the members of the media operating under liberal privilege finally get a history lesson from someone who doesn't hate white people. It would be even nicer to see more of it.

5. Christopher Columbus Says, "You're Welcome!"

Every year on Columbus Day, we hear and see the Left endlessly bash the explorer who braved the seas and became the first European Christian to set foot in the New World. Sure, the Vikings had reached Canada centuries earlier, but they lacked the follow-through of the Spanish and their lead Italian explorer, Christopher Columbus.

Thank God for the Catholic patriarchy that brought civilization to one of the most savage dumps on planet Earth!

We hear the Left moan endlessly about Columbus's sins, real and imagined, but there will be *zero discussion* of what he found when he got here. The pre-Columbian Americans have been sanitized and rewritten into some sort of idyllic paradise in which oppression and disease did not exist. Humans lived in perfect harmony with nature and each other, peacefully gazing at the stars, devising advanced Mayan calendars, building great astronomical observatories in the desert in Chaco Canyon, constructing ornate Aztec pyramids in what is now Mexico and Guatemala, and engineering those fabulous Inca cities in the clouds in the Andes.

All was well, beautiful, and peaceful until Columbus came along, just a couple of continents full of artistic villages and scientific communities, or so we're told. Misogyny, racism, and hate all arrived with the Europeans.

Yeah…about that.

The Spanish arrived in America after centuries of bloody and brutal warfare with the Muslim Moors who had taken over much of the Iberian Peninsula by force of arms. They had just finished pushing the oppressive Moors out in 1492, not coincidentally the same year Columbus sailed the ocean blue. The Spanish arrived with both religious and practical reasons to make Christians of those they encountered. A few centuries of direct contact with Islam suggested coexistence could be done on a future Ann Arbor left-winger's bumper sticker but was much more problematic in the real world.

When he arrived in the New World, Columbus documented some of the horrors he found. Rape of women was commonplace, as were murder, slavery, and even cannibalism. Early encounters were dramatic as both peoples came to grips with new realities.

Decades later, when the Spanish arrived in the Aztec empire,[251] they found both an incredible and advanced civilization and an imperial power loathed by those it had spent centuries oppressing. A few hundred Spaniards were able to defeat that mighty empire not purely by having more advanced weapons, and not just by the spread of disease, but also by the fact that the Aztecs' many victims saw the arrival of the Spanish as their chance to overthrow their hated rulers. Those pyramids had flowed with the blood of the vanquished long before Columbus arrived.

If you've heard anything about the pre-1492 Incas, it's probably that they built the amazing Machu Picchu up on an Andean mountaintop,[252] and that we still know little about how or why they built it. You may have also heard about the legendary Inca gold the Spanish plundered. The Great Inca Rebellion has gotten a lot of ink over the years as a story of noble natives rising up to fight their horrible Spanish overlords, but recent scholarship on this series of events suggests a far more complex truth.

Like the Aztecs to their north, the Inca had spent centuries building their empire on the backs and blood of their neighbors. The arrival of the Spanish under Francisco Pizarro was a godsend to those oppressed peoples, and they allied with the alien conquistadors to overthrow the Inca. In fact, it was an Inca princess married to Pizarro who called in Indian reinforcements during the Siege of Lima to break the Inca forces and save the Spanish. The Incas might have crushed the Spanish in 1536 if they'd simply been nicer to their neighbors.

All of this is chronicled in a 2020 National Geographic documentary called *Skeletons of the Inca Rebellion,* which airs infrequently—perhaps because it bucks the woke dominant anti-European narrative.

As for the astronomically inclined Chaco Canyon people, they never came into contact with Europeans at all. They rose, built their amazing desert cities and observatories, and dispersed before Columbus ever arrived.[253] But the latest research suggests they did have contact and trade with the Mayans to their southeast and learned from them about devising caste systems by which the rulers could consolidate their power and oppress their own people. This brutal system may have been a reason for their mysterious demise. People get fed up with being oppressed, as the woke zombies are already finding out.[254]

We'll never know what the Americas would have become if Columbus never arrived. We do know, based on science, that oppression and brutality were part of the human condition in the New World long before any Vikings or other Europeans stepped anywhere in the hemisphere. After all, human beings tend to be, in comedian Bill Maher's words, "generally atrocious."[255]

But for all their faults, the Europeans did expand scientific knowledge, the Christian faith, and the freedom that we enjoy today, in part by learning from English history, particularly the English Civil Wars,[256] and even from the Iroquois system of governance.[257] America's founders were keen students of history and human nature.

So, thanks to the patriarchy and those wicked Europeans and their thirst for knowledge, you're free to bash or praise Christopher Columbus as you see fit. Thank the patriarchy. You're welcome!

6. Playing Catch with a Ghost

No sooner had the World Series between the Houston Astros and the Philadelphia Phillies begun than the craven media tried to make it about race. Not achievement. Not success. Not even the pleasure of watching the New York Yankees get humiliated in a sweep. The media made it all about race.

Ben Walker of the Associated Press set the tone with a report on the absence of black players in the series this year.[258] Like lemmings, media outlets either published the AP's piece uncritically or piled on with their own hot takes, even though Major League Baseball has had plenty of black stars since Jackie Robinson broke the color barrier. Hank Aaron, Ken Griffey Sr. and Jr., Willie Mays, Barry Bonds, Jimmy Rollins, and Rickey Henderson are just a few of the many baseball heroes America has embraced over the years who happened to be black.

Walker qualified his piece somewhat, saying there are no "US-born Black players" in the 2022 World Series. That's some qualification! The fact is, if diversity matters, the Major Leagues are as diverse as they've ever been, with more than a quarter of their players having been born outside the United States.[259] America's pastime is now global.

Walker avoided discussion of the racial makeup of the NBA and NFL. They're predominantly black. Baseball—and hockey—are getting beat up because they're not. But even presuming this is a fault, is it the fault of the sport or does responsibility lie elsewhere?

Most of MLB's international players come from Latin America, and many of them are black. They just weren't born in the United States. Do Hispanics and especially black Hispanics no longer count in the diversity sweepstakes? Are they all "white adjacent,"[260] or is the media cherry-picking to get clicks and politicize everything they possibly can?

One of MLB's best players is Shohei Ohtani of Japan. He's baseball's best two-way player in one hundred years. Another of baseball's best is Aaron Judge, who blasted the American League home run record this season. Neither of them made the World Series (through no fault of their own), and importantly to the diversity police, neither is white, but they have a lot in common outside baseball.

Ohtani and Judge both come from very strong families. Ohtani's family introduced him to baseball as a kid, and he and his brother took to it immediately. Judge was adopted by a white family who brought him up with morals as strong as his hitting power. Ohtani and Judge come from a culture of family first. Strong families are very important to one's success in life, in whatever field they choose.

Most baseball players from Latin America come from a culture where Catholicism dominates and encourages large, intact families. Such families tend to have present fathers who engage in raising their children. That includes getting out in the yard or nearest park with a bat, ball, and gloves and teaching a kid to hit and catch. You can't play catch with someone who is not there.

Here's a hard, cold fact about modern life in America's predominantly black cities: fathers are absent. According to the Casey Foundation, 66 percent of black kids in America were raised without fathers in 2010. Many of those kids would be of age to play professional baseball now. The fatherless percentage has held steady over the years, standing at about 64 percent in the most recent survey.

The disadvantages of fatherlessness have been well documented. Kids who grow up without fathers are far more likely to struggle with employment; lack education; are more likely to use drugs, commit crimes, and end up in prison. This isn't racial at all. It's a product of not being brought up with strong morals and a strong sense of your own value as a person. Kids in that environment are also far less likely to want to play a sport that lacks the razzle-dazzle hip-hop culture that has saturated professional football and, especially, basketball.

Sports are cultural. It's undeniable. Baseball careers tend to be longer and can pay better over time than basketball and football careers, so it isn't about money. Baseball doesn't even have a salary cap. A kid without a father can easily pick up a basketball and play hoops alone or with friends. He can learn football with a buddy or from a decent high school coach. But a kid without a father just isn't likely to learn the intricacies of using a big leather glove and a big stick to hit a ball on a lazy Sunday afternoon.

Baseball takes more than raw athleticism. It takes the patience and the skill that a father is most likely to help provide. The baseball diamonds in urban America aren't being used to learn the sport—they're filled with needles, not with kids playing catch with their fathers. And they're in cities run by a party that prioritizes criminals over victims and has created urban hellscapes in which no kid should have to grow up.

Rather than blame the Major Leagues, anyone who cares about the present and future of black America should look at ways to strengthen families. That's better for everyone, whether they play any sport or no sport at all.

7. Can I Still Be a Black Guy for Halloween?

As a child growing up in Philadelphia in the 1980s, my usual Halloween costumes mostly consisted of three black guys: Julius Erving ("Dr. J"), Charles Barkley, and Darth Vader. Could I do this today in unhinged cancel-culture America? Could I be Jalen Hurts of the Philadelphia Eagles? Or Adonis Creed, from the Rocky spin-off boxing franchise? Who makes the rules?

The obvious answer for an Irishman with blonde hair is not just no, but Halloween no!

But why?

As a hardcore Philadelphian, my heroes mostly came from sports.

Julius Erving graced the courts for the Philadelphia 76ers during the team's glory years.[261] In the NBA era, before everybody liked Mike, and wore Mike's shoes, and made Mike a billionaire, Dr. J was one of the most elegant and incredible basketball players on the planet. He had few, if any, challengers.

Dr. J seemed to defy gravity when he leaped from the free throw line to slam the ball through the rim. These were the days before twenty-four-hour sports channels and YouTube and finding highlights anytime you want just by going onto social media. My father and I would watch every game live if we could and stay up late for the eleven o'clock news just to see Dr. J's highlight reel. He'd always do something spectacular every game. I'd always watch. Dr. J was one of my first heroes.

A few years later, Charles Barkley started lighting up the NBA. The Round Mound of Rebound wasn't the flying type like Dr. J, but he was a force of nature on the boards and especially in the paint. Like Dr. J, Sir Charles was a hero, and I'd stay up past my bedtime to catch his highlights.

On the football side, I grew up an Eagles fan and could never get enough of wide receiver Harold Carmichael flying down the sidelines and making Cowboys defensive backs look like clowns. For thirteen incredible seasons, Carmichael tore up the NFC East, one amazing highlight after another. Hero. Full stop.

I'd love to go out for Halloween and dress like Dr. J, Sir Charles, Carmichael, or any of several other of my sports heroes, but there's one problem, and it's a big one: they're all black and I'm white.

I never for one second cared that any of my heroes were black. It never occurred to me to care. They're my heroes; that's all that mattered. Anything I did to emulate them was entirely out of respect and honor.

I tried to play like them on the playground, but they had talents I never had. Could I dress like them? Sure, I could buy a jersey with their name and number on it, but that's not really dressing like them. Dr. J, for one, sported the classic Afro during his early days in the league. That was one of the things that made him so cool. He had a suave baller aspect to him, a smile that always lit things up. He seemed otherworldly cool whether he was dunking a basketball or just talking to fans.

If I, as a blonde Irish guy, put on an Afro wig and tried to make my skin look even close to his, what would happen? We all know, don't we?

You and I both know *exactly* what would happen. Despite my meaning the costume as nothing but a heartfelt tribute to one of my all-time idols and heroes, a legend of the game and a gentleman for all the time since he retired, I would go viral for wearing blackface and be canceled immediately. I would be shunned and cast into the outer darkness where there is weeping and gnashing of teeth, and you can only watch Hulu with ads.

I had another hero when I was a kid. He was tall and powerful; in fact, he had such a high rank, he ruled a whole galaxy, far, far, away. He could choke you from across the stars and was the best laser swordsman around. He'd been a pretty good pilot in his day too. He was also jet black.

Could I dress up as Darth Vader for Halloween and stay out of trouble?

Of course, I could. People just like me do it every year. They do it at sci-fi cons and comic book shows and just for fun. Black, white, whatever, it doesn't matter; anyone can be Darth Vader. Because the guy inside the mask started out as white (until Obi-Wan Kenobi left him burnt to a crisp, anyway).

But what about kids dressing up as Black Panther from the Marvel comics and movies? If you listen to the woke cultural scolds out there, not anyone can dress up as Black Panther. If you decide to tread this path anyway, you'd best be careful.

Get a load of this one from *Chatelaine*: "[T]here can be absolutely no Blackface. If you have even the slightest inclination of taking your child's costume to the next level by adding a Chadwick Boseman low afro wig or grabbing some brown body paint to tint your child's hands or face, don't do it. Dressing as Black Panther for Halloween is fine.

Blackface, the act of using make-up or a costume to impersonate a Black person, is not."[262]

The perpetually offended folks at *The Nation* agree: "All uses of blackface, all of them, come from a deeply biased place where other people's races and cultures can be used as a prop in some white fantasy narrative. That's why it's always wrong."[263]

Fatherly is also not on board: white kids would be "appropriating" if they dress up as Black Panther. "A white child dressed as Black Panther might not represent a provocation but does represent blithe appropriation. Ignorance, whether it stems from youth or carelessness, is not an excuse."[264]

What actual ignorance are we talking about here? We live in a time when a movie about a black superhero can cut across all remaining racial lines in an ever more integrated world and make a billion in bank from a whole lot of white people and inspire kids to play with toys of a black superhero and dress up as one too. How is any of this bad?

Who is appropriating what, exactly, when Black Panther's creators, Stan Lee and Jack Kirby, were both white and Jewish? That's right.

The current thinking is, maybe you can do the character in tribute to him and the late actor who portrayed him, but you're not allowed to actually look like him if you weren't born looking like him. Does this make any actual, logical sense?

The accusation that this is "blackface" runs up against the history of *actual blackface*. The blackface we're more familiar with originated in minstrel shows more than a century ago and was negative. It was making fun of people who had no power.

Black Panther has *lots* of power. He's a superhero who rules his own technologically advanced kingdom. He's benevolent. He stops bad guys of all colors. Everybody who knows anything about the character knows this.

Making yourself black to look like Black Panther is emphatically not about making fun of anyone. Lee and Kirby made him nothing but a hero. Being Black Panther is about being powerful and looking cool—and also getting the look right. It really is about honoring the character and Chadwick Boseman. A white kid in a Black Panther costume whose face and hands remain white doesn't look much more like Black Panther than I would if I walked around wearing a 76ers Dr. J jersey and shorts but didn't otherwise make myself look like him.

We've come a long way since the old minstrel shows, which no one living has ever even seen except on old film, to this point where white (and Asian, and Hispanic, and so forth) kids want to dress up as Black Panther because he is so cool. We have a universally loved black superhero. Kids want to emulate him, be him, be cool like him, look like him. Shouldn't that be considered? Shouldn't this even be encouraged?

Does intent matter, or is everything in the hands of the most easily offended and those who stand to profit in some way by being offended?

Let's work on making the phony rules make sense, please.

XI.
November Privilege

*"Someone has to be the villain in the cartoon
world that woke leftists believe is reality."*

1. Joe Biden's Crayola Army

The US military used to be everything that Thomas Jefferson—and Martin Luther King Jr.—thought America should be.

Our military used to be everything George S. Patton—arguably one of America's greatest generals—*demanded* it be.

And what was that? A meritocracy in which people rose according to their talents and initiative, as opposed to having privileged status on account of some other consideration, such as family name or wealth. Or skin color. Or sex.

Patton demanded excellence and initiative. He did not care what color wrapper it came in. It is why his Third Army rolled over the German Wehrmacht in Europe, racking up victory upon victory.

Patton earned his four stars.

The Biden administration is determined to make the US military more like the America it has been working overtime to turn into the antithesis of a meritocracy—one in which what matters most isn't what you've done or how hard you've worked to get it done but whether your color (or sex or sexual preferences) check the necessary boxes.

These policies basically turn the US Marine Corps into a United Colors of Benetton ad.

Biden in the summer of 2023 came out against merit-based promotions that do not take the candidate's race into consideration.[265]

This is absolutely *fascinating*, as Mr. Spock from *Star Trek* might have put it. Weren't Democrats once upon a time the party that opposed checking people off the list on account of their race? The liberal crooner Bruce Hornsby sang a whole song about it, "The Way It Is."

Well, it's of a piece with the Left's parking brake 180 on free speech, which it also claimed to favor once upon a time. But that was a time when leftists objected to their speech being suppressed. Once the Left acquired control over speech—via the Left's control of the federal government, colleges, and major media—it no longer favored free speech.

Well, not for those who questioned leftist speech, anyway.

It's the same story with "choice." The Left says—militantly—that a woman has the absolute right to choose to abort her baby, because it is her body the growing baby happens to be inside of. But if men—or women—want to choose whether to wear a mask, well, so much for their choice.

"The administration strongly opposes...sweeping attempts [by the GOP-controlled House] to eliminate the [Defense Department's] longstanding DEIA efforts and related initiatives to promote a cohesive and inclusive force," said the Biden regime's Office of Management and Budget in a written statement.

This statement is even more fascinating—in that the "efforts" to force-feed diversity, equity, inclusion, and accessibility criteria on the military are not "longstanding." They only came into force after Joe Biden took the oath of office in January 2021.

I'm not sure US Army general William Tecumseh Sherman was worried about DEI when he burned Atlanta to the ground.

"Promote a cohesive and inclusive force"?

How do you promote *cohesion* by separating out people according to how they look? And how is it inclusive to kick *certain* people out—or shunt them aside—on account of how they *look*? Will a white male captain who didn't get his earned promotion to major because he was passed over in favor not of someone more qualified but someone of the politically correct sex feel respect for the person who got promoted because of *their* sex or color?

And how about "people of color," as the Left styles everyone who isn't the one *wrong* color?

The military used to be the place where black Americans especially didn't have to worry that their color would hold them back. The military—once upon a time—did not indulge doctrines that thwarted the promotion of people who had shown they were right for the job—because it wasn't just a *job*.

If a mediocre student is allowed to graduate law school while a better student is denied admittance to law school, the legal profession is subtly degraded. If people in the military are advanced—or held back—according to any other standard than excellence, America's ability to fight and win wars is degraded, and it won't be so subtle when we lose.

The Russians and the Chinese do not consider "diversity, equity, inclusion, and accessibility." They consider intelligence, drive, and capability. Because if there's a war, they want to *win*. They want to beat us. There's no moral victory for your armed forces looking like the Crayola 64 box.

Patton understood this. Because he didn't like to lose.

"DoD's strategic advantage in a complex global security environment is the diverse and dynamic talent pool from which we draw," continued the OMB's statement. It is a statement as counterfactual as "safe and effective," regarding the assertions made about the vaccines that neither prevented anyone from getting COVID or spreading it.

The "talent pool" referenced is no such thing when talent is excluded on the basis of color or sex.

"Wokeness is a cancer that will destroy our military from the inside out if we don't stop it," said Representative Jim Banks, an Indiana Republican who is among those leading the fight in the House to rid the military of diversity considerations.

"What we're trying to do is move to a colorblind, race-neutral worldview, where we're focused on building a national defense and a military that is focused on, you know, blowing things up and killing people, not on social engineering wrapped in a uniform," added Texas Republican Chip Roy.

In other words, the things the military used to focus on in Patton's time—back in the days when it was the most meritocratic institution in America.

2. Yogi Bear's Darkest Secret Has Been Exposed

Yogi Bear, the lovable grizzly who debuted on TV way back in 1958, taught generations about going outside and "touching grass" before that phrase became a way for people to tell others to get off their phones and computers. Yogi and his sidekick, Boo-Boo Bear, got up to all kinds of shenanigans in Jellystone National Park.

One time, Yogi and Boo-Boo tried to escape their park paradise. Why he would want to do that is still a mystery. "Every day it's the same old thing," Yogi told Boo-Boo. "Look at da bear! Look at da bear!" So, Yogi wanted out. "I am gonna get out of this park!" he resolved. He was done with people of whatever background looking at "da bear."

Yet no matter what disguise he put on, which tree he used to launch himself, Yogi Bear couldn't get past wily Ranger Smith.[266] He stayed put in Jellystone until he went off the air in 1988.

All that time, across all those decades, while he was holed up in that famous fictitious park, Yogi was harboring a secret that, if it had been exposed, would surely have gotten the big bear tossed on the cancel heap of history.

Here's the truth, at last, according to the Minnesota Department of Natural Resources: Yogi Bear was a racist who was trying to keep BIPOC people out of the very same park he tried to escape.

The park in which he was constantly stealing picnic baskets…the park in which he wooed his bear girl while neither of them ever wore pants (what was that about?), was a secret den of rampant racism!

It's the bear truth. Minnesota's intrepid race rangers of whatever indeterminate gender and number of spirits are on the case. They announced recently that they're going to crush the bear's blatant bias, which they found in a totally unscientific volunteer study of who goes to Minnesota's parks. Yogi may be smarter than the average bear, but he's not smarter than the average state bureaucrat, who is smart enough to make up statistics they can use to do whatever they totally wanted to do anyway.

Minnesota is one of the whitest states in America, clocking in at more than 80 percent melanin-deprived. That doesn't leave a lot of room for BIPOCS—black, indigenous, or people of color—to make a dent in the state park system's stats.

As Yogi Berra, not the bear, famously said, "Nobody goes there anymore. It's too crowded." And so it seems Minnesota's parks are too crowded with Caucasians. Leave it to the parks to figure out that this is a problem and write up an expensive taxpayer-funded study about it. They launched a task force in 2020 a few months before the riots, which reported in 2021 that it's past time to make diversity, equity, and inclusion more prominent features of parks where people used to go to get away from politics and catch a breath of fresh air.

No more of that. Go to the state's parks, and you'll be taught the birds and bees of racism, equity, and closet Minnesota Marxism.[267]

Here's how the game works:[268] leftist group makes demands of state bureaucrats, who are lavishly-funded leftists themselves, and the bureaucrats gladly do what the leftists demand. In this case, the leftist group is PolicyLink out of California (where else?).[269] They're pushing everyone including parks to get political. The parks are obliging. So are the media, the corporations, and just about every nonprofit in America. They're injecting this racism straight into their veins.

And just like that, hey Boo-Boo, Yogi is a racist who's been standing in the park gates deliberately keeping BIPOCS from touching grass. It's not that Minnesota's overwhelmingly white population is reflected in who visits its parks. It's not that wealthier people with kids just tend to go to parks more often than less wealthy people without kids. And it's not that anyone should be commended for using the parks that are available to them without regard to accidents of birth, which include being born white until Ibram X. Kendi made being born white an original sin.

Someone has to be the villain in the cartoon world that woke leftists believe is reality. In Minnesota, that villain is every white person who goes to the park, and the fictional Yogi Bear has been their secret racist leader this whole time.

3. I Miss My Aunt Jemima and My Uncle Ben...

Mr. Clean—and the Quaker Oats guy—are still *slaving away* on store shelves all over the country, their exploited images used to sell products.

Oh, the humanity! The Society of Friends and the follically challenged should be *pissed*!

How can this be tolerated? Why is no one boycotting the companies that insist on stereotyping people to sell their products?

Perhaps because almost no one considers *characters* to be people— excepting people looking for an excuse to make an issue of it.

Aunt Jemima and Mrs. Butterworth are also characters. Uncle Ben too. They are as "black" as Mr. Clean and the Quaker Oats guy are "white," in that none are real.

In that the *affront* is fake.

Who was actually "offended" by Aunt Jemima, Uncle Ben, or Mrs. Butterworth? Or—for that matter—the now ex-Washington Redskins? Certainly—as regards the latter—not native Americans. Polling of actual Native Americans—as opposed to "activists" claiming to represent them—reveals the *opposite*.

This ought not to be surprising given the Redskin's stylized Indian Brave mascot was a symbol of native American pride that *everyone* could take pride in. There is a massive effort underway by actual Native Americans to bring back the Redskins name and mascot[270]—because it is much harder to take pride in—or feel much of anything about—the Washington Football Team. The Washington "Commanders" is a name as soporifically generic as the Pearl Milling Company, which is what Aunt Jemima is now.

"Pearl Milling Company" sounds like a business address for a drywall company. Not very appetizing. It is as faceless as Ben's Original[271]—which is what Uncle Ben's rice is now that wokeness has effaced his face.

There is something interesting in this whiting-out of people (well, characters) "of color."

Aunt Jemima and Uncle Ben—and Mrs. Butterworth too—have all disappeared, like the famous airbrushed photos of Stalin without the people who'd been disappeared by him.

Stalin had the images of his enemies effaced for political reasons. And the same has happened, for politically correct reasons, to the images of Aunt Jemima, Uncle Ben, and Mrs. Butterworth.

Three black people that were part of everyone's day are now gone. The Left thinks no black people is better than three.

Notwithstanding the fact that these characters were *appealing*—to people of all colors—because of the long association with home-cooked breakfast, as regards Aunt Jemima. Just as Uncle Ben's rice was esteemed for its deliciousness—and its distinctiveness.

Not because people were mocking either character—or people.

People like to feel they know what they're buying and like familiar things. If this is "racist," then Johnny Walker Black Label *must* be the KKK's favorite libation.

Equating the Aunt Jemima or Uncle Ben character with some supposed agenda to demean people of a certain color is as absurd as claiming the Quaker Oats character was designed to mock people of a certain religion. Except no one—*including the Quakers*—is pretending to be upset about the Quaker Oats guy.

For the same reason, no one cares—or rather, no one is pretending to be upset—about Mr. Clean either.

But maybe there *is* something to be "concerned" about. Mr. Clean looks awfully *funny*. Why does he wear a *ring* in his ear? At one time, the wearing of an earring by a man was considered *code* for that man being *gay*. And what's up with his white outfit? Is he going to clean the floors—or put you in a rubber room?

It's all very silly, of course.

Actually, it's all very sinister. Aunt Jemima, Mrs. Butterworth, and Uncle Ben were exactly like Mr. Clean and the Quaker Oats guy in that they were familiar faces people came to associate with products they liked. If there is something sinister in that then there is something sinister about the Burger King and Ronald McDonald.

Rather, what's sinister is the imputation of "racism" where no such thing exists but which is being fomented. The idea seems to be to set us at each other's throats—so as to keep our hands off the throats of our real oppressors, who use color to divide us in order to rule us.

Ironically, Quaker Oats (the company) owns what used to be Aunt Jemima and is now sold under the drywall (whoops, Pearl Milling Company) brand. To salve the wounds caused by a century of people pouring Aunt Jemima syrup over their Aunt Jemima pancakes, the Quaker Oats company "pledged" $5 million to "support the black community." This probably means the money will go to support racist activists such as the ones who organized the Black Lives Matter riots of 2020—and profited from them.

A "civil rights activist" named Ja'Mal Green explained on social media:

> 130 years ago two white men created "Aunt Jemima" syrup. Took a black slave archetype & made her the face of their syrup for profit. Today, that ends. Aunt Jemima is finally being replaced. Those white men made billions appropriating blackness & hopefully rotting in hell.[272]

And so we get drywall paste for breakfast instead.

"It's the start of a new day," says the company's website, where you can read all about how the company "made a commitment to change the name and image of Aunt Jemima, recognizing that they do not reflect our core values."[273] Those "core values" can be found on the company's P.E.A.R.L. page, where you can read all about the company's "commitment to Black women and girls all across America."[274]

No mention of other women and girls of a different color. Because, of course, it's *not* "racist" to exclude them from the P.E.A.R.L pledge—that "black girls can."

Apparently, white (and Asian and Latino) girls *can't*.

How much longer before the Quaker Oats guy is "finally replaced"? And Mr. Clean too? Probably not ever—because no one is pretending to be affronted by these characters that aren't any more real than Aunt Jemima, Uncle Ben, or Mrs. Butterworth.

They're just not as useful—for riling us all up like a pack of dummies.

4. America's Idi Amin: The Last King of Clyburn

He helped Joe Biden win the South Carolina primary in 2020, and now his fiefdom's junta gets to go first in the Democratic nominating process in 2024.[275]

He helped Joe, Joe helped him, and Joe said, "You're welcome."

Historic inflation is making Americans poorer every day. There's chaos on the border and a demoralized, overwhelmed Border Patrol. A deadly fentanyl epidemic is killing a 9/11's worth of Americans every single day. A violent war in Europe could go nuclear. China is threatening to unleash its military on our allies in Asia. North Korea is launching missiles and ramping up its nuclear arsenal. Our woke military is becoming ever more hostile to the beliefs and values of everyday Americans. And, to top it off, we have a feeble president who can often barely complete a sentence and frequently seems not to know where he is while the world around us inches toward catastrophe.

Responsibility for all of this lies at the feet of one man. That man is a divisive, election-denying hyperpartisan who dumped nuclear waste on his own state.[276]

In the 2020 Democratic presidential primary race, Joe Biden was dead in the water. Trump was cruising to reelection against an awful Democrat field. Then COVID happened. The confirmed plagiarist and partisan hack from Delaware was floundering against ridiculously weak opposition despite having spent a lifetime in the Senate and two terms as Obama's vice president. Obama himself sat on the sidelines while his veep suffered in the polls, his notorious quote about Joe "f-ing things up" haunting the campaign.[277]

Into the breach stepped liberalism's military officer Rep. James Clyburn of South Carolina.

Clyburn's endorsement changed the game and catapulted the clownish Biden from the pack to the top, just in time. He essentially foisted the woke, incompetent buffoon Joe Biden on an unsuspecting nation.

And then he insisted that Biden make his vice presidential pick on two criteria: sex and skin color.[278] He forced the foolish Biden into picking a black woman on that basis, as opposed to leadership qualities and actual experience. That's how we got the wildly terrible Kamala Harris.

Clyburn's history of opposing Americans' rights to question Democrats,[279] opposing our right to self-defense, lying about his party's wish to defund police across the country,[280] trashing elections, and undermining America to benefit his political party is no joke.

It's all the rage now to ostracize so-called election deniers, since doing so benefits Democrats and silences their opponents, but Clyburn was an election denier before anyone had coined the term. Way back in 2000, during and after the close presidential contest between George W. Bush and Al Gore, Clyburn went out of his way to undermine the election and then undermine the man who legally won it.

Weeks after the last vote had been cast, as the Bush campaign fought for every vote to count, and the Gore campaign openly battled for selective and biased recounts, Clyburn stepped up and said what Bush wanted was illegal, and he shouldn't be in the race at all.[281] This was *after* the votes had been cast!

Courts disagreed with Clyburn and Gore and insisted that recounts should be fair and based on the law as written before the election, not cynically twisted afterward to benefit the Democrats. Bush won. Gore went off to spread disinformation that the polar ice caps would be gone by 2013[282] and building on earlier false predictions that New York City's west side would be underwater by now.[283] He's a genius like Joe, if you somehow can't smell it.

None of that happened, of course, but Clyburn and the Democrats keep pushing their false climate prophecies to foist disastrous economic and anti-liberty regimes on the American people. Clyburn leads the Democratic pack as their number three in the House, one of the most powerful posts in the country and kingmaker to the president. Clyburn championed the dishonestly named Inflation Reduction Act, which did nothing to reduce inflation and everything to make Americans suffer and put the good life farther out of reach for his own constituents.[284]

Clyburn went on a tear in 2022, when he argued that America was somehow becoming Nazi Germany.[285] The analogy he made—a government allowing no opposition and controlling the media—might have made a little sense, but he was slamming so-called election deniers (remember, he's been one himself for decades when Democrats lose) and ignoring the reality that at the time he said it, the Democrats controlled the White House and Congress and without question dominated the media and were using social media to crush all dissent.

Clyburn himself has fought to silence opposition through the Fairness Doctrine, another dishonestly named bit of government disinformation. He hates the First Amendment and doesn't care who knows it.

"I myself consider myself the most powerful figure in the world," said Idi Amin, the Ugandan dictator and Clyburn clone.

This is the core problem with today's Democrats, including Clyburn. With massive media assists, they present an image of being for the little guy, the farmer that Clyburn often cites in his speeches, the plucky American who's just trying to get by, the black American trying to build a business and community. But then Clyburn does everything he can to make life harder. He leads the march in Congress for higher taxes, for lawless cities, for destroying the First and Second Amendments, for shackling America to international institutions dominated by demagogues and dictators, and ultimately for crushing what's left of the American dream for everyone.

The South Carolina kingmaker who gave us Biden gave us all of that. Your dollars are worth less, you're paying more just to flip the lights on, and your country is weaker with war threatening the world because a gerrymandered lifetime politician[286] who hasn't worked a real job since the 1990s endorsed a hapless hack whose last original thought was sometime before the raid on Entebbe.[287]

5. Meet the Patron Saint of Fentanyl

Far more black people are killed by prescription drugs such as fentanyl than by police brutality. That includes George Floyd.

As it turns out, Floyd wasn't necessarily killed by Derek Chauvin, the ex-Minneapolis police officer who was convicted of killing him back in 2020 and who is now in prison serving hard time for a crime he was merely an accomplice to.

Former Fox TV commentator Tucker Carlson says Chauvin was the victim of a kind of rebooted Soviet-era show trial based on lies—and suppressed truths. Specifically, that Floyd's death was not the result of anything *Chauvin* did to him but rather what *fentanyl* abuse did to him. An autopsy found that Floyd died as a consequence of "decades of drug use, as well as the fatal concentration of fentanyl that was in his system on his final day."

But what *is* fentanyl?

When *prescribed*, it is a legal synthetic opioid drug used for pain relief that is "100 times more potent than morphine and 50 times more potent than heroin," according to the DEA.[288]

The problem is that it's regularly used illegally, by Floyd and millions of others, to get high. That high cost an estimated 67,325 people their lives in 2021,[289] the year after fentanyl caused the death of George Floyd, according to his autopsy report. The number of deaths attributed to fentanyl in 2021 was up *26 percent* from the year prior, when Floyd was just one of the estimated 53,480 people killed by this drug.

Apparently, all those lives—many of them black—do not matter.

At least, they matter a lot less than making a false case against a white police officer in order to increase racial tensions and make a lot of money in the process of ruining a lot of lives, both black and white. All of those businesses and neighborhoods trashed—and burned—by people not-so-peacefully protesting Floyd's death were *used* by the people who purposely misrepresented the cause of Floyd's death in order to profit from it.

Black Lives Matter became a multimillion-dollar shakedown operation, and its leadership cadre became wealthy by fomenting black rage and white guilt over the death of a black man who killed himself.

It's interesting to read the DEA's explanation of the effects of fentanyl abuse:

> Overdose can cause stupor, changes in pupil size, clammy skin, cyanosis, coma, and *respiratory failure* leading to death. The presence of a triad of symptoms

such as coma, pinpoint pupils, and respiratory depression strongly suggests opioid intoxication.[290]

George Floyd fit the bill.

"I can't breathe"—which became a kind of mantra for the Woke Left (both black and white)—wasn't due to Floyd being restrained by Chauvin. It was due to the drugs in Floyd's system, as determined but suppressed in the official autopsy report.

Floyd's arrest for trying to pass a counterfeit twenty-dollar bill increased the stress on his *already strained system*. If a man with heart trouble dies in the course of exertion, we don't generally blame the *exertion* for causing his death. We blame the fact that the man had heart trouble—and probably should not have been exerting himself.

Floyd's arrest caused him stress, no doubt. But that he deserved to be arrested is not in doubt. Chauvin did not select him at random, much less because he was black.

Chauvin arrested Floyd because he committed a crime. But he did not kill Floyd for committing it.

As Tucker Carlson put it, "This was not a killing, it was yet another narcotics OD in a country that records more than 100,000 of them every year. The medical examiner clearly understood that and, in fact, articulated it."

But those findings were suppressed in order to create a narrative of a white cop brutalizing a black victim.

Dr. Andrew Baker, the medical examiner who performed Floyd's autopsy, stands accused of deliberately withholding his findings about the real cause of death because he "feared the public's reaction," according to accusations leveled by Hennepin County Prosecutor Amy Sweasy.[291]

Sweasy alleged in a deposition that Baker told her that "there were no medical findings that showed any injury to the vital structures of

Mr. Floyd's neck. There were no medical indications of asphyxia or strangulation...."[292]

Well, never mind that.

Sweasy also alleged Baker said: "Amy, what happens when the actual evidence doesn't match up with the public narrative that everyone's already decided on?"

So let's *lie* about it and give the public an officially endorsed reason to believe that what they've decided on is righteous and true.

And leave others to pick up the pieces.

Others still—such as the leadership cadre of the Black Lives Matter movement—pick up dollars. They have made millions from the death of George Floyd, who is merely one of many victims of leftism, which isn't interested in black people except insofar as they are useful to advance leftism.

Carlson interviewed our friend Vince Everett Ellison (author of the foreword of this book), who is a black superman.[293] Ellison told him that Floyd is "the perfect black man," as far as the Left is concerned. Floyd's death was useful to the Left.

Never mind that it's all a tragic lie. Never mind that the victims of that lie have had to pay for it.

Including Derek Chauvin, who doesn't himself appear to be a model human being but who is serving a twenty-years-to-life sentence thanks to fentanyl. For his trouble, Chauvin was stabbed and nearly died in federal prison on November 24, 2023—Black Friday.

6. The Era of Pretendians

I think we finally found Elizabeth Warren's secret grandmother.

It turns out Elizabeth Warren told 1/1024th of the truth when she laid claim to being a Native American back in 2020.

Well, maybe it was 1/64th true—according to the results of the DNA test she took to back up those claims.[294]

Warren's cultural appropriation of Native American identity *pales* beside that of Sacheen Littlefeather, though. For decades, Maria Louise Cruz—her real name—claimed to be of White Mountain Apache heritage. She dressed the part in full Land O' Lakes regalia—even though her heritage was Mexican-Canadian, as explained by her sister, Rosalind Cruz.

"It's a fraud. It's disgusting to the heritage of tribal people. And it's just insulting to my parents."

"Sacheen Littlefeather" even had the effrontery to lecture the audience at the 1973 Academy Awards about the maltreatment of American Indians—on behalf of Marlon Brando, who protested the awards that year by not showing up to accept his award for best actor in the timeless masterpiece, *The Godfather*.

"Sacheen Littlefeather's" other sibling, Trudy Orlandi, thinks the motive for playing Indian was profit. She "found it more prestigious to be an American Indian than it was to be Hispanic."

It's hard for me to keep track of how liberals calculate which fake race hustle earns them the most money.

The actress-activist's sisters believe that Deb—which is what they called "Sacheen"—got her pretendian name from the Sacheen Ribbon Company, which "made the thread they used to make clothes as children."

"Sacheen"—who died in October 2022—lived long enough to get an apology from the Academy of Motion Picture Arts and Sciences for the "treatment she received for refusing Brando's Oscar for him."[295]

Another appropriator is Rachel Dolezal, a 100 percent white woman who "identified" as a black one—and became president of the Spokane, Washington, chapter of the NAACP, until she was forced to resign in the wake of revelations that she's even less black than Warren is Cherokee.[296]

These events are all of a piece with Joe Biden's claims, such as the one about his son having died in Iraq and—prior to that—of having been "sort of raised in the Puerto Rican community."

Emphasis on *sort of.*

When Biden entered politics in 1970, people of Puerto Rican background constituted just 0.39 percent of the population in Delaware.[297] It's hard to be "raised" in a "community" of less than 1 percent of anything.

These claims are every bit as insulting as it is to assume the heritage and culture of others for political (and pocket-lining) purposes. But liberals not only feel no shame in doing just that, they seem to have a penchant for doing it. This is how identity politics is played. It tells us something about how liberals really feel about the "people of color" for whom they feign respect.

As the *Guardian* put it with regard to the Dolezal fiasco: [She] "changed her appearance, revised her history and constructed a new family. She adopted a series of African-American 'dads' and presented to the world a black son, who turned out to be her brother."

This amounted to a worse-than-blackface "skit," because it was meant to fool black people into believing she actually was black—just as Warren attempted to fool her supporters about her "Native American" heritage. This goes beyond mockery into something far more contemptuous of the people they tried to fool. It smacks of "stolen valor"—the term for appropriating a military record (and decorations) the individual doesn't have—and didn't earn.

Ever heard of Barry Dunham? He was the forty-fourth president of the United States. How about Robert Francis O'Rourke? Are you smelling what I'm stepping in?

Yet, even when caught in actual blackface—as in the case of the former governor of Virginia, Ralph "Coonman" Northam—liberals invariably give other liberals a pass. Northam wasn't forced to resign when photos of him doing the "mammy" routine surfaced. He was *defended* by his fellow liberals, who cited "an extraordinary effort to connect with black constituents across Virginia, a process that

Northam says broke him down and built him back a better person—more aware of the ugly reality of race in America."[298]

Let that sink in.

The man who dressed like Al Jolson and mocked black people "connect(s)" with black people and is "more aware of the ugly reality of race in America." Such as his mocking of black people, perhaps?

That, by the way, is something his Republican successor, Glenn Youngkin, has never done. Liberals, on the other hand, tried to portray Youngkin as a "racist" by sending fake racists to stage a fake tiki torch-lit rally at one of his campaign stops.[299]

These cigar-store "racists" were almost as real as Elizabeth Warren's claims about her "Native American" heritage—the "evidence" of which her "Fact Squad" appears to have systematically scrubbed from the record in anticipation of a long shot presidential run in 2024.[300]

Warren's "triumphant" tweets, web page assertions of Native American kinship, and YouTube videos have been whited out, too, so to speak.

She subsequently boarded the mea culpa express and did the usual rounds, making apologies to those whose identity she attempted to appropriate. "Senator Warren has reached out to us and apologized to the tribe," said Cherokee Nation spokeswoman Julie Hubbard. "We are encouraged by this dialogue and understanding that being a Cherokee Nation tribal citizen is rooted in centuries of culture and laws, not through DNA tests."[301]

Especially when those tests reveal as much Cherokee DNA as Rachel Dolezal's "African American" heritage.

Warren was eventually forced to concede the self-evident. "I am not a person of color; I am not a citizen of a tribe."

Who'd have guessed?

"We are encouraged," Hubbard went on, "by her action and hope that slurs and mockery of tribal citizens and Indian history and heritage will now come to an end."

Which they won't—until white liberals such as Elizabeth Warren, "Sacheen Littlefeather," Rachel Dolezal, and Joe Biden stop pretending they are what they are not—mocking all of us along the way.

7. For Thanksgiving, the Pilgrims Say, "You're Welcome!"

During the height of the COVID-19 pandemic in 2020, my wife was walking our late French bulldog through a tony neighborhood in northern Virginia. As she walked, she happened upon two women arguing about how racist the Pilgrims likely were—two lily-white, woke members of the pumpkin spice mafia.

These two knew the Pilgrims were absolutely white supremacists, the debate was only a matter of degree.

This is what the DC swamp is all about: a virtue-signaling debate by the whitest women in America, about pilgrims, *in June*.

Let that sink in.

The nation that has done more than any other before its existence to further human rights and civil rights is under sustained attack. Its plight is existential. If those who are assaulting it get their way, it's the death penalty for that nation and major, permanent problems for anyone who has the courage to support it.

Simply put: America is under attack from the Woke Left. Its foundation, including its earliest history, is being torn apart, misrepresented, and lied about for the purpose of destroying the country itself.

Or do you not hear the cultural Marxists when they say they seek to "dismantle the systems" that they claim "sustain and perpetuate systemic racism"? The systems they're referring to are the systems by which America operates, on which it is founded, and how it exists, and dismantling them means nothing less than taking America apart. That is the entire point of the woke project. They have seized control of the Democratic Party, academia, and our culture to carry their diabolical plans out.

The woke hordes have to discredit America to accomplish their goals, and since America is famously a nation not built on tribe or geography but on ideas, those ideas must be discredited.[302] That's why our history is under attack, from the pseudo historical 1619 Project to the leftist attack on the Alamo all the way back to the very first Thanksgiving.

That moment has been twisted from a day of cooperation between bedraggled Europeans and Native Americans to a day of rage and oppression. It's wokeism run wild, attacking dead Pilgrims who are not here to defend themselves.

That's a hallmark of the Left's strategy. They worship the likes of dead white men such as Karl Marx, whose terrible ideas have led to the enslavement and deaths of millions, while denigrating the achievements of other dead white men and women who mostly just sought and found a better life free from kings and tyrants.

Such were the Pilgrims of the first Thanksgiving. They fled England because they were persecuted for their religious beliefs. England in the seventeenth century was a monarchy with a state-approved church that the king controlled. If you didn't agree with that church, you ran afoul of the king, and you could be imprisoned or even executed. The very freedoms we take for granted—freedom of religion, freedom of speech—did not exist as legally recognized rights yet. Brave individuals were starting the fight for those rights. Their success was not guaranteed. Whole armies stood in their way.

The Pilgrims sailed from Southampton, England, in 1620,[303] braving the harrowing Atlantic journey, leaving their lives behind, risking everything to carve out lives in a world unknown to them—to be free. Leftists today would unfairly and dishonestly call them oppressors because they were white. And yet, the Pilgrims were among the oppressed themselves.

Were they perfect by the ever-changing standards of the twenty-first century? No, but who is? No one is woke enough to satisfy the most radical. A certain Frenchman who led a revolution would find out how impossible it is to be radical enough a couple of centuries later.

But in America, the Pilgrims carved out lives in a wild, dangerous land for the sake of freedom. Not just their own but for their progeny and for those who followed them. Roger Williams, founder of Providence, Rhode Island, established one of the first legal systems that recognized religious freedom.[304] He had to be in America to do that, as it was impossible and could be fatal just about anywhere in Europe. And in Asia, for that matter, where the Buddhist dictatorship of feudal Japan suppressed Christianity brutally for centuries. Most Americans aren't even aware of Japan's mass-scale crucifixion of Christians or of the rebellions fought for religious freedom[305]—and savagely suppressed by the shoguns. The age of the Pilgrims was an age of souls seeking the light of free faith.

In America, in a city on a hill, a whole new thing was growing. It was just a tiny spark in a dark world at the time. But it grew. That spark became a little flame, and by the 1760s, it was a raging bonfire. When America rebelled against the tyrants in faraway London, her founders wrote this radical concept of religious and intellectual liberty into the new nation's founding documents. This was one of the most courageous acts in human history, and it has freed more people of all backgrounds all over the world ever since.

The people who would destroy America now use this very freedom to undermine her. Attacks on "white privilege" are a cruel lie that only promises to eradicate freedom and empower a very few while enslaving or eliminating everyone else.

As for the Pilgrims the Left despises, they would just have one thing to say on Thanksgiving to Americans enjoying football, freedom, turkey, and even the right to trash their country now: "You're welcome!"

They set the world on a path toward freedom. The question now is, can we keep it?

XII.
December Privilege

"Cancel culture—the threat of destroying someone's life for stepping out of line with the Far Left in any way, at any time—creates a climate of fear the Left cannot win without.... What they cannot win at the ballot box, and what they cannot win through lawfare and malicious prosecutions in court, they seek to win through the raw force of intimidation and silencing of anyone who stands in their way."

1. The Covidians Found Another Excuse to Muzzle You: Equity

Before COVID-19, only three kinds of people wore masks outside of a surgical suite: stick-up men, Klansmen, and mumbling schizophrenics pushing grocery carts around.

It's why wearing masks outside of a surgical suite—inside a place of business—was illegal in many places as recently 2020, such as in Virginia.[306]

People are recovering their senses about "masks" as COVID hysteria recedes—even though the elites haven't forgotten. In fact, they recently met at the G20 summit to push worldwide vaccine passports in the form of digital "health certificates."

Unsurprisingly, some people are saying that if you don't wear a mask, you're a racist. Not just any people either. It's the *New England Journal of Medicine*, which once upon a time concerned itself with, well, *medicine*.

Times change.

Now the *Journal* concerns itself with being medically woke. In particular, a November 2022 "study" was more chock full of misinformation than an Anthony Fauci press conference.[307] It urged the return of mass masking for the sake of "equity" and to "mitigate the effects" of "structural racism in schools."

That is how "masks work," according to the *Journal*.

Remember, this is from what was once one of the most respected American medical journals. One that has since become *very* political.

Since when did medical doctors concern themselves with "mitigating the effects of structural racism"? Isn't that the bailiwick of "doctors" such as Dr. Jill Biden, whose doctorate has nothing to do with medicine?

Of course, masks do "work"—just not in the sense most people think of when they are told they must wear them. Read the box they come in, for openers. It says right there in plain English that they do not protect against respiratory viral particles, which are so small they easily pass through (and around) the flimsy, porous, throw-away masks that kids in schools were forced to wear.

It's telling that while mask mandates abounded during the pandemic, there were never any standards defining which masks made the cut. So long as a person had something over his face—even a dirty old bandana—it permitted entry to any place where "masks" were mandated.

Mask wearing was never about "stopping the spread." It was about obedience.

But people grew tired of obeying—just because they were told they had to. Because they knew that granny wasn't dying because they weren't wearing it. Wearing masks only "stopped the spread" of sanity.

So now, you have to be race-guilted into wearing them.

If you object, you support "structural racism."

The *Journal's* basis for this claim is that "people of color" are more likely to get COVID more severely. "Black, Latinx, and Indigenous children and adolescents are more likely to have had severe Covid-19."

Which is true, in that these groups are more likely to have comorbidities, especially obesity,[308] which is strongly correlated with sickness generally. But mask-wearing doesn't cure obesity. Nor does it make an obese person, white, black, or any other race, any less likely to get COVID. But the *Journal* insists it does, by omitting these several key variables from its "study."

As the *New York Post* notes in its dissection of the *Journal's* conclusions:

> The study centers on two Massachusetts school districts that didn't remove their mask mandates as soon as the state allowed, in March 2022, but kept them until June. A few months later, they saw slightly lower COVID rates than other districts.[309]

Evidence that masks "work," right?

Wrong.

The *Journal* omits the fact that "COVID rates in all the schools" in Massachusetts—not just the two districts' schools—"were higher before anyone took off their masks." Also, contacts of kids who tested positive were exempted from further testing while unmasked contacts continued to be tested. In other words, the "researchers" found what they weren't looking for[310]—and probably on purpose to reach the conclusion they wanted.

Nor did the *Journal* study adjust its findings to consider critically relevant factors such as comorbidities that correlate closely with sickness and which aren't treatable by wearing a cheap, Chinese-made, throw-away mask.

But now, the *Journal* says, those who don't want to wear them are "structural racists," which sounds like a really bad name for a really bad Klan band.

But the worst consequence is that woke virtue signaling is discrediting medicine and formerly respectable medical publications that would never have published misinformation such as this.

The damage is immense and possibly irreparable. People have rightly come to distrust institutional medicine, as manifested in the person of the discredited Anthony Fauci, the *New England Journal of Medicine*, and many more.

It's not merely that they are quacks and purveyors of quackery. They are quacks with the power to "mandate" adherence to their woke (and wrong) prescriptions.

Unsurprisingly, the equally discredited organs of the *Lügenpresse*—German for "the lying press"—are touting the study in order to tout a return to mandatory masking, which they know works very well—at keeping people in line. The *New York Times* reported, as if it were true, that "masking mandates were linked with significantly reduced numbers of COVID cases in schools."[311]

Except they weren't.

And just saying they were doesn't make it true. Just as pointing it out—and refusing to "mask up"—does not make one a "racist" either. "Structurally" or otherwise.

2. Long Live the King of White Male Christmas Patriarchy

Have you noticed the death of the great Christmas movie? Jon Favreau's *Elf* is probably the last major Christmas movie made in Hollywood to spread joy and cheer.[312] Will Farrell's "Buddy" character captured the wild-eyed wonder, along with some of the lighthearted absurdity, of the holiday season in a film that makes us laugh and cry. That was in 2003. Has anything since reached critical mass? Has anything else been put into the Christmas rotation? Fan favorite *Love, Actually* came out in the same year.

Today? We get Seth Rogen cynically trashing Christmas and then calling anyone who criticizes him a racist.[313] If you're getting the sense that Hollywood hates Christmas and anyone who celebrates it, you may be onto something. It wasn't always this way. Not too long ago, from Danny Kaye to Kevin McCallister, before *Elf*, the Christmas movie was a major part of Hollywood's annual offerings.

Chevy Chase helmed 1989's *National Lampoon's Christmas Vacation*, a film Hollywood would *never* make today. Like most Christmas films, *Christmas Vacation* had a stellar cast that included Beverly D'Angelo, Juliette Lewis, Johnny Galecki, Julia Louis-Dreyfus, Diane Ladd, Brian Doyle-Murray, Doris Roberts, Randy Quaid...so many huge talents. But what do they all have in common?

They're all white, suburban, heteronormative, middle-class people outside of Chicago.

No one cared at the time that *Christmas Vacation* ruled the box office. Everyone across the country saw it and loved the universal themes of comedy and story. Well, regular people loved it. It has an

86 percent positive rating on Rotten Tomatoes[314] but just 67 percent from critics. The media disconnect is real.

Now Hollywood absolutely forbids having a cast that isn't shoe-horned to "look like America," even though the country is still about 76 percent white. If a film doesn't bow to racial quotas,[315] it won't get any love come awards season, no matter how great the performances are and no matter how great the story is. None of that matters to Hollywood as much as whether diversity and equity are clearly and visibly on display.

There's nothing wrong with having a diverse cast when the story calls for it. Many films and stories do need a mix of people from various backgrounds, such as the Jon Favreau-helmed *Mandalorian* series on the very woke Disney+.[316] But it's not forced (see what I did there?); it's natural. So it works.

Christmas Vacation shows us something Hollywood won't show in a major film now: an intact family. Granted, the Griswolds are chaotic. But they're together. Clark works hard as the family patriarch and protector. Ellen is his long-suffering wife, who stands by him no matter how many times he launches the car into a snowbank, sets something on fire, or falls off the roof. The two kids tend to mock their father, but they also love him. And the kids aren't obviously smarter than their parents. They have their flaws too.

Chase's Clark is also an unquestionably straight man who reacts to beautiful women, including his wife. In the original *National Lampoon's Vacation*, he's gobsmacked by the stunning Christie Brinkley. Hey, who wasn't? In *Christmas Vacation*, it's the lovely young woman in red, Mary (Nicolette Scorsese), at the shopping mall who catches his eye.[317] Men and women are wired to notice each other. That's science.[318] *Trust the science.*

Clark is a goofball in a Chicago Bears hat, but he's good-hearted. He provides the family with a very nice home and all the latest stuff they want. He'll do anything to get his family together in the car (or plane) to take them on adventures together. He brings a special lubricant home from work to make the sled rocket down the hill. He'll show off and suffer visits from the extended family to make Christmas—not "the holidays" but *Christmas*—special. What's his plan for the Christmas bonus? To buy himself a flashy car? No, he wants to buy a swimming pool for the kids. The bonus sets up one of the most memorable strings of insults in cinematic history[319] and then a latter-day Christmas miracle.

Despite the mockery from pretty much everyone around him, and despite his own tendency to bumble his way into disaster, Clark is never cynical or riddled with middle-aged angst. He's a happy doofus who's just trying to be a good, if often dangerous (though never outright villainous, even when wielding a chainsaw), dad. But he's also a white, male patriarch.

The Griswolds make a plausible family too. Not because they're all white, but because they don't seem forced together to make a skin color-counter happy. Ellen is a beautiful blonde and so is Griswold's daughter, Audrey. Clark is tall, dark, and clumsy, and son Russ looks like he's cut from the same cloth. The Griswolds work as a unit despite the fact that Clark's schemes don't.

"I dedicate this house to the Griswold family Christmas," Clark proudly says as his family gives him a hilarious drumroll. Then, when he ostentatiously plugs in the power, nothing happens. When Grandma mocks him, it's cynical teenage daughter Audrey who defends her father the most. Because they're a family, and that means something.

What would Hollywood do with Clark nowadays? He wouldn't stammer, "It's a bit nipply out!" to Mary because he and writer John Hughes would be hauled off for Maoist #MeToo struggle sessions. College kids would call him a creep, storm out, and demand that the film never be allowed to be seen on campus again. Antifa would dig up the late Hughes so they could knock him over. CNN would have Jeffrey Toobin on set[320] while one of its so-called news anchors inveighed against the film's "tone" and found a way to blame Trump.

Hollywood doesn't make happy, cheerful Christmas movies anymore because it sees nothing to celebrate—not the holiday, not the culture, and certainly not the family. It makes cynical, bitter films that mock faith and family—see Seth Rogen's dud, for instance.

Clark Griswold was the king of the white male Christmas movie patriarchy in the tradition of *Elf*, *Miracle on 34th Street*, and *It's a Wonderful Life*. But we'll never see his like again. Enjoy *Christmas Vacation* while you can—because you can bet it's going down the memory hole soon.

3. Elon Musk: African American of the Year

Remember when Elon Musk was the darling of the Left for his stylish electric cars and his devil-may-care attitude? It was in 2021, but in Joe Biden's dystopian America, it seems like an eternity has passed.

If you happen to have been on X (formerly Twitter) lately, you've seen startling news: prominent attorneys are investigating the platform's owner and CEO over his US citizenship application from years ago after he emigrated from South Africa. Tweets about it were hard to miss, as is the fact that such tweets all used the same wording to describe the so-called investigation. Here are a few:

> BREAKING: Prominent attorneys are investigating whether Elon Musk lied on his application for U.S. citizenship. If it shows that he lied anywhere on the application, its [sic] likely he could be stripped of his of U.S. citizenship and deported.
> —Erica Marsh (@ericareport) December 13, 2022

> Breaking: Atorneys [sic] are investigating whether Elon Musk lied on his application for U.S. citizenship.

If it shows that he lied anywhere on the application, its [sic] likely he could be stripped of his of U.S. citizenship and deported back to Africa.

—Ted Hartung (@tednsocal) December 14, 2022

Breaking: Atorneys are investigating whether Elon Musk lied on his application for U.S. citizenship. If it shows that he lied anywhere on the application, its likely he could be stripped of his of U.S. citizenship and deported back to Africa.

—I Smoked The J6 Committee's Criminal Referrals (@BlackKnight10k) December 13, 2022

That isn't an error. The last two are the same post by two different people. It's common on X for leftists and media hacks to copy and paste identical posts, even without spellcheck.

Note, too, that the identities of the "prominent attorneys" are never mentioned. The posts insinuate but never define any wrongdoing. Oh, and one of the aforementioned tweets hails from a former Biden campaign employee. If it all feels a bit oily and from the shadows, that's because it is.

The left-wing dumpster divers are on the move.

Either Elon Musk still hasn't quite succeeded in killing off Twitter's rampant spambot problem, or someone is sending out talking points[321] with marching orders to wage war against him.[322] Why would that be? Why would actress Alyssa Milano—who tweeted praise for Musk as recently as a couple of years ago[323]—give up her Tesla for a car that's the product of a company founded by Nazis?[324]

Elon Musk is under attack now by the same people who used to fawn over him and promote his cars because he is no longer their man. Musk has declared his independence, and in so doing has brought down the wrath of the media, the Left, and before long, the Democratic Party and the White House.

Even my old friend Matt Drudge,[325] or whoever is sitting behind the terminal now,[326] is after Musk.

Musk accomplished even more than what Senator Kyrsten Sinema of Arizona did when she distanced herself from the increasingly deranged Democratic Party.[327] Musk has been doing that incrementally over the past couple of years. He moved Tesla to Texas from California, explicitly blaming the Democrats' hostility to business on his way out. But he's one of many CEOs to have moved from blue to red states over the past several years. In 2022, he went further and declared that at this point, he's voting Republican and supporting Florida governor Ron DeSantis for president in 2024.[328] None of those are unforgivable sins, though. CEOs can move from blue states to red states and even support a Republican from time to time. As long as they say woke things their lawyers and human resources departments write for them, they will stay out of the Left's crosshairs.

Musk, however, bought Twitter. This, more than anything before, has made him an object of hate on the Left. In buying the social media giant, Musk poses a threat to those such as Meidas Touch,[329] who use the platform to engage in cancel campaigns against anyone it decides to attack.

Cancel culture—the threat of destroying someone's life for stepping out of line with the Far Left in any way, at any time—creates a climate of fear the Left cannot win without. A non-leftist buying Twitter—it didn't have to be Musk, but few can raise the billions needed to complete the sale—poses an existential threat to how the Left in America and around the world operates. What they cannot win at the ballot box, and what they cannot win through lawfare and malicious prosecutions in court, they seek to win through the raw force of intimidation and silencing of anyone who stands in their way. Before Musk, Twitter was silencing anyone who objected to the trans pronoun issue and a host of other deeply divisive discussions.

But Musk went even further than just buying one of the Left's shiniest toys. He has opened up the vaults to show what was really going on inside the company when it morphed from a software platform to a publisher with an extreme leftist and activist point of view.

The Twitter Files, published by Bari Weiss, Matt Taibbi, and Michael Shellenberger—also once darlings of the Left but now targets of leftist ire for having the gall to think for themselves—prove what millions suspected: Twitter was a hive of left-wing activism and deliberately changed its internal processes and policies to justify censorship of the Hunter Biden laptop revelations in the crucial weeks leading up to the 2020 elections. The files on that laptop show how the younger Biden traded his father's influential positions in government for foreign cash and that Joe Biden profited and was fully aware of what his son was doing. It's all there.

But Twitter (and Facebook) blocked the story and suspended the *New York Post*'s account for reporting it. These platforms are where Americans tend to get their news. The censorship undoubtedly had consequences, as it was designed to do. Why would Twitter's activists have blocked the story if they didn't expect that to affect the world outside their lavish San Francisco headquarters?

Americans across the political spectrum should be alarmed at the prospect that a sitting president may be compromised by undisclosed foreign deals about which the evidence in his son's possession says he has lied to us.

But for disclosing Twitter's machinations in this and in deplatforming former President Trump, Musk isn't being universally applauded or thanked. He's being attacked relentlessly even on the platform he owns. And that's by people who know the truth but despise it. Most of the media outside of Fox News, Newsmax TV, and other conservative outlets didn't bother to report on the Twitter Files.[330] It's fair to say that more than a year after those revelations appeared, most Americans still don't know it's a serious story. That's one way censorship works. The establishment media might not block a story entirely, but declining to cover it signals that isn't worth the audience's time.

Musk wasn't born an American, but he's proven that he lives by American principles more strongly than millions of people who were born here do. He believes so strongly in freedom of speech that he leveraged himself to buy Twitter and restore the bedrock rights that had been so badly damaged on the platform. He believes so strongly in the rule of law that he's made himself subject to Twitter's new fact-check system and has prioritized getting predators who used Twitter to exploit children off the platform permanently. He has also gone after the bots that swarm and distort the public conversation.

For all these things he's being attacked, but the immigrant who dreams of restoring America's space dominance and occupying Mars deserves to be feted with a title. *Time* magazine chooses its "Person of the Year" based on a number of factors, and Musk was one of the nominees but didn't get the nod this time. He's actually something better and more profound.

He emigrated legally from Africa. He built businesses and created thousands of jobs. He has restored free speech, and with that, the hope of a free tomorrow.

Elon Musk is the African American of the year.

4. It's the Magical Time of Year, When White Liberals Celebrate Kwanzaa

Two questions: How many black people do you know who celebrate Kwanzaa? I'll wait. Next question: Who's buying the Kwanzaa decorations at Lowe's, Party City,[331] Target,[332] or any of the other panderers?

Let's be honest: Kwanzaa is a jolly batch of virtue signaling by corporate America and the nearest lily-white humanities department deployed to alleviate liberal guilt.

If liberals in Hollywood still had a sense of humor, they would hire Jason Alexander to do a Festivus-esque spoof of Kwanzaa—the

"African American" alternative to Christmas invented by '60s-radical and convicted felon Ronald McKinley Everett, who changed his name to the more "African" sounding Maulana Karenga back in the 1960s.

Festivus is as fictitious as Kwanzaa,[333] which is about as African as Jason Alexander. Or Everett-Karenga, for that matter.

The latter was born in Parsonsburg, Maryland—not Africa.

Similarly, Kwanzaa was born in the mind of Everett-Karenga. The only thing African about it is the corruption of a Swahili phrase, "matunda y kwanza," which translates as "first fruits of the harvest."

Everett-Karenga even got the *spelling* wrong.

But it's the meaning that Everett-Karenga warped. From an innocuous and apolitical phrase, he created a celebration, not of "first fruits" but of communism. And of division based on race, of course. Christmas, for whites, is a celebration of "white supremacy" (as characterized by Everett-Karenga) and never mind that Jesus was Middle Eastern and preached salvation for all mankind.

Kwanzaa, for blacks, is a repudiation of Christmas.

The left-wing *Guardian* of London made the former explicit in a 2020 story: Kwanzaa is an "opportunity [for black people] to celebrate themselves and their history rather than indulge in the customary traditions of a *white Christmas*."[334] (Italics added.)

NPR blithely styled Kwanzaa as "a mainstream holiday like Christmas and Hanukkah" that "celebrate(s) African-American culture."[335]

The *Los Angeles Times* asserted the invented (and misspelled) holiday is a way to "honor African heritage and bring Black families and communities together."[336]

Because, of course, the birth of Jesus Christ *never* did that.

Instead, Kwanzaa encourages a "celebration" of ideas such as "cooperative economics." An idea straight out of the *Communist Manifesto*, which was written by a white man from Europe who plagiarized the ideas of another white man (Plato, also from Europe) re-sold to black Americans as something African by a man who wasn't born there.

And there is nothing "cooperative" about communism.

The ideas propagated by Marx-channeling-Plato (who first described the ideal communist state in his *Republic*) and rebranded as African by Everett-Karenga in the '60s are imposed by force when people decline to "cooperate." Liberals—leftists—always shy away from discussing the violence that lies at the core of their ideas—that is the dark heart of communism, without which it cannot impose its ideas. Because absent force, most people want nothing to do with communism. Because it is a terrible idea.

One that has led to mass murder and mass enslavement of whole populations.

You'd think a black American such as Everett-Karenga would be opposed to slavery, especially of Africans, who have suffered horribly under the yoke of "cooperative economics."[337] See, for example, the reigns of Robert Mugabe of Zimbabwe, of Sani Abacha of Nigeria, and—perhaps most infamously—Idi Amin of Uganda.

But then, Everett-Karenga does have something in common with these African tyrants—in that they all practiced violence, including torture.

In 1971, Everett-Karenga was convicted for doing just that to two women—Deborah Jones and Gail Davis[338]—who had been part of his United Slaves group of left-wing radicals.[339] According to a May 1971 story in the *Los Angeles Times* about Everett-Karenga's trial and subsequent conviction, Jones "testified that a hot soldering iron was placed in Miss Davis' mouth and placed against Miss Davis' face and that one of her own big toes was tightened in a vise. Karenga, head of US, also put detergent and running hoses in their mouths."

The article goes on to state that "the victims said they were hit on the heads with toasters."

Everett-Karenga also reportedly told the women, "Vietnamese torture is nothing compared to what I know."

He meant, of course, the North Vietnamese Communists, who also practiced "cooperative economics."

Everett-Karenga was eventually convicted of felony assault and false imprisonment and sentenced to prison for his crimes. He was paroled in 1975, after which he became a tenured professor of—what else?—Africana Studies (the new term for what was formerly Black Studies)[340] at California State University in Long Beach, California.

Today's *Los Angeles Times* does not mention the history or background of Kwanzaa's founder when covering the fake holiday.

FrontPage writer Paul Mulshine wrote about this memory-holing of Everett-Karenga's background, which he says has "disappeared into an Orwellian time warp"—just like the picture of the disgraced Inner Party members attending a conference that proved the party was lying about them, which Winston Smith (in Orwell's novel about "cooperative economics," *1984*) quickly throws into the fire.

Mulshine wrote that Kwanzaa has "nothing to do with Africa and everything to do with California in the '60s," by which he means the radical leftist politics of the '60s.

Sixties radicalism has morphed into the woke politics of the '20s—largely embraced by white liberals, such as the ones writing hagiographies about Kwanzaa's origins and whitewashing the ugly history of its felonious inventor. I wonder if any of these big box stores know the garbage they are pushing in their stores.[341]

For all of that, not many black Americans seem much interested in Kwanzaa.

A recent survey conducted by the National Retail Federation notes that only 1.6 percent of the entire American public actually celebrates Kwanzaa. That puts it on par with Festivus, the fictitious holiday evangelized by George, the fictitious character portrayed by Jason Alexander in the hit sitcom *Seinfeld*.

Of course, one big difference is that George wasn't a convicted felon—and Festivus was an original invention—unlike the retreaded fraud that is Kwanzaa.

5. A Peer Contagion to Erase America : An Epilogue

"Wokeness is a contagion."

I described it as a mind virus in my number-one bestselling book, *The Woking Dead*, long before Elon Musk did. I think Musk likely read it. He must have, because fighting wokeness is among one of the many reasons he decided to leverage his empire to buy Twitter.

In *The Woking Dead*, I argued that in order for cultural Marxists to overthrow the West, they could not do it on the backs of blue-collar workers. They will never unite the working class to overthrow the government. There will be no peasant revolt like so many communist dumps of the twentieth century. And the plumbers, longshoremen, lumberjacks, and coal miners of America have no love for radical left-wing politics.

And so around the time of World War I, the cultural Marxists began infecting our public schools, teacher unions, academia, early radio, Broadway, silent pictures, newspapers, and, of course, the Democratic Party of Woodrow Wilson and Margaret Sanger. Fast forward one hundred years, the peer contagion has spread due to the long march through the institutions, and the erasing of America's past, present, and future has only intensified.

African American of the year Elon Musk gets all of this, and he bought then leftist woke Twitter (now called X) to fight back. And that is why the Biden administration is going after Musk with questionable (at best) investigations.

There's the Department of Justice investigation of Musk's SpaceX for—I'm not making this up—not hiring enough asylum-seekers.

They're not citizens of the United States. Their asylum claims have not been vetted, because the Biden administration chooses not to vet them properly. Their citizenship and even identities have not been vetted, again because the Biden administration doesn't want to. If they're terrorists bent on killing Americans, Biden and his cronies just shrug. They don't care. Just look at the Woke Left's support for defunding police. Has Soros or any other woke leader shed a tear for the victims piling up in every woke city in the country?

The Biden-Garland Justice Department announced that it would investigate Musk's rocket company anyway.[342] "Our investigation found that SpaceX failed to fairly consider or hire asylees and refugees because of their citizenship status and imposed what amounted to a ban on their hire regardless of their qualification, in violation of federal law," Kristen Clarke, assistant attorney general of the DOJ's Civil Rights Division, said in a statement.

According to Musk, SpaceX was told repeatedly by the federal government that it couldn't even hire verified Canadian citizens because the company's technology is sensitive to US national security. The Department of Justice itself doesn't hire asylum seekers. But it's demanding Musk violate government guidance anyway.

This isn't incompetence on the Biden DOJ's part. It's how wokeness works. The law doesn't matter, the process is the punishment. Musk and his company will be vilified as racist xenophobes and dragged through a hostile media, forced to spend millions on lawyers to defend themselves. The Democrat online woke hivemind will support this to the hilt, because they're mean and that's wokeness.

In fact, Musk recognized that wokeness isn't the nice, fair philosophy it claims to be. It never was. That's a disguise, a skin suit like the one the aliens wore in the first *Men in Black* film.[343] Underneath that skin is a toxic alien viciousness.

Musk said as much: "Wokeness gives people a shield to be mean and cruel, armored in false virtue."

Wokeness is the ultimate in self-righteousness, a kind of Marxist inquisition, without even the belief in a God that instructs in right and wrong and puts limits on the inquisitors.

In Mao's China, wokeness brought innocent people down, humiliated them. Millions were murdered or starved to death. In Cambodia, the woke Khmer Rouge destroyed families, eradicated knowledge, and killed a quarter of their own countrymen. Today's wokeness is philosophically akin to these earlier genocidal movements and is no less insidious than they were.

This same woke self-righteousness is underneath the Biden administration's prioritization of illegal aliens of all stripes over American citizens. This creates negative pressure that keeps wages low and creates competition for homes and apartments that makes them more expensive, because the woke puppet masters atop the Biden administration have deemed America irredeemably racist and evil. Anything they can do to weaken it is justified in their minds. Any way they can hurt Americans is the moral and right thing to do.

Again, see their reaction to the blood that flowed from their decision to defund police. Americans died. They haven't even bothered to lie about it.

Leaving the border wide open, allowing violent drug cartels to take operational control of the frontier between the United States and Mexico, is morally right in their view because it prioritizes brown non-Americans above any and all Americans. The endgame for this is, of course, votes—especially in Arizona and Texas, to turn them blue and give the woke total power forever. But between now and that goal, there's the goal to weaken Americans' faith in work, an honest day's wage, and the American dream of home ownership. If you can't afford it, you won't buy it—whether it's a house, or a car, or even that nice dinner out. If you lose faith in the American dream, if you believe you can't get ahead no matter what you do, if you think the land of the free is just a land of unending oppression and misery, eventually you lose faith in the free market and in America itself.

And this is the goal of the woke—to spread their toxic peer contagion beyond academia and media to every mind in the country. Once the virus takes hold, it can turn an average American bitter and vengeful, no longer a believer in the great and noble experiment in self-government that has powered our republic for generations and centuries.

In zombie films and movies, the contagion is spread with a bite. Once a victim gets chomped, they begin to turn, and before long, they're slogging with the hordes looking for more victims' brains to consume.

So it is with the woke contagion. But it's more insidious. You can see a zombie coming at you, you can defend yourself against the fatal bite. But wokeness spreads through the air, in books, on the network news, in nearly every prime-time drama, in classrooms from kindergarten through doctoral programs, and in corporate "diversity, equity, and inclusion" (DEI) programs that teach everyone to judge and rank everyone else according to their intersectionality points and race. The next woke zombie you encounter may be your boss or co-worker, or your child who the zombified public education system has taken over.

The good news is, there are more and more leaders out there— Elon Musk, Joe Rogan, Bill Maher, Jerry Seinfeld, Donald Trump, Dave Chappelle, Vivek Ramaswamy, and me—who get it.

And we're fighting back. Merry Christmas.

ENDNOTES

1   Michael Jackson, "Black or White," YouTube, October 2, 2009, https://www.youtube.com/watch?v=F2AitTPI5U0.
2   Nicola Dall'Asen, "Lizzo's *Vogue* Cover Helps Validate Including Fat Women in Fashion," *Allure*, September 25, 2020, https://www.allure.com/story/lizzo-vogue-cover.
3   American Medical Association, "AMA Adopts New Policy Clarifying Role of BMI as a Measure in Medicine," June 14, 2023, https://www.ama-assn.org/press-center/press-releases/ama-adopts-new-policy-clarifying-role-bmi-measure-medicine.
4   Tori L. Cowger et al., "Lifting Universal Masking in Schools—Covid-19 Incidence among Students and Staff," *New England Journal of Medicine*, November 24, 2022, https://www.nejm.org/doi/full/10.1056/NEJMoa2211029?query=featured_home.
5   Peter Kasperowicz, "Racism Raises Alzheimer's Risk for Non-White Americans, HHS Claims in New Report," Fox News, December 20, 2022, https://www.foxnews.com/politics/racism-raises-alzheimers-risk-non-white-americans-hhs-claims-in-new-report?intcmp=tw_fnc.
6   "Cultural Responsiveness," The Institute for Child Welfare Innovation, https://forchildwelfare.org/resources/cultural-competence/.
7   Martin J. Schreiber, "Don't Let Alzheimer's Rob You of Holiday Joy," Fox News, December 18, 2022, https://www.foxnews.com/opinion/dont-let-alzheimers-rob-you-holiday-joy.
8   Zachary Rogers, "Not Wearing a Mask Is a 'Manifestation' of Racism, Illinois Professor Says," CBS Iowa, September 2, 2022, https://cbs2iowa.com/news/nation-world/not-wearing-a-mask-is-a-manifestation-of-racism-illinois-professor-says-ableism-jahred-adelman-young-america-foundation-yaf-campus-bias-covid-coronavirus-maskless-university-niu-northern-physics.

9   A. J. Rice, "Un-Scientific Un-American," BizPac Review, January 19, 2023, https://www.bizpacreview. com/2023/01/19/un-scientific-un-american-1325902/.

10 Tracie Canada, "Damar Hamlin's Collapse Highlights the Violence Black Men Experience in Football," *Scientific American*, January 6, 2023, https://www.scientificamerican.com/article/damar-hamlins-collapse-highlights-the-violence-black-men-experience-in-football/.

11 Dave Manuel, "Joe Theismann Never Played Again after Suffering Injury to Right Leg," Sports-King.com, September 11, 2022, https://www.sports-king.com/joe-theismann-injury-3423/.

12 Ryan Gaydos, "Tony Dungy Rips Article Examining Black Athletes' Injuries in Football: 'Absolutely Ridiculous,'" Fox News, January 8, 2023, https://www.foxnews.com/sports/tony-dungy-rips-article-examining-black-athletes-injuries-football-absolutely-ridiculous.

13 Elizabeth Wolfe, Jacob Lev, and Adrienne Broaddus, "'Keep praying for me': Damar Hamlin, Breathing on His Own, Posts on Instagram for the First Time since Collapse," CNN, January 7, 2023, https://www.cnn.com/2023/01/07/sport/damar-hamlin-collapse-bills-status-saturday/index.html.

14 National Association for the Advancement of Colored People, "NAACP Issues Travel Advisory in Florida," May 20, 2023, https://naacp.org/articles/naacp-issues-travel-advisory-florida.

15 Associated Press, "Chicago Mayor Lori Lightfoot: I'm Only Granting One-on-One Interviews to Journalists of Color," *USA Today*, May 20, 2021, https://www.usatoday.com/story/news/nation/2021/05/20/chicago-mayor-lori-lightfoot-journalists-interviews/5192857001/.

16 Matt Masterson, "Chicago Homicides Declined in 2022, but Total Still among Highest Since '90s," WTTW PBS, January 4, 2023, https://news.wttw.com/2023/01/04/chicago-homicides-declined-2022-total-still-among-highest-90s.

17 *CST* Editorial Board, "Endorsement: Lori Lightfoot for Mayor—and a New Chicago Way," *Chicago Sun-Times*, February 8, 2019, https://chicago.suntimes.com/2019/2/8/18317392/endorsement-lori-lightfoot-for-mayor-and-a-new-chicago-way.

18 Bridgette Matter, "Miami Police Reports Violent Crimes Continue to Decrease," Local10.com, February 18, 2023, https://www.local10.com/news/local/2023/02/18/miami-police-reports-violent-crimes-continue-to-decrease/.

19 Michael Lee, "BLM Paid Execs Millions Despite Being Nearly $9M in the Red: Tax Documents," Fox News, May 24, 2023, https://www.foxnews.com/us/blm-paid-execs-millions-despite-being-nearly-9m-in-red-tax-documents.

20 Sam Dorman, "Oregon Promotes Teacher Program That Seeks to Undo 'Racism in Mathematics,'" Fox News, February 12, 2021, https://www.foxnews.com/us/oregon-education-math-white-supremacy.

21 Sonia Michelle Cintron et al., "A Pathway to Equitable Math Instruction," May 2021, https://equitablemath.org/wp-content/uploads/sites/2/2020/11/1_STRIDE1.pdf.

22 Thomas Sowell, *Black Rednecks and White Liberals* (New York: Encounter Books, 2006).

23 Thomas SowellTV, "The Origin of Black American Culture and Ebonics," YouTube, April 23, 2022, https://www.youtube.com/watch?app=desktop&v=FT4NQ9D0M6w.

24 A. J. Rice, *The Woking Dead: How Society's Vogue Virus Destroys Our Culture* (New York: Post Hill Press, 2022).

25 John McWhorter, *Woke Racism: How a New Religion Has Betrayed Black America* (New York: Penguin Publishing Group, 2021).

26 Chris Gardner, "Super Bowl LVI: Megan Thee Stallion on Sampling 'OG Hot Girls' Salt-N-Pepa for Flamin' Hot Cheetos Ad," *Hollywood Reporter*, February 11, 2022, https://www.hollywoodreporter.com/lifestyle/lifestyle-news/super-bowl-2022-megan-thee-stallion-flamin-hot-cheetos-ad-1235091482/.

27 Quote from the motion picture *The Terminator* (dir. James Cameron, 1984), said by Kyle Reese portrayed by Michael Biehn.

28 "Executive Order on Further Advancing Racial Equity and Support for Underserved Communities through the Federal Government," White House Briefing Room, Presidential Actions, February 16, 2023, https://www.whitehouse.gov/briefing-room/presidential-actions/2023/02/16/executive-order-on-further-advancing-racial-equity-and-support-for-underserved-communities-through-the-federal-government/.

29 Lucas Nolan, "Joe Biden Releases Executive Order Promoting Woke AI," Breitbart, February 22, 2023, https://www.breitbart.com/tech/2023/02/22/joe-biden-releases-executive-order-promoting-woke-ai/.

30 Shaad D'Souza, "Obama Blames Rap for Trump's Purported Increase in Black Male Vote," *Fader*, November 16, 2020, https://www.thefader.com/2020/11/16/obama-blames-rap-for-trump-increase-in-black-male-vote.

31 Clarence Page, "America's First Hip-Hop President Isn't Who You Think," *Chicago Tribune*, https://digitaledition.chicagotribune.com/tribune/article_popover.aspx?guid=66842d63-64c2-4656-9c13-08fcb8b4c3ca.

32 Steven Nelson and Bruce Golding, "'I Love What They Did': Snoop Dogg on Trump Granting Clemency to Pal," *New York Post*, January 19, 2021, https://nypost.com/2021/01/19/i-love-what-they-did-snoop-dogg-on-trump-granting-clemency-to-pal-harry-o/.

33 Alex Isenstadt, "The Inside Story of How Ice Cube Joined Forces with Donald Trump," *Politico*, October 15, 2020, https://www.politico.com/news/2020/10/15/ice-cube-trump-partnership-429713.

34 Brett Samuels, "Trump Tells Rapper A$AP Rocky to 'Get Home ASAP' after Release in Sweden," *Hill*, August 2, 2019, https://thehill.com/homenews/administration/455950-trump-tells-rapper-aap-rocky-to-get-home-asap-after-release-in-sweden/.

35 Donald J. Trump (@realDonaldTrump), "A$AP Rocky released from prison and on his way home to the United States from Sweden. It was a Rocky Week, get home ASAP A$AP!," Twitter (now X), August 2, 2019, https://twitter.com/realDonaldTrump/status/1157345692517634049?ref_src=twsrc%5Etfw.

36 Callie Patteson, "Trump Threatened Trade War with Sweden over A$AP Rocky's Arrest in 2019: Report," *New York Post*, July 1, 2022, https://nypost.com/2022/07/01/trump-threatened-trade-war-with-sweden-over-aap-rocky-arrest/.

37 Donald J. Trump (@realDonaldTrump), "Just had a very good call with @SwedishPM Stefan Löfven who assured me that American citizen A$AP Rocky will be treated fairly. Likewise, I assured him that A$AP was not a flight risk and offered to personally vouch for his bail, or an alternative...." Twitter (now X), July 20, 2019, https://twitter.com/realDonaldTrump/status/1152577020594917376?s=20.

38 Cocoa Brovaz feat. Raekwon, "Black Trump Music Video," Cyclone7Spoiler, YouTube, May 30, 2010, https://www.youtube.com/watch?v=AeYHRY6Q5qg.

39 "Ice Cube Tells Tucker Carlson…'Nothing Changed' with Obama or BLM," TMZ, July 26, 2023, https://www.tmz.com/2023/07/26/ice-cube-tucker-carlson-president-barack-obama-stay-in-your-lane/.

40 C-SPAN, "President Biden: 'If You Are Fully Vaccinated, You No Longer Need to Wear a Mask.," YouTube, May 13, 2021, https://www.youtube.com/watch?v=4SkzTa8HRDk.

41 Gil Kaufman, "Ice Cube Tells Tucker Carlson He Refused 'Rush Job' COVID Vaccine: 'I Didn't Feel Safe,'" *Billboard*, July 26, 2023, https://www.billboard.com/music/rb-hip-hop/ice-cube-tucker-carlson-didnt-take-rush-job-covid-vaccine-1235379258/.

42 Michelle Watson, "Black Lives Matter Executive Accused of 'Syphoning' $10M from BLM Donors, Suit Says," CNN, September 5, 2022, https://www.cnn.com/2022/09/04/us/black-lives-matter-executive-lawsuit/index.html.

43 Monique C. Valeris and Leena Kim, "President Obama Has Canceled His 60th Birthday Bash at His Martha's Vineyard Mansion," *Town & Country*, August 4, 2021, https://www.townandcountrymag.com/leisure/real-estate/a30169311/barack-michelle-obama-buy-marthas-vineyard-house/.

44 Andrew Lisa, "Barack Obama's Net Worth in 2023: How He Made His Money," GO Banking Rates, April 11, 2023, https://www. gobankingrates.com/net-worth/politicians/barack-obama-net-worth/.

45 Barry Mehler, "The Viral Video That Started It All (Week I Gen Intro 010922)," YouTube, January 16, 2022, https:// www.youtube.com/watch?v=RrOzY86YcEM.

46 The Muppets, "Pigs in Space, 'The Gravity of the Situation,'" YouTube, December 16, 2016, https://www.youtube.com/watch?v=SN0wK-wXqY0.

47 Adam Sabes, "Washington University in St. Louis: 'Professionalism' Is Racist," Fox News, January 23, 2022, https://www.foxnews.com/ us/washington-university-in-st-louis-professionalism-is-racist.

48 Adam Sabes, "University of Chicago Student Organization Hosts 'BIPOC-Only' Discussion about Race on Campus," Fox News, October 2, 2022, https://www.foxnews.com/us/university-chicago-student-organization-hosts-bipoc-only-discussion-about-race-campus.

49 Sergio Arau and Sergio Guerrero, dir., *A Day without a Mexican* (Plural Entertainment, 2004), https://www. imdb.com/title/tt0377744/?ref_=tt_mv_close.

50 Emily Crane, "Pelosi Ripped for Saying Florida Needs Migrants to 'Pick the Crops,'" *New York Post*, September 30, 2022, https://nypost. com/2022/09/30/nancy-pelosi-says-florida-needs-migrants-to-pick-crops/.

51 A. J. Rice, *The Woking Dead: How Society's Vogue Virus Destroys Our Culture* (New York: Post Hill Press, 2022).

52 Tom Lasseter et al., "Slavery's Descendants," Reuters, June 27, 3023, https://www.reuters.com/investigates/special-report/usa-slavery-lawmakers/?utm_source=Sailthru&utm_medium=Newsletter&utm_campaign=Daily-Briefing&utm_term=062723.

53 Annie Linskey and Amy Gardner, "Elizabeth Warren Apologizes for Calling Herself Native American," *Washington Post*, February 5, 2019, https://www.washingtonpost.com/politics/elizabeth-warren-apologizes-for-calling-herself-native-american/2019/02/05/1627df76-2962-11e9-984d-9b8fba003e81_story.html.

54 Townhall.com (@townhallcom), "BIDEN: 'White families gathered to celebrate' lynching. 'Some people still want to do that. [video clip of Joe Biden included],'" Twitter (now X), February 16, 2023, https://twitter.com/i/status/1626381322976460800.

55 Julia Ward Howe, "Battle Hymn of the Republic," 1861, https://www. digitalhistory.uh.edu/disp_textbook.cfm?smtID=3&psid=4010.

56 "William Wilberforce," *Encyclopedia Britannica*, https:// www.britannica.com/biography/William-Wilberforce.

57 "English Civil Wars," *Encyclopedia Britannica*, https:// www.britannica.com/event/English-Civil-Wars.

58 "Battle of Alesia," *Encyclopedia Britannica*, https://www. britannica.com/event/Battle-of-Alesia-52-BCE.

59 "Cols. Robin Olds & Chappie James," National Museum of the United States Air Force, https://www.nationalmuseum. af.mil/Upcoming/Photos/igphoto/2000270914/.

60 Atira Winchester, "The History of Ethiopian Jewry," My Jewish Learning, https://www.myjewishlearning.com/article/the-history-of-ethiopian-jewry/.

61 "President Gerald R. Ford's Message on the Observance of Black History Month," February 10, 1976, https://www. fordlibrarymuseum.gov/library/speeches/760074.htm.

62 "Rubenstein Gives $10 Million to Restore Madison's Plantation," Philanthropy News Digest, November 7, 2014, https://philanthropynewsdigest.org/news/ rubenstein-gives-10-million-to-restore-madison-s-plantation.

63 Mary Kay Linge, "Woke Board Proposes National Slavery Monument at James Madison's Home," *New York Post*, September 24, 2022, https://nypost.com/2022/09/24/woke-board-proposes-national-slavery-monument-at-james-madisons-home/.

64 Mary Kay Linge and Jon Levine, "Founding Father James Madison Sidelined by Woke History in His Own Home," *New York Post*, July 16, 2022, https://nypost.com/2022/07/16/james-madison-sidelined-by-woke-history-in-his-own-home/?sp_amp_linker=1*54k5a*amp_id*b0YwOUtTRnhU-VC1PdlRneXFhVnNsOEFPYkJpQVJHY1BBeDdkVDR0NU d4RVJzX3hGWDBKNkRGOElYNk9mcldyWg..&_gl=1*ujae7d*_ ga*elZCXy1Wdm54TEVYZWx4LS1xNDhPMG9BZEk5OHNzQ2Z-RaS1jaVp5Rn l3aGpqeWVqc3Mxc1RXejA5emVMZW9rWg.

65 Douglas MacKinnon, *The 56: Liberty Lessons from Those Who Risked All to Sign the Declaration of Independence* (New York: Post Hill Press, 2022).

66 Sheelah Kolhatkar, "What Happens When Investment Firms Acquire Trailer Parks," *New Yorker*, March 8, 2021, https://www.newyorker.com/magazine/2021/03/15/ what-happens-when-investment-firms-acquire-trailer-parks.

67 Brandon Drey, "Only 1% of Hispanics Prefer the So-Called Gender-Neutral Term 'Latinx': Report," Daily Wire, October 31, 2022, https://www.dailywire.com/news/ only-1-of-hispanics-prefer-the-so-called-gender-neutral-term-latinx-report.

68 Culture Club, "Karma Chameleon (Official Music Video)," YouTube, February 28, 2009, https://www.youtube.com/watch?v=JmcA9LIIXWw.

69 Brandon Drey, "Hispanic Voters Believe Nation Heading in Wrong Direction: Report," Daily Wire, October 24, 2022, https://www.dailywire.com/news/ hispanic-voters-believe-nation-heading-in-wrong-direction-report.

70 Benjamin Ryan, "Bush Demanded Billions for AIDS in Africa at His 2003 State of the Union. It Paid Off.," NBC News, February 7, 2023, https://www.nbcnews.com/nbc-out/out-news/bush-demanded-billions-aids-africa-2003-state-union-paid-rcna69555.

71 Melody Schreiber, "George W. Bush's Anti-HIV Program Is Hailed as 'Amazing'—and Still Crucial at 20," NPR, February 28, 2023, https://www.npr.org/sections/goatsandsoda/2023/02/28/1159415936/george-w-bushs-anti-hiv-program-is-hailed-as-amazing-and-still-crucial-at-20.

72 Gabriel Range, dir., *Death of a President* (FilmFour and Borough Films, 2006), Wikipedia, https://en.wikipedia.org/wiki/Death_of_a_President_(2006_film).

73 "Former President George W. Bush Speaks on 20th Anniversary of Presidential AIDS Relief Plan, Part 2 [video]," C-SPAN, February 24, 2023, https://www.c-span.org/video/?526266-1/president-george-w-bush-speaks-20th-anniversary-presidential-aids-relief-plan-part-2.

74 Melody Schreiber, "George W. Bush's Anti-HIV Program Is Hailed as 'Amazing'—and Still Crucial at 20," NPR, February 28, 2023, https://www.npr.org/sections/goatsandsoda/2023/02/28/1159415936/george-w-bushs-anti-hiv-program-is-hailed-as-amazing-and-still-crucial-at-20.

75 A. J. Rice, *The Woking Dead: How Society's Vogue Virus Destroys Our Culture* (New York: Post Hill Press, 2022).

76 "Vince Everett Ellison: It Is a Privilege to be Black," *Tucker Carlson Tonight*, February 23, 2023, https://www.foxnews.com/video/6321090265112.

77 Emerald Robinson, "New Documentary Shows the Evil of the Democratic Party," Rumble, February 2023, https://rumble.com/v2d4htc-new-documentary-shows-the-evil-of-the-democratic-party.html.

78 Ibid.

79 Laurel Duggan, "Media Twists Itself into Knots Covering Transgender School Shooter," Daily Caller, March 28, 2023, https://dailycaller.com/2023/03/28/media-transgender-school-shooter-pronouns-audrey-hale/.

80 Awr Hawkins, "Nashville Shooting Suspect Texted Friend: 'I'm Planning to Die Today,'" Breitbart, March 28, 2023, https://www.breitbart.com/2nd-amendment/2023/03/28/nashville-shooting-suspect-texted-friend-im-planning-die-today/.

81 Hannah Grossman, "Pentagon Doctors Claim 7-Year-Olds Can Make Decisions to be Injected with Hormones, Puberty Suppressants," Fox News, March 22, 2023, https://www.foxnews.com/media/pentagon-doctors-claim-7-year-olds-can-make-decisions-injected-hormones-puberty-suppressants.

82 Nicole Russell, "Disgusting: New York Not Only Legalized Late-Term Abortions, but Also Celebrated Like It Won the Super Bowl," *Washington Examiner*, January 23, 2019, https://www.washingtonexaminer.com/?p=2174512.

83 Ashley Carnahan, "'The Democratic Party is controlled by a cabal of liars,' Christian author tells Tucker," Fox News, January 25, 2023, https://www.foxnews.com/media/vince-everett-ellison-sneak-peek-new-documentary-guts-democrats-controlled-cabal-liars.

84 "Will You Go to Hell for Me?," *Tucker Carlson Tonight*, February 24, 2023, https://www.facebook.com/watch/?v=1576378479502080.

85 "Democrats: Wokeness First, Americans Last," Republican National Committee, September 23, 2022, https://gop.com/research/democrats-wokeness-first-americans-last-rsr/.

86 Joseph Simonson, "Woke Agenda Survives: These House Republicans Are Sticking with 'Diversity and Inclusion,'" Washington Free Beacon, January 20, 2023, https://freebeacon.com/latest-news/woke-agenda-survives-these-house-republicans-are-sticking-with-diversity-and-inclusion/.

87 Rick Rubin, "Phil Jackson," *Tetragrammaton*, April 2023, https://open.spotify.com/episode/6Keik5RZkQiRE2HeUaMe0e.

88 Nick Selbe, "ESPN's Jalen Rose Blasts Phil Jackson for Controversial Social Justice Comments," *Sports Illustrated*, April 23, 2023, https://www.si.com/nba/2023/04/23/espn-jalen-rose-blasts-phil-jackson-controversial-comments-social-justice.

89 Marty Fenn, "Shaquille O'Neal's Net Worth in 2023: How Much Is Shaquille O'Neal Worth?," ClutchPoints, October 19, 2023, https://clutchpoints.com/shaquille-oneal-net-worth.

90 "Rockets' General Manager's Hong Kong Comments Anger China," Associated Press, October 6, 2019, https://apnews.com/general-news-0a660e9e10664e31bf6ee359c22058cf.

91 Laura He, "China Suspends Business Ties with NBA's Houston Rockets over Hong Kong Tweet," CNN Business, October 7, 2019, https://www.cnn.com/2019/10/07/business/houston-rockets-nba-china-daryl-morey.

92 J. Clara Chan, "LeBron James Deletes Tweet Saying 'You're Next' to Officer Who Shot Ma'Khia Bryant," The Wrap, April 21, 2021, https://www.thewrap.com/lebron-james-deletes-tweet-saying-youre-next-to-officer-who-shot-makhia-bryant/.

93 Joe Grobeck, "The NBA's Choice of Jerry West as Its Iconic Logo Remains Controversial," FanBuzz, February 27, 2023, https://fanbuzz.com/nba/jerry-west-nba-logo/.

94 Enes Freedom (@EnesFreedom), "#China cannot invade the U.S. from the outside, but they can do it from the inside and the #NBA is just a very, very small example of it.," Twitter (now X), October 1, 2022, https://twitter.com/EnesFreedom/status/1576312524072714240.

95 Brad Kolberg, "The Humble Superstar: New Giannis Antetokounmpo Biography Explores Champion's Family Life, Legacy," *Wisconsin Life*, October 14, 2021, https://wisconsinlife.org/story/giannis-the-improbable-rise-of-an-nba-mvp/.

96 Gerald Baria, "Giannis Is Grateful," YouTube, July 21, 2021, https://www.youtube.com/watch?v=3-_0Dj9TlQM.

97 Doug Kezirian, "2022–23 NBA Betting Preview: Can Joel Embiid Finally Win MVP?," ESPN, October 11, 2022, https://www.espn.com/chalk/story/_/id/34773467/2022-23-nba-betting-preview-mvp-award-joel-embiid-luka-doncic.

98 Jelani Scott, "76ers' Joel Embiid Becomes United States Citizen," *Sports Illustrated*, September 29, 2022, https://www.si.com/nba/2022/09/29/76ers-joel-embiid-becomes-united-states-citizen.

99 Jackson Frank, "Joel Embiid Becomes American Citizen," SB Nation, September 29, 2022, https://www.libertyballers.com/2022/9/29/23379425/joel-embiid-becomes-american-citizen-philadelphia-76ers-nba.

100 Max Tani, "Stephen A. Smith Says Trump Is Not Racist, but Will Not Vote for Him," Semafor, April 10, 2023, https://www.semafor.com/article/04/10/2023/stephen-a-smith-semafor-media-summit.

101 Warner Todd Huston, "VIDEO: ESPN's Stephen A. Smith Says He Knows Trump Is Not 'Racist' from Personal Experience," Breitbart, April 11, 2023, https://www.breitbart.com/sports/2023/04/11/video-espns-stephen-a-smith-says-he-knows-trump-not-racist-personal-experience/.

102 Bobby Burack, "Sage Steele's Lawsuit against Disney Revived by Trial Court," OutKick, January 12, 2023, https://www.outkick.com/analysis/sage-steeles-lawsuit-against-disney-revived-by-trial-court.

103 Gilbert McGregor, "What Happened to Michele Tafoya? NBC's Former NFL Sideline Reporter Sets Sights on Politics," *Sporting News*, September 8, 2022, https://www.sportingnews.com/us/nfl/news/michele-tafoya-nbc-nfl-reporter-politics/xxny62qfo8r6dph3dzlk6zxj.

104 Bloomberg, "Max Schmeling, Joe Louis's Friend and Foe, Dies at 99," International Raoul Wallenberg Foundation, February 4, 2005, https://www.raoulwallenberg.net/es/prensa/2005-prensa/max-schmeling-joe-louis-s/.

105 Ken Burns, dir., *Baseball* (National Endowment for the Humanities, 1994), https://www.pbs.org/kenburns/baseball/.

106 "Apr 15, 1947 CE: Jackie Robinson Day," *National Geographic* Education, https://education.nationalgeographic.org/resource/jackie-robinson-day/.

107 Kristine Parks, "Colin Kaepernick Accuses His White Adoptive Parents of 'Problematic' Upbringing, Perpetuating Racism," Fox News, March 9, 2023, https://www.foxnews.com/media/colin-kaepernick-accuses-white-adoptive-parents-problematic-upbringing-perpetuating-racism.

108 News the world, "NBA: The Rise, Fall, and Eventual Disappearance of Allen Iverson," YouTube, June 8, 2020, https://www.youtube.com/watch?v=ydGY_Ea57fQ.

109 A. J. Rice, "All Rise for Aaron Judge's Parents," American Greatness, October 8, 2022, https://amgreatness.com/2022/10/08/all-rise-for-aaron-judges-parents/.

110 A. J. Rice, *The Woking Dead: How Society's Vogue Virus Destroys Our Culture* (New York: Post Hill Press, 2022).

111 Aaron Judge All Rise Foundation, https://www.aaronjudgeallrisefoundation.org/.

112 Nancy Rosenhaus, "Yankees' All-Star Aaron Judge Was Adopted," Adoptions with Love, June 14, 2022, https://adoptionswithlove.org/adoptive-parents/aaron-judge-adopted.

113 Jaclyn Hendricks, "Aaron Judge's Parents, Patty and Wayne, Celebrate as Yankees Star Hits 62nd Home Run," *New York Post*, October 4, 2022, https://nypost.com/2022/10/04/aaron-judges-parents-patty-and-wayne-celebrate-his-62nd-home-run/.

114 Roger Maris (@RogerMarisJr), "Congratulations to Aaron Judge and his family on Aaron's historic home run number 62! It has definitely been a baseball season to remember. You are all class and someone who should be revered. For the MAJORITY of the fans, we can now celebrate a new CLEAN HOME RUN KING!!," Twitter (now X), October 4, 2022, https://twitter.com/rogermarisjr/status/1577451107516809216.

115 Jenna Lemoncelli, "Who Are Aaron Judge's Parents? Meet Patty and Wayne Judge," *New York Post*, September 30, 2022, https://nypost.com/article/who-are-aaron-judge-parents-patty-wayne/.

116 "Magic Johnson," Basketball Reference, https://www.basketball-reference.com/players/j/johnsma02.html.

117 "Air Jordan Jumpman Logo," 1000 Logos, January 24, 2024, https://1000logos.net/air-jordan-logo/.

118 Lee Habeeb, "'Air' Celebrates Risk-Taking, Grit, Parental Love—and Capitalism Itself," *Newsweek*, May 30, 2023, https://www.newsweek.com/air-celebrates-risk-taking-grit-parental-love-capitalism-itself-1803445.

119 Daniel Schorr, "A New, 'Post-Racial' Political Era in America," NPR, January 28, 2008, https://www.npr.org/templates/story/story.php?storyId=18489466.

120 Giselle Ruhiyyih Ewing, "Biden Calls White Supremacy 'Most Dangerous Terrorist Threat' in Speech at Howard," Politico, May 13, 2023, https://www.politico.com/news/2023/05/13/biden-howard-university-white-supremacy-terrorism-00096811.

121 Tom Withers, "All-Time NFL Great Running Back, Social Activist Jim Brown Dies at 87," PBS News Hour, May 19, 2023, https://www.pbs.org/newshour/politics/all-time-nfl-great-running-back-social-activist-jim-brown-dies-at-87.

122 Rob Goldberg, "Jim Brown on Donald Trump: 'I Find Myself Really Pulling for the President,'" Bleacher Report, August 21, 2018, https://bleacherreport.com/articles/2792118-jim-brown-on-donald-trump-i-find-myself-really-pulling-for-the-president.

[123] Brandon Jackson, "A Tale of Unwanted Disruption: My Week without Amazon," Medium, June 4, 2023, https://medium.com/@bjax_/a-tale-of-unwanted-disruption-my-week-without-amazon-df1074e3818b.

[124] Kevin Armstrong, "Tesla Sentry Mode: What It Is, How to Use It and Battery Drain," Not a Tesla App, April 5, 2023, https://www.notateslaapp.com/tesla-reference/1303/tesla-sentry-mode-what-it-is-how-to-use-it-and-battery-drain.

[125] Brian Lloyd, "Yes, Your Samsung Smart TV Has Been Listening In on Your Conversations," Entertainment.ie, February 2015, https://entertainment.ie/trending/yes-your-samsung-smart-tv-has-been-listening-in-on-your-conversations-340669/.

[126] Andrea Vacchiano, "Amazon Customer Claims Company Locked Him Out of Smart Home Devices over Bogus Racism Allegations," Fox Business, June 14, 2023, https://www.foxbusiness.com/technology/amazon-customer-claims-company-locked-him-out-smart-home-devices-over-bogus-racism-allegations.

[127] State of California Department of Justice Office of the Attorney General, "Chapter 16: Recommendation for California to Apologize," Final Draft Report Material for Task Force Consideration, May 6, 2023, https://oag.ca.gov/system/files/media/ab3121-agenda9-ch16-recomm-apologize-05062023.pdf.

[128] Josh Levin, "The Welfare Queen," Slate, December 19, 2013, https://www.slate.com/articles/news_and_politics/history/2013/12/linda_taylor_welfare_queen_ronald_reagan_made_her_a_notorious_american_villain.html.

[129] "Sippenhaft," Jewish Virtual Library, https://www.jewishvirtuallibrary.org/sippenhaft.

[130] Matt Delaney, "California Task Force Suggests Paying $223,000 in Reparations to Black Residents," Washington Times, December 4, 2022, https://www.washingtontimes.com/news/2022/dec/4/california-task-force-suggests-paying-223000-repar/.

[131] Katy Grimes, "California's Ludicrous Slave Reparations Bill," California Globe, December 15, 2022, https://californiaglobe.com/articles/californias-ludicrous-slave-reparations-bill/.

[132] "California Panel Sizes Up Reparations for Black Citizens," New York Times, December 1, 2022, https://www.nytimes.com/2022/12/01/business/economy/california-black-reparations.html.

[133] Allie Griffin, "California Panel Estimates $569 Billion in Reparations Is Owed to Black Residents," New York Post, December 2, 2022, https://nypost.com/2022/12/02/california-panel-estimates-569-billion-in-reparations-is-owed-to-black-residents/.

[134] Jesse Greenspan, "California's Little-Known Role in the American Civil War," History, December 14, 2021, https://www.history.com/news/california-civil-war.

135 "The Historical Legacy of Juneteenth," Smithsonian, https:// nmaahc.si.edu/explore/stories/historical-legacy-juneteenth.

136 "George B. McClellan—1864 Election Broadside," American Battlefield Trust, https://www.battlefields.org/learn/ primary-sources/george-b-mcclellan-1864-election-broadside.

137 Kerry J. Byrne, "On This Day in History, March 20, 1854, Republican Party Founded to Oppose Expansion of Slavery," Fox News, March 20, 2023, https://www.foxnews.com/lifestyle/this-day-history-march-20-1854-republican-party-founded-oppose-expansion-slavery.

138 National Education Association, "Read Across America," https://www.nea. org/professional-excellence/student-engagement/read-across-america.

139 William Shakespeare, "Hath Not a Jew Eyes?," *The Merchant of Venice*, https://www.shakespearesglobe.com/discover/ blogs-and-features/2022/04/08/hath-not-a-jew-eyes/.

140 Daniel Pollack-Pelzner, "All of Shakespeare's Plays Are about Race," *The Atlantic*, March 10, 2023, https://www.theatlantic.com/culture/ archive/2023/03/white-people-in-shakespeare-book-plays-race/673341/.

141 Shakespeare Network, "Falstaff—Chimes at Midnight, Orson Welles, Jeanne Moreau, John Gielgud, 1966, Trailer," YouTube, July 24, 2022, https://www.youtube.com/watch?v=tKlUBoM1kZw.

142 Technicalmark, "Henry V—Speech: Eve of Saint Crispin's Day," YouTube, May 3, 2009, https://www.youtube.com/watch?v=A-yZNMWFqvM.

143 "Famous Quotes: A List of Quotes from Othello," Royal Shakespeare Company, https://www.rsc.org.uk/othello/about-the-play/famous-quotes.

144 A. J. Rice, *The Woking Dead: How Society's Vogue Virus Destroys Our Culture* (New York: Post Hill Press, 2022).

145 Alejandra Marquez Janse, Patrick Jarenwattananon, and Asma Khalid, "Which Skin Color Emoji Should You Use? The Answer Can Be More Complex Than You Think," NPR, February 9, 2022, https://www.npr. org/2022/02/09/1078977416/race-chat-emoji-skin-tone-colors.

146 Greg Botelho, "Ex-NAACP Leader Rachel Dolezal: 'I Identify as Black,'" CNN, June 17, 2015, https://www.cnn.com/2015/06/16/ us/washington-rachel-dolezal-naacp/index.html.

147 Christian Toto, "'Black Panther: Wakanda Forever' Can't Recover from Star's Absence," Hollywood in Toto, November 8, 2022, https://www. hollywoodintoto.com/black-panther-wakanda-forever-review/.

148 Frederick Douglass, "What to the Slave Is the Fourth of July? (1852)," National Constitution Center, https://constitutioncenter. org/the-constitution/historic-document-library/detail/ frederick-douglass-what-to-the-slave-is-the-fourth-of-july-1852.

149 Ryan Coogler, dir., *Black Panther: Wakanda Forever* (Marvel, 2022), https://www.marvel.com/movies/black-panther-wakanda-forever.

150 "Lieutenant Governor of Virginia Winsome Earle-Sears,"
Official Website of the Commonwealth of Virginia, accessed
March 2023, https://www.ltgov.virginia.gov/.

151 Sky News Australia, "Watch the Moment Dave Chappelle Is
Attacked on Stage during Comedy Show," YouTube, May 4,
2022, https://www.youtube.com/watch?v=IoPkT8JQj-I.

152 Tim Scott, US Senator South Carolina, https://www.scott.senate.gov/.

153 The Honorable Michael L. Williams, Texas State Directory, https://
www.txdirectory.com/online/person/?id=44258&office=7136.

154 Wallace B. Jefferson, Alexander Dubose Jefferson, https://
adjtlaw.com/attorney/wallace-b-jefferson/.

155 Leo Terrell, Fox News, https://www.foxnews.com/person/t/leo-terrell.

156 "Clarence Thomas Blasts Ketanji Brown Jackson's 'Racist' Worldview:
'Cancerous to Young Minds,'" Daily Wire, June 29, 2023, https://
www.dailywire.com/news/clarence-thomas-blasts-ketanji-brown-
jacksons-racist-worldview-cancerous-to-young-minds.

157 Ketanji Brown Jackson, "'A Tragedy for Us All': Justice Ketanji
Brown Jackson's Dissent," Nation, June 29, 2023, https://www.
thenation.com/article/society/kbj-dissent-affirmative-action/.

158 Glimpses of Reich, "Horst Wessel Lied," YouTube, July 10, 2023,
https://www.youtube.com/watch?v=raQNyM_M3OA.

159 Mark Oliver, "Death by Tire Fire: A Brief History of 'Necklacing'
in Apartheid South Africa," All That's Interesting, May
19, 2018, https://allthatsinteresting.com/necklacing.

160 Ian Miles Cheong (@stillgray), "South African EFF leader Julius Malema
calls for his supporters to go out and kill white farmers. 'You must never
be scared to kill. A revolution demands that at some point there must be
killing because the killing is part of a revolutionary act.' [video]," X, August
6, 2023, https://twitter.com/stillgray/status/1688202450262790144.

161 British Movietone, "Party Day at Nuremberg—Sound," YouTube, July
21, 2015, https://www.youtube.com/watch?v=WRRG43WBbig.

162 Paul Farrell, "Black Diversity, Equity and Inclusion Director Fired
from Woke California College Was Accused of Disrespecting
BLM Founder and 'Whitesplaining' after Asking for Definition
of Anti-Racism," Daily Mail, March 11, 2023, https://www.
dailymail.co.uk/news/article-11849241/Dr-Tabia-Lee-fired-
woke-California-college-asking-anti-racism-definition.html.

163 Sean Campbell, "Black Lives Matter Secretly Bought a $6 Million
House," New York Magazine, April 4, 2022, https://nymag.com/
intelligencer/2022/04/black-lives-matter-6-million-dollar-house.html.

164 Charlie Daniels, "Uneasy Rider," YouTube, November 7, 2014,
https://www.youtube.com/watch?v=EJrRwTTqm0o.

165 Students for Fair Admissions, Inc. v. President and Fellows of Harvard College, June 29, 2023, https://www.supremecourt.gov/opinions/22pdf/20-1199_hgdj.pdf.

166 Dr. Tabia Lee, "Dr. Tabia Lee: Accused of 'Whitesplaining.' Told Students Are Either 'Victims' or 'Oppressors.' And Then Fired as Diversity Chief…My Grim Story of How Woke Extremists Are Taking Over America's Colleges," *Daily Mail*, March 25, 2023, https://www.dailymail.co.uk/news/article-11902095/DR-TABIA-LEE-fired-diversity-chief-Woke-extremists-taking-Americas-colleges.html.

167 Richard D. Kahlenberg, "Liberal Suburbs Have Their Own Border Wall," *The Atlantic*, July 23, 2023, https://www.theatlantic.com/ideas/archive/2023/07/wealthy-liberal-suburbs-economic-segregation-scarsdale/674792/.

168 "Scarsdale, NY," Realtor.com, https://www.realtor.com/realestateandhomes-search/Scarsdale_NY/overview.

169 Josh Boswell, "Exclusive: Listen as Hunter Biden Bragged That He Would Regularly Smoke Crack with Late D.C. Mayor Marion Barry at a Georgetown Bar When He Was a Student in Recorded Phone Call with a Friend," *Daily Mail*, May 28, 2021, https://www.dailymail.co.uk/news/article-9627185/Hunter-Biden-bragged-smoked-crack-late-DC-Mayor-Marion-Barry-recorded-call.html.

170 Josh Christenson and Steven Nelson, "Hunter Biden Ducked $1.2M Tax Bill over 2017, 2018: IRS Whistleblower," *New York Post*, June 28, 2023, https://nypost.com/2023/06/28/hunter-biden-prosecutor-made-obstruction-crystal-clear-whistleblower/.

171 Universal Pictures, "Scarface—Push It to the Limit," YouTube, May 2, 2020, https://www.youtube.com/watch?v=Olgn9sXNdl0.

172 German Lopez, "The Controversial 1994 Crime Law That Joe Biden Helped Write, Explained," Vox, September 29, 2020, https://www.vox.com/policy-and-politics/2019/6/20/18677998/joe-biden-1994-crime-bill-law-mass-incarceration.

173 Future, "Tony Montana (Explicit Video Version)," YouTube, October 27, 2011, https://www.youtube.com/watch?v=CNdySYdVe0E.

174 Movieclips, "Scarface (1983)—Say Hello to My Little Friend Scene (8/8)," YouTube, June 16, 2011, https://www.youtube.com/watch?v=a_z4IuxAqpE.

175 Larry Elder, "The Trump Charlottesville Lie Just Won't Die," May 26, 2022, Creators, https://www.creators.com/read/larry-elder/05/22/the-trump-charlottesville-lie-just-wont-die.

176 Leading against White Supremacy Act of 2023, H.R. 61, 118th Cong. (2023), https://www.congress.gov/bill/118th-congress/house-bill/61/text.

177 "Robert Mugabe," *Encyclopedia Britannica*, https://www.britannica.com/biography/Robert-Mugabe.

178 Ciara O'Rourke, "Sheila Jackson Lee Says There Are Two Vietnams: North and South," Politifact, July 21, 2010, https://www.politifact.com/factchecks/2010/jul/21/sheila-jackson-lee/sheila-jackson-lee-says-there-are-two-vietnams-nor/.

179 Houston Keene, "Rep. Sheila Jackson Lee Introduces Bill Criminalizing Some Forms of 'Hate Speech,'" Fox News, January 16, 2023, https://www.foxnews.com/politics/sheila-jackson-lee-introduces-bill-criminalizing-hate-speech.

180 Frankie Stockes, "Congressional Democrat Moves to End Free Speech for White People," National File, January 15, 2023, https://nationalfile.com/congressional-democrat-moves-to-end-free-speech-for-white-people/.

181 Kelsey Koberg, "Minneapolis Teachers Union Agreement Protecting Minorities from Layoffs Faces Outcry on Twitter: 'Illegal,'" Fox News, August 17, 2022, https://www.foxnews.com/media/minneapolis-teachers-union-agreement-protecting-minorities-layoffs-faces-outcry-twitter-illegal.

182 "Protocols of the Elders of Zion," United States Holocaust Memorial Museum, https://encyclopedia.ushmm.org/content/en/article/protocols-of-the-elders-of-zion.

183 Kelsey Koberg, "Minneapolis Teachers Union Agreement Stipulates White Teachers Be Laid Off First, Regardless of Seniority," Fox News, August 15, 2022, https://www.foxnews.com/media/minneapolis-teachers-union-agreement-stipulates-white-teachers-laid-off-first-regardless-seniority.

184 Kelsey Koberg, "Minneapolis Policy to Lay Off White Teachers First Could Go to the Supreme Court: Leo Terrell," Fox News, August 17, 2022, https://www.foxnews.com/media/minneapolis-policy-lay-off-white-teachers-first-could-supreme-court-leo-terrell.

185 Koberg, "Minneapolis Teachers Union Agreement Protecting Minorities from Layoffs.

186 "Yorktown: Siege of Yorktown," American Battlefield Trust, https://www.battlefields.org/learn/revolutionary-war/battles/yorktown.

187 Barack Obama, *Dreams from My Father* (New York: Times Books, 1995).

188 David Samuels, "The Obama Factor: A Q&A with Historian David Garrow," Tablet, August 2, 2023, https://www.tabletmag.com/sections/arts-letters/articles/david-garrow-interview-obama.

189 David Garrow, *Rising Star: The Making of Barack Obama* (New York: HarperCollins, 2017).

190 Nick Robertson, "Gannett Sued for Alleged 'Discrimination against Non-Minorities,'" *Hill*, August 24, 2023, https://thehill.com/regulation/court-battles/4170321-gannett-sued-for-alleged-discrimination-against-non-minorities/.

191 Intellectual Dark Web, "Jordan Peterson & Ben Shapiro—Postmodernism, The Leftist Ideology," YouTube, December 4, 2018, https://www.youtube.com/watch?v=UhX2h3QrX9I.

192 Students for Fair Admissions, Inc. v. President and Fellows of Harvard College, June 29, 2023, https://www.supremecourt.gov/opinions/22pdf/20-1199_hgdj.pdf.

193 James Reinl, "Progressive Insurance Sued for 'Patently Unlawful' Racism by Offering $25,000 Grants to Help Black-Owned Businesses Buy Vehicles, but Ruling Out Whites, Asians, Latinos, and Others," *Daily Mail*, August 18, 2023, https://www.dailymail.co.uk/news/article-12421139/Progressive-insurance-sued-patently-unlawful-racism-offering-25-000-grants-help-black-owned-businesses-buy-vehicles-ruling-whites-Asians-Latinos-others.html.

194 Max Zahn, "Starbucks Discrimination Lawsuit Awarded White Employee $25 million: Legal Experts Weigh In," ABC News, June 16, 2023, https://abcnews.go.com/Business/starbucks-discrimination-lawsuit-awarded-white-employee-25-million/story?id=100104620.

195 "A Culture of Belonging: An Interview with Lori Costew, Chief Diversity Officer and Director, People Strategy, Ford Motor Company," *Leaders Magazine*, July 3, 2021, https://www.leadersmag.com/issues/2021.3_Jul/Diversity_Inclusion/LEADERS-Lori-Costew-Ford.html.

196 Ben Ashford, "How 29-Year-Old Kamala Harris Began an Affair with Powerful San Francisco Politician Willie Brown, Then 60 and Married, Who Appointed Her to Two Lucrative Positions Only to Dump Her after He Was Voted First Black Mayor of the City," *Daily Mail*, August 13, 2020, https://www.dailymail.co.uk/news/article-8623781/Kamala-Harris-affair-San-Franciscos-black-mayor-Willie-Brown.html.

197 Esme Mazzeo, "The Life and Death of Anna Nicole Smith," Business Insider, May 17, 2023, https://www.businessinsider.com/anna-nicole-smith-life-death-2023-5.

198 ABC News (@ABC), "Potential 2020 presidential candidate Kamala Harris shares advice for young women: 'Don't let anybody tell you who you are, you tell them who you are.,'" Twitter (now X), January 17, 2019, https://twitter.com/ABC/status/1085851247297654784.

199 Sara Higdon, "Makeup and Tampon Companies Erase Women by Pushing Sexist Trans White House Guest Dylan Mulvaney," Human Events, October 25, 2022, https://humanevents.com/2022/10/25/ultas-embrace-of-transgender-white-house-guest-dylan-mulvaney-as-a-woman-is-offensive.

200 "White adjacent," Urban Dictionary, https://www.urbandictionary.com/define.php?term=white%20adjacent.

201 Naseeb Bhangal, MEd and OiYan Poon, PhD, "Are Asian Americans White? Or People of Color?," *Yes!*, January 15, 2020, https://www.yesmagazine.org/social-justice/2020/01/15/asian-americans-people-of-color.

202 Jennifer Lee, "Are Asian Americans People of Color or the Next in Line to Become White?," Brookings, October 11, 2022, https://www.brookings.edu/articles/are-asian-americans-people-of-color-or-the-next-in-line-to-become-white/.

203 Kenny Xu, "Critical Race Theory Has No Idea What to Do with Asian Americans," *Newsweek*, July 13, 2021, https://www.newsweek.com/critical-race-theory-has-no-idea-what-do-asian-americans-opinion-1608984.

204 Andrew Mark Miller, "Democratic Strategists Respond to Conservative Latino Swing to GOP: 'They Don't Like Socialists,'" Fox News, October 15, 2022, https://www.foxnews.com/politics/democratic-strategists-respond-conservative-latino-swing-gop-dont-like-socialists.

205 John B. Judis and Ruy Teixeira, *The Emerging Democratic Majority* (New York: Simon & Schuster, 2002).

206 Brandon Gillespie, "Hispanics Rejecting Democratic Party for GOP over Concerns about Economy, Crime and Family Values," Fox News, October 6, 2022, https://www.foxnews.com/politics/hispanics-rejecting-democratic-party-gop-concerns-economy-crime-family-values.

207 Jemele Hill (@jemelehill), "That proximity to whiteness is a real thing. Also reminds me of an adage I heard a long time ago about how the oppressed begin to take on the traits of the oppressor.," Twitter (now X), October 22, 2022, https://twitter.com/jemelehill/status/1583841333965246464.

208 Iris Kuo, "The 'Whitening' of Asian Americans," *The Atlantic*, August 31, 2018, https://www.theatlantic.com/education/archive/2018/08/the-whitening-of-asian-americans/563336/.

209 "What's in a Name? King Charles III's Name Has Loaded History," Associated Press, September 10, 2022, https://apnews.com/article/queen-elizabeth-ii-king-charles-iii-4bed0301fb638e0e6ffb9527ab4597f1.

210 Raechal Shewfelt, "'The View' Host Sunny Hostin Talks Death of Queen Elizabeth II: 'We Can Mourn the Queen and Not the Empire,'" Yahoo! Entertainment, September 9, 2022, https://www.yahoo.com/entertainment/the-view-sunny-hostin-queen-elizabeth-death-reparations-012228619.html.

211 Johnny Dodd, "A Lifelong Supporter of Hundreds of Charities, Queen Elizabeth's Death Marks 'The End of an Era,'" *People*, September 9, 2022, https://people.com/human-interest/the-queens-tireless-charity-work/.

212 Chris Donaldson, "Long Island Town Offers to Take Historic Statues of Former Presidents NYC Dems Want Removed," BizPac Review, September 20, 2023, https://www.bizpacreview.com/2023/09/20/long-island-town-offers-to-take-historic-statues-of-former-presidents-nyc-dems-want-removed-1397453/.

213 "Amerigo Vespucci," *Encyclopedia Britannica*, https://www.britannica.com/biography/Amerigo-Vespucci.

214 "Martin Luther King Jr. Authorship Issues," *Wikipedia*, last modified January 6, 2024, https://en.wikipedia.org/wiki/Martin_Luther_King_Jr._authorship_issues.

215 Boston University, "Center for Antiracist Research," via Internet Archive, https://web.archive.org/web/20230731134850/https:/www.bu.edu/antiracism-center/the-center/teams/.

216 Jason Rantz, "Rantz: School District Says Your Baby Is Racist—Their CRT Propaganda Will Fix It," AM 770 KTTH, March 7, 2022, https://mynorthwest.com/3358368/rantz-school-district-says-your-baby-is-racist/.

217 M. Night Shyamalan, dir., *The Sixth Sense* (Hollywood Pictures, 1999).

218 Staff, "Amid Mass Layoffs, BU Center for Antiracist Research Accused of Mismanagement of Funds, Disorganization," *Daily Free Press*, September 21, 2023, https://dailyfreepress.com/2023/09/21/amid-mass-layoffs-bu-center-for-antiracist-research-accused-of-mismanagement-of-funds-disorganization/.

219 "Tuition and Fees," Boston University Admissions, https://www.bu.edu/admissions/admitted/tuition-and-fees/.

220 Mike Damiano and Hilary Burns, "Following Layoffs, Boston University Announces 'Inquiry' into Ibram Kendi's Antiracist Center," *Boston Globe*, September 20, 2023, https://www.bostonglobe.com/2023/09/20/metro/following-layoffs-boston-university-announces-inquiry-into-ibram-kendis-antiracist-center/.

221 Staff, "Amid Mass Layoffs, BU Center for Antiracist Research Accused of Mismanagement of Funds, Disorganization," *Daily Free Press*, September 21, 2023, https://dailyfreepress.com/2023/09/21/amid-mass-layoffs-bu-center-for-antiracist-research-accused-of-mismanagement-of-funds-disorganization/.

222 Caitlin Doornbos, "Mandela Effect: Biden Again Brings Up Debunked South Africa Story," *New York Post*, October 24, 2022, https://nypost.com/2022/10/24/biden-again-brings-up-debunked-south-africa-nelson-mandela-story/.

223 Glenn Kessler, "Biden's Ridiculous Claim He Was Arrested Trying to See Mandela," *Washington Post*, February 25, 2020, https://www.washingtonpost.com/politics/2020/02/25/bidens-ridiculous-claim-he-was-arrested-trying-see-mandela/.

224 Veronica Stracqualursi and Sarah Mucha, "Biden Acknowledges He Wasn't Arrested in South Africa Despite Earlier Claims," CNN, February 28, 2020, https://www.cnn.com/2020/02/28/politics/joe-biden-south-africa-arrest-cnntv.

225 Janell Ross, "Joe Biden Didn't Just Compromise with Segregationists. He Fought for Their Cause in Schools, Experts Say.," NBC News, June 25, 2019, https://www.nbcnews.com/news/nbcblk/joe-biden-didn-t-just-compromise-segregationists-he-fought-their-n1021626.

226 Editorial Board, "Biden's 'Jim Crow 2.0' Dies in Georgia," *Wall Street Journal*, November 9, 2022, https://www.wsj.com/articles/joe-bidens-jim-crow-2-0-dies-in-georgia-voters-midterm-election-raphael-warnock-brian-kemp-stacey-abrams-11668035286.

227 E. J. Dionne Jr., "Biden Admits Plagiarism in School but Says It Was Not 'Malevolent,'" *New York Times*, September 18, 1987, https://www.nytimes.com/1987/09/18/us/biden-admits-plagiarism-in-school-but-says-it-was-not-malevolent.html.

228 Jake Tapper, "VP Biden Says Republicans Are 'Going to Put Y'All Back in Chains,'" ABC News, August 14, 2012, https://abcnews.go.com/blogs/politics/2012/08/vp-biden-says-republicans-are-going-to-put-yall-back-in-chains.

229 Catherine Herridge and Graham Kates, "Copy of What's Believed to Be Hunter Biden's Laptop Data Turned Over by Repair Shop to FBI Showed No Tampering, Analysis Says," CBS News, November 21, 2022, https://www.cbsnews.com/news/hunter-biden-laptop-data-analysis/.

230 Steve Cortes, "Trump Didn't Call Neo-Nazis 'Fine People.' Here's Proof," RealClearPolitics, March 21, 2019, https://www.realclearpolitics.com/articles/2019/03/21/trump_didnt_call_neo-nazis_fine_people_heres_proof_139815.html. Emphasis added.

231 Natasha Korecki, "Biden defiantly defends remarks about Trump and white supremacists," Politico, August 8, 2019, https://www.politico.com/story/2019/08/08/joe-biden-trump-white-supremacy-1453521.

232 Jessica Chasmar, "Biden repeats debunked claim he 'used to drive a tractor-trailer,'" Fox News, December 1, 2021, https://www.foxnews.com/politics/biden-debunked-claim-used-drive-tractor-trailer.

233 Jon Greenberg, "Fact check: Biden says he 'used to drive a tractor trailer,'" WRAL News, December 9, 2021, https://www.wral.com/story/fact-check-biden-says-he-used-to-drive-a-tractor-trailer/20026445/.

234 Valuetainment, "'I Was WRONG!' - Michael Rapaport Admits Being Wrong About Donald Trump," YouTube, February 9, 2024, https://www.youtube.com/watch?v=6b8StTGxSEE.

235 S, "Bill Maher Confronts Jimmy Kimmel on Masks Hypocrisy," YouTube, November 10, 2022, https://www.youtube.com/watch?v=UrxKpb9b1Uo.

236 Kendall Tietz, "BLM Chapter Sparks Outrage after Posting Pro-Palestinian Cartoon Referencing Hamas Terrorists," Fox News, October 11, 2023, https://www.foxnews.com/media/blm-chapter-sparks-outrage-posting-pro-palestinian-cartoon-referencing-hamas-terrorists.

237 Jessica Schladebeck, "Teen Wanted for Journalist Josh Kruger's Murder Had Been in a Drug-Fueled Relationship with Him, Family Says," *New York Daily News*, October 12, 2023, https://www.nydailynews.com/2023/10/12/josh-kruger-murderer-robert-davis-relationship-philadelphia/.

238 Isaac Schorr, "Black Lives Matter Chapters Celebrate Terrorist Attack in Israel, Revel in Slaughter at Music Festival," Mediaite, October 10, 2023, https://www.mediaite.com/news/black-lives-matter-chapters-celebrate-terrorist-attack-in-israel-revel-in-slaughter-at-music-festival/.

239 Karol Markowicz (@karol), "Take a good look, liberal Jews. This is the shit you supported.," X, October 10, 2023, https://twitter.com/karol/status/1711803163324416052.

240 Frank James, "Sotomayor's 'Wise Latina' Line Maybe Not So Wise," NPR, May 27, 2009, https://www.npr.org/sections/thetwo-way/2009/05/sotomayors_wise_latina_line_ma.html.

241 PBS News Hour, "President Obama Nominates Merrick Garland for Supreme Court," YouTube, March 16, 2016, https://www.youtube.com/watch?v=t6EHfK_FEiE.

242 Kerry Picket, "Liberals at Koch Protest: Hang Justice Thomas," *Washington Times*, February 3, 2011, https://www.washingtontimes.com/blog/watercooler/2011/feb/3/lberals-koch-protest-call-lynching-justice-clarenc/.

243 Philip Rucker, "Joe Biden: When a Woman Alleges Sexual Assault, Presume She Is Telling the Truth," *Washington Post*, September 17, 2018, https://www.washingtonpost.com/politics/joe-biden-when-a-woman-alleges-sexual-assault-presume-she-is-telling-the-truth/2018/09/17/7718c532-badd-11e8-a8aa-860695e7f3fc_story.html.

244 Jane Mayer, "What Joe Biden Hasn't Owned Up to about Anita Hill," *New Yorker*, April 27, 2019, https://www.newyorker.com/news/news-desk/what-joe-biden-hasnt-owned-up-to-about-anita-hill.

245 Andrew Brennan, "Biden Refuses to Condemn Kavanaugh Assassination Attempt, Again," GOP Blog, June 9, 2022, https://gop.com/blog/biden-refuses-to-condemn-kavanaugh-assassination-attempt-again-az/.

246 "African American Workers at Ford Motor Company," Henry Ford Museum of American Innovation, February 26, 2013, https://www.thehenryford.org/explore/blog/african-american-workers-at-ford-motor-company/.

247 Detroit Historical Society, "Model T," Encyclopedia of Detroit, https://detroithistorical.org/learn/encyclopedia-of-detroit/model-t.

248 Budgie97, "Biggie Smalls: Warning (Lyrics)," YouTube, August 5, 2011, https://www.youtube.com/watch?v=ktyuNv9X-PA.

249 "Beastmode: Brit Smacks Down Don Lemon on Reparations," Washington Free Beacon, September 20, 2022, https://freebeacon.com/media/beastmode-brit-smacks-down-don-lemon-on-reparations/.

250 Michael Haskoor, "Bill Maher Says It's 'Stupid' to Judge Past Behaviors Using Today's Social Values," Decider, September 17, 2022, https://decider.com/2022/09/17/bill-maher-says-its-stupid-to-judge-past-behaviors-on-current-social-values/.

251 Karen Juanita Carrillo, "How Hernán Cortés Conquered the
Aztec Empire," History, updated June 26, 2023, https://www.
history.com/news/hernan-cortes-conquered-aztec-empire.

252 "Machu Picchu," *Encyclopedia Britannica*, https://
www.britannica.com/place/Machu-Picchu.

253 National Park Service, "Chaco Culture: A Brief History of Chaco
Culture National Historical Park," US Department of the Interior,
https://www.nps.gov/chcu/learn/upload/Chaco-Brief-History.pdf.

254 A. J. Rice, *The Woking Dead: How Society's Vogue Virus Destroys
Our Culture* (New York: Post Hill Press, 2022).

255 Michael Haskoor, "Bill Maher Says It's 'Stupid' to Judge Past
Behaviors Using Today's Social Values," Decider, September
17, 2022, https://decider.com/2022/09/17/bill-maher-says-its-
stupid-to-judge-past-behaviors-on-current-social-values/.

256 "English Civil Wars," *Encyclopedia Britannica*, https://
www.britannica.com/event/English-Civil-Wars.

257 Terri Hansen, "How the Iroquois Great Law of Peace Shaped U.S.
Democracy," PBS, December 13, 2018, https://www.pbs.org/native-america/
blog/how-the-iroquois-great-law-of-peace-shaped-us-democracy.

258 Ben Walker, "No US-Born Black Players on Expected World
Series Rosters," Associated Press, October 26, 2022, https://
apnews.com/article/world-series-black-players-astros-phillies-f77
68955507758abf3af00552d4ba9b7.

259 "Opening Day Rosters Feature 275 Internationally-Born Players,"
MLB.com, April 8, 2022, https://www.mlb.com/press-release/
press-release-opening-day-rosters-feature-275-internationally-born-players.

260 A. J. Rice, "How Long Until Hispanics Are 'White Adjacent?,'" Human
Events, October 26, 2022, https://humanevents.com/2022/10/26/
aj-rice-how-long-until-hispanics-are-white-adjacent.

261 "Julius Erving," Basketball Reference, https://www.
basketball-reference.com/players/e/ervinju01.html.

262 Kearie Daniel, "Yes, It's OK for Any Child to Dress as Black Panther
This Halloween—With One Big Caveat," *Chatelaine*, October 11, 2018,
https://chatelaine.com/opinion/black-panther-halloween-costume/.

263 Elie Mystal, "Some Advice for White People on
Halloween," *Nation*, October 29, 2020, https://www.
thenation.com/article/society/halloween-costume/.

264 Joshua David Stein, "Hey Van Jones, Can My White Kid
Dress Up as Black Panther for Halloween?," Fatherly, updated
July 19, 2018, https://www.fatherly.com/entertainment/
van-jones-white-kid-black-panther-costume-halloween.

265 Caitlin Doornbos, "Biden Admin Objects to Merit-
Based Military Promotions, No Race Quotas," *New*

York Post, July 11, 2023, https://nypost.com/2023/07/11/biden-admin-objects-to-merit-based-military-promotions-no-race-quotas/.

266 "Yogi Bear," Hanna-Barbera Wiki, https://hanna-barbera.fandom.com/wiki/Yogi_Bear.

267 "Minnesota Outdoor Recreation Task Force Recommendations," March 24, 2021, https://files.dnr.state.mn.us/aboutdnr/outdoor-rec-taskforce/minnesota-outdoor-recreation-task-force-recommendations03-24-21-final.pdf.

268 Corinne Murdock, "Minnesota Dept of Natural Resources Concerned with Bringing More Non-White Visitors to State Parks," Daily Wire, August 16, 2023, https://www.dailywire.com/news/minnesota-dept-of-natural-resources-concerned-with-bringing-more-non-white-visitors-to-state-parks.

269 "The Equity Manifesto," PolicyLink, https://www.policylink.org/about-us/equity-manifesto.

270 Kerry J. Byrne, "Native Americans Leading Redskins Petition Outraged That a Washington Commanders Rep Called Them 'Fake group,'" Fox News, August 29, 2023, https://www.foxnews.com/sports/native-americans-leading-redskins-petition-outraged-washington-commanders-rep-called-fake-group.

271 Ben's Original, https://www.bensoriginal.com/.

272 Ja'Mal Green (@JaymalGreen), Twitter (now X), February 9, 2021, https://twitter.com/JaymalGreen/status/1359315956955234305.

273 "Brand Origins," Pearl Milling Company, https://www.pearlmillingcompany.com/our-history.

274 "P.E.A.R.L. Pledge," Pearl Milling Company, https://www.pearlmillingcompany.com/pearlpledge.

275 Alex Seitz-Wald, "Democrats Make South Carolina First Presidential Primary Voting State," NBC News, February 4, 2023, https://www.nbcnews.com/politics/2024-election/democrats-make-south-carolina-first-presidential-primary-voting-state-rcna68918.

276 David Schmidt, "Clyburn Has His Own Nuclear Problem," *State*, https://www.thestate.com/opinion/letters-to-the-editor/article167996592.html.

277 "Barack Obama Reportedly Said: 'Don't Underestimate Joe's Ability to (Expletive) Things Up,'" CBS19 News, August 16, 2020, https://www.cbs19news.com/story/42501205/barack-obama-reportedly-said-dont-underestimate-joes-ability-to-expletive-things-up.

278 Tanya A. Christian, "Clyburn Urges Biden to Choose Stacey Abrams, Another Black Woman as Running Mate," *Essence*,

updated December 6, 2020, https://www.essence.com/news/
politics/clyburn-biden-black-woman-running-mate/.

[279] Keach Hagey, "Rep. Clyburn: Bring Back Fairness Doctrine," Politico,
January 10, 2011, https://www.politico.com/blogs/onmedia/0111/
Rep_Clyburn_Bring_back_Fairness_Doctrine.html.

[280] Chandelis Duster, "Clyburn Says He Does Not Support Defunding
the Police," CNN, June 14, 2020, https://www.cnn.com/2020/06/14/
politics/james-clyburn-defund-police-cnntv/index.html.

[281] "User Clip: Rep James Clyburn (D-SC) Said That the Bush
Campaign Claiming to Have Won the Election Has 'No Ground'
and If Laws Were Enforced, He Would Be 'Out of' the Race
'All Together.,'" C-SPAN, November 15, 2000, https://www.c-
span.org/video/?c5018059/user-clip-rep-james-clyburn-bush-
campaign-claiming-won-election-no-ground-laws-enforced.

[282] FORA.tv, "Al Gore Warns Polar Ice May Be Gone in Five Years," YouTube,
December 16, 2009, https://www.youtube.com/watch?v=MsioIw4bvzI.

[283] Suzy Hansen, "Stormy Weather," Salon via Internet Archive,
October 23, 2001, https://web.archive.org/web/20110202162233/
https://www.salon.com/books/int/2001/10/23/weather/.

[284] James E. Clyburn (@RepJamesClyburn), "Climate change is real and its
evidence is all around us. The Paris Agreement was an important first
step toward holding countries accountable and we cannot allow this
president to remove us from it.," Twitter (now X), May 2, 2019, https://
twitter.com/RepJamesClyburn/status/1124007260013965314?lang=en.

[285] Transcript: Fox News Sunday, November 6, 2022, https://www.
foxnews.com/transcript/fox-news-sunday-november-6-2022.

[286] Representative James E. Clyburn, https://www.congress.
gov/member/district/james-clyburn/C000537.

[287] Irvin Kershner, dir., Raid on Entebbe (20th Century Fox Television,
1977), https://en.wikipedia.org/wiki/Raid_on_Entebbe_(film).

[288] "Fentanyl," United States Drug Enforcement Administration,
https://www.dea.gov/factsheets/fentanyl.

[289] "Drug Overdoses," National Safety Council, https://injuryfacts.nsc.org/
home-and-community/safety-topics/drugoverdoses/data-details/.

[290] "Fentanyl," Department of Justice/Drug Enforcement Administration
Drug Fact Sheet, https://www.dea.gov/sites/default/files/2023-06/
Fentanyl%202022%20Drug%20Fact%20Sheet-update.pdf.

[291] Nicole Silverio, "'Everyone Lied': Tucker Carlson Points to
Shocking, Untold Details about George Floyd's Death," Daily

Caller, October 20, 2023, https://dailycaller.com/2023/10/20/tucker-carlson-george-floyd-death-coroner-lawsuit/.

292 Tom Norton, "Fact Check: Tucker Carlson Says New Evidence Clears Derek Chauvin of Murder," *Newsweek*, October 25, 2023, https://www.newsweek.com/tucker-carlson-new-evidence-derek-chauvin-murder-george-floyd-1836953.

293 TheLibertyDaily, "Tucker Carlson: Everything You Have Been Told about George Floyd's Death Was a Lie, the Truth Hidden," Rumble, https://rumble.com/v3qo5o0-tucker-carlson-everything-you-have-been-told-about-george-floyds-death-was-.html.

294 Joseph Wulfsohn, "Elizabeth Warren Apparently Scrubs DNA-Test Rollout from Campaign Site, Twitter," Fox News, October 16, 2019, https://www.foxnews.com/media/elizabeth-warren-completely-scrubs-dna-results.

295 Theresa Braine, "Sacheen Littlefeather, Indigenous Activist Who Refused Marlon Brando's 'Godfather' Oscar, Dies at Age 75," *New York Daily News*, October 2, 2022, https://www.nydailynews.com/2022/10/02/sacheen-littlefeather-indigenous-activist-who-refused-marlon-brandos-godfather-oscar-dies-at-age-75/.

296 Chris McGreal, "Rachel Dolezal: 'I Wasn't Identifying as Black to Upset People. I Was Being Me,'" *Guardian*, December 13, 2015, https://www.theguardian.com/us-news/2015/dec/13/rachel-dolezal-i-wasnt-identifying-as-black-to-upset-people-i-was-being-me.

297 "General Social and Economic Characteristics Delaware," US Census, 1970, https://www2.census.gov/library/publications/decennial/1970/population-volume-1/1970a_de-02.pdf.

298 Gregory S. Schneider, "'A Wounded Healer': Ralph Northam Wraps Up Term in Office, Forged by Scandal into a Governor of Lasting Consequence," *Washington Post*, January 9, 2022, https://www.washingtonpost.com/dc-md-va/2022/01/09/governor-northam-blackface-scandal-legacy/.

299 Natalie O'Neill and Samuel Chamberlain, "Lincoln Project Claims Responsibility for Fake 'White Supremacists' at Glenn Youngkin Event," *New York Post*, October 29, 2021, https://nypost.com/2021/10/29/glenn-youngkin-aide-accuses-terry-mcauliffe-team-of-fake-white-supremacist-stunt/.

300 Jim Treacher, "Warren Campaign Scrubs DNA-Test Announcement Video from Internet," PJ Media, October 16, 2019, https://pjmedia.com/jim-treacher/2019/10/16/warren-campaign-scrubs-dna-test-announcement-video-from-internet-n69697.

301 Asma Khalid, "Warren Apologizes to Cherokee Nation for DNA Test," NPR, February 1, 2019, https://www.npr.org/2019/02/01/690806434/ warren-apologizes-to-cherokee-nation-for-dna-test.

302 A. J. Rice, *The Woking Dead: How Society's Vogue Virus Destroys Our Culture* (New York: Post Hill Press, 2022).

303 "The Day the Mayflower Left Southampton for America," Mayflower 400, https://www.mayflower400uk.org/education/who-were-the-pilgrims/2019/ august/the-day-the-mayflower-left-southampton-for-america/.

304 "Roger Williams," Free Speech Center at Tennessee State University, https://firstamendment.mtsu.edu/article/roger-williams/.

305 "Shimabara Rebellion," *Encyclopedia Britannica*, https:// www.britannica.com/event/Shimabara-Rebellion.

306 "Is It Legal to Wear a Mask in Public in Virginia?," Greenspun Shapiro PC, https://www.greenspunlaw.com/blog/is-it- legal-to-wear-a-mask-in-public-in-virginia.cfm.

307 Tori L. Cowger et al., "Lifting Universal Masking in Schools— Covid-19 Incidence among Students and Staff," *New England Journal of Medicine*, November 24, 2022, https://www.nejm.org/ doi/full/10.1056/NEJMoa2211029?query=featured_home.

308 "Obesity, Race/Ethnicity, and COVID-19," Centers for Disease Control and Prevention, https://www.cdc. gov/obesity/data/obesity-and-covid-19.html.

309 Karol Markowicz, "'Masks Reduce Racism' Study Is Latest Sign US Medical Establishment Is Insanely, Perilously Woke," *New York Post*, November 11, 2022, https://nypost.com/2022/11/11/ us-medical-establishment-has-gone-woke-with-masking-racism-study/.

310 Neeraj Sood et al., "Association between School Mask Mandates and SARS-CoV-2 Student Infections: Evidence from a Natural Experiment of Neighboring K-12 Districts in North Dakota," *Research Square*, July 1, 2022, https://assets.researchsquare.com/files/rs-1773983/v1/ e13a2526-72ff-459b-a988-37ef6eb6eadf.pdf?c=1656708065.

311 Roni Caryn Rabin, "Masks Work to Cut Covid Spread, a Study of Boston School Districts Finds," *New York Times*, November 11, 2022, https:// www.nytimes.com/2022/11/10/health/covid-schools-masks.html.

312 Jon Favreau, dir., *Elf* (New Line Cinema, 2003), https:// www.imdb.com/title/tt0319343/?ref_=tt_mv_close.

313 Rachael O'Connor, "Seth Rogen Says 'Thousands of White Supremacists' Are Posting Bad Reviews about His New Christmas Show," Metro, updated December 5, 2021, https://

metro.co.uk/2021/12/04/seth-rogen-says-white-supremacistsare-posting-bad-reviews-of-show-15715203/.

314 "National Lampoon's Christmas Vacation," Rotten Tomatoes, https://www.rottentomatoes.com/m/national_lampoons_christmas_vacation.

315 "Academy Announces Next Phase of Equity and Inclusion Initiatives," A.frame, June 12, 2020, https://www.oscars.org/news/academy-announces-next-phase-equity-and-inclusion-initiatives.

316 *The Mandalorian* (Lucasfilm Fairview Entertainment Golem Creations, 2019–), https://www.imdb.com/title/tt8111088/.

317 Movieclips, "A Bit Nipply Out—Christmas Vacation," YouTube, May 26, 2011, https://www.youtube.com/watch?v=GxGkcC1VrhU.

318 Lindsay Dodgson, "12 Biological Factors That Make You Attracted to Someone," Business Insider, September 27, 2023, https://www.businessinsider.com/biological-reasons-youre-attracted-to-someone-2018-10.

319 Movieclips, "Clark Freaks Out—Christmas Vacation," YouTube, May 26, 2011, https://www.youtube.com/watch?v=TQXuazYI_YU.

320 Gabrielle Fonrouge, "Jeffrey Toobin Back on CNN after Masturbation Scandal, Admits It Was 'Moronic,'" *New York Post*, June 10, 2021, https://nypost.com/2021/06/10/jeffrey-toobin-back-on-cnn-after-masturbation-scandal/.

321 RedpillPatriot (@redpill2138), "Do you all get a daily script emailed to you?," Twitter (now X), December 13, 2022, https://twitter.com/redpill2138/status/1602874243045154816.

322 (((DeanObeidallah))) (@DeanObeidallah), "As a lawyer Im going to do research to see if @elonmusk in any way lied on his application for US citizenship. I'll be making a FOIA request for his immigration application. If he lied anywhere on application we will move to strip him of US citizenship. Stay tuned.," Twitter (now X), October 31, 2022, https://twitter.com/DeanObeidallah/status/1587048259758989313?ref_src=twsrc%5Etfw%7Ctwcamp%5Etweetembed%7Ctwterm %5E158704 8259758989313%7Ctwgr%5Ec22756e54b686d3f62afe 301c73b 5d3246bcc489%7Ctwcon%5Es1_&ref_url=https%3A%2F%2Fwww.foxbusiness.com%2Fmedia%2Ffrequent-msnbc-guest-ripped-plotting-strip-elon- musk-us-citizenship-stupid-incompetent.

323 Alyssa Milano (@Alyssa_Milano), "Thank you, @elonmusk for helping this city! And thank you, @LittleMissFlint for your tireless work and advocacy. You inspire me on a@daily basis.," Twitter (now X) March 23, 2019, https://twitter.com/alyssa_milano/status/1109664114907856896.

[324] Alyssa Milano (@Alyssa_Milano), "I gave back my Tesla. I bought the VW ev. I love it. I'm not sure how advertisers can buy space on Twitter. Publicly traded company's products being pushed in alignment with hate and white supremacy doesn't seem to be a winning business model.," Twitter (now X), November 26, 2022, https://twitter.com/Alyssa_Milano/status/1596502100066045952?ref_src=twsrc%5Etfw.

[325] Ariel Zilber, "Drudge Report Slams Elon Musk over Twitter Bans: 'Is He Tripping on Drugs?,'" *New York Post*, December 16, 2022, https://nypost.com/2022/12/16/drudge-report-slams-elon-musk-over-twitter-bans-blame-the-ambien/.

[326] Joe Concha, "Tucker Carlson: 'Matt Drudge Is Now Firmly a Man of the Progressive Left,'" *Hill*, July 25, 2020, https://thehill.com/homenews/media/509017-tucker-carlson-matt-drudge-is-now-firmly-a-man-of-the-progressive-left/.

[327] Jeremy Herb, "Sinema Leaving the Democratic Party and Registering as an Independent," CNN, December 9, 2022, https://www.cnn.com/2022/12/09/politics/kyrsten-sinema-leaves-democratic-party/index.html.

[328] Jared Gans, "Musk Says He Would Support DeSantis in 2024," *Hill*, November 26, 2022, https://thehill.com/policy/technology/3750864-musk-says-he-would-support-desantis-in-2024/.

[329] MeidasTouch, YouTube, https://www.youtube.com/channel/UC9r9HYFxEQOBXSopFS61ZWg.

[330] Nikolas Lanum, "Twitter Files: CNN, ABC, NBC, CBS Blackout Coverage of Elon Musk Leaks," Fox News, December 13, 2022, https://www.foxnews.com/media/twitter-files-cnn-abc-nbc-cbs-blackout-coverage-elon-musk.

[331] "Kwanzaa Party Supplies," Party City, https://www.partycity.com/kwanzaa-party-supplies.

[332] "Kwanzaa: Decorations," Target, https://www.target.com/c/decorations-party-supplies/kwanzaa/-/N-5xt1zZmkp3f.

[333] "Happy Festivus…for the Rest of Us!," Festivus! The Website, https://festivusweb.com/.

[334] Kehinde Andrews, "Happy Kwanzaa! It's So Much More Than a 'Black Christmas,'" *Guardian*, December 25, 2020, https://www.theguardian.com/lifeandstyle/2020/dec/25/happy-kwanzaa-its-so-much-more-than-a-black-christmas.

[335] *Tell Me More*, "Is Kwanzaa Still a Thing?," NPR, December 28, 2012, https://www.npr.org/2012/12/28/168202864/is-kwanzaa-still-a-thing.

336 Lisa Boone, "9 Ways to Celebrate Kwanzaa in Los Angeles in 2020," *Los Angeles Times*, December 21, 2020, https://www.latimes.com/lifestyle/story/2020-12-21/how-to-celebrate-kwanzaa-la-2020.

337 Stephanie Schoppert, "10 Most Corrupt African Dictators in Modern History," History Collection, October 8, 2016, https://historycollection.com/ten-corrupt-african-dictators-modern-history/2/.

338 Eric Owens, "REMINDER: Kwanzaa Was Concocted by a Deranged Felon Who Tortured Naked Women with a Karate Baton and a Toaster," Daily Caller, December 24, 2017, https://dailycaller.com/2017/12/24/reminder-kwanzaa-was-concocted-by-a-deranged-felon-who-tortured-naked-women-with-a-karate-baton-and-a-toaster/.

339 J. Lawrence Scholer and the editors of *Dartmouth Review*, "The Story of Kwanzaa," January 15, 2001, http://www.hartford-hwp.com/archives/45a/767.html.

340 "Black Studies," *Wikipedia*, updated February 2, 2024, https://en.wikipedia.org/wiki/Black_studies.

341 "Kwanzaa Decorations," Kirkland's Home, https://www.kirklands.com/category/Seasonal-Gifts/Kwanzaa-Decorations/pc/2289/3251.uts.

342 Michael Sheetz, "DOJ Sues SpaceX, Alleging Hiring Discrimination against Refugees and Asylum Recipients," NBC News, August 24, 2023, https://www.nbcnews.com/tech/tech-news/doj-sues-spacex-alleging-hiring-discrimination-refugees-asylum-seekers-rcna101634.

343 Barry Sonnenfeld, dir., *Men in Black* (Amblin Entertainment, 1997), https://www.imdb.com/title/tt0119654/?ref_=fn_al_tt_1.

344 Publius PR, https://publiuspr.com/.

345 The Publius National Post, https://publiusnationalpost.substack.com/.

ACKNOWLEDGMENTS

I want to begin with a moment of silence for The Very Fine People. After reading this masterpiece, you know who you are now; and you are on Both Sides.

Great thinkers, from Pablo Picasso to Woody Allen, have quipped, "If you're going to steal, steal from the best." I couldn't agree more, but to steal from talented people, you must surround yourself with talented people. That has been not only my mission in life but my professional mission throughout my career: to become a collector of valuable, brilliant, talented people. But don't just be a coach—also be a player. No one respects a coach who hasn't played the game. Surround yourself with enough geniuses and you can swim in their wake, or possibly create your own. True wisdom doesn't come from what you know, it comes from what you don't know, so be brave enough to not know a great many things.

This is why the first person I want to thank is me. That's right, *me*. For not knowing what it would take and for failing until I did. You see, in the beginning there was an idea called Publius PR. The idea was to bring together a group of remarkable people to see if they could become something more. To see if they could work together when we needed them to, to fight the battles that we never could. Since the 2016 election, many patriots have been cancelled, investigated, and imprisoned—some have even died—fighting for the ideals of liberty.

These are the clients of Publius PR. These are not "summer soldiers." They are the heroes in our existential battle against tyranny, *The Woking Dead*, globalism, and the deep state. I honor them all.

There will be no sophomore slump in this content collection. A book like this involves many layers of talented people, I would like to express my gratitude to all those who fought for Volume 2 and helped to midwife it into existence. A sequel was never guaranteed, but now a trilogy must follow.

I want to thank my publisher, Anthony Ziccardi and Post Hill Press, for allowing me a second crack at unleashing hilarious political madness on the world. A very special shoutout to Vince Everett Ellison for contributing the foreword to the book, as well as my editors and collaborators Ben Boychuk, Bryan Preston, and Eric Peters.

Shoutout to the Publius PR cavalry, including Drew Allen, Sutton Porter, and Ilaria Thompson-Davoli.

As someone who grew up and played sports in the 1980s and 1990s, no single athlete dominated the public consciousness more than Michael Jordan. He is The GOAT of the NBA and someone I used as motivational fodder for this book. He even makes an appearance.

I was living in the suburbs of Philadelphia and watching MJ light up the hapless 76ers regularly when a family from Chicago moved in down the street. I became fast friends with this family and played little league baseball and CYO basketball with their oldest son. I had never met Midwesterners before, and they extended their hospitality for many years of my childhood. It was a philosophical adoption, and it allowed me to literally adopt Michael Jordan as my own because they were, of course, Bulls fans. It was in this milieu that I learned how to be a winner and more importantly how to transmit losses into productive learning from failure. I would like to give a huge shoutout to that Chicago family, the Law Family: Gary, Jill, Matt and Dan... You helped create a monster... Say *you're welcome*!

Commanding Publius PR is like commanding the Death Star from *Star Wars*. It involves long and bizarre hours away from family time, and when you add book-writing into the mix, it can get hectic. My wife Kelly is a certified superhero. A mother, a thinker, a friend, and an ass kicker. I love you.

To my brother Christopher and my parents John and Elizabeth, thank you for always keeping me grounded while also letting me dream.

And finally, to my son Archer: I love you 3000.

ABOUT THE AUTHOR

A.J. Rice is America's publicist, and the undisputed GOAT of conservative public relations—a columnist, humorist, and impresario.

Officially Rice serves as president and CEO of Publius PR,[344] editor-in-chief of The Publius National Post on Substack,[345] and author of the number-one Amazon bestseller, *The Woking Dead: How Society's Vogue Virus Destroys Our Culture.*

Rice is a brand manager, star-whisperer, media influencer, and literary agent who has produced, promoted, or represented Laura Ingraham, Judge Jeanine Pirro, Donald Trump Jr., Monica Crowley, Congresswoman Marjorie Taylor Greene, Senator Marsha Blackburn, Vivek Ramaswamy, Congresswoman Tulsi Gabbard, Kari Lake, Dan Bongino, Charles Krauthammer, Congressman Steve Scalise, George P. Bush, Dr. Ben Carson, Congressman Michael Waltz, The Hodgetwins, Roger L. Simon, Buck Sexton, Ben Stein, Steve Hilton, Alan Dershowitz, Bobby Kennedy Junior, Dr. Peter Navarro, Congresswoman Lauren Boebert, Dr. Naomi Wolf, Dr. Robert Malone, Pete Hegseth, Newt Gingrich, Victor Davis Hanson, and many others.

Rice served as the executive producer of *The Laura Ingraham Show* for four years, and *The Monica Crowley Show* for two years. Following that, he produced an investigative news show at the *Washington Times* for John Solomon for three years called *America's Morning News*, and later was brought in by Glenn Beck's team to help launch The Blaze Radio Network. Some of his current or former clients are the groups that represent the core of the conservative movement, like the Federalist Society, America First PAC, FreedomWorks, CO2 Coalition, and Gun Owners of America.

In addition to running Publius, Rice writes as a columnist for over thirty national media outlets that include *Investor's Business Daily*, *The Hill*, *Epoch Times*, Newsmax, PJ Media, American Greatness, Townhall.com, TheBlaze.com, RealClearMarkets, and the *Washington Examiner*.